LEADERSHIP EDUCATION 200:
COMMUNICATION, AWARENESS, AND LEADERSHIP

Second Edition

Empower People

Inspire People

"CUSTOM EDITION FOR THE US AIR FORCE JUNIOR RESERVE OFFICER TRAINING CORPS"

AIR FORCE J.R.O.T.C.

Lead Change

Shared Vision

C² Technologies

www.C2TI.com

LEADERSHIP

C² Technologies, Inc.
1921 Gallows Road, Suite 1000
Vienna, VA 22182-3900
703-448-7900
www.c2ti.com

Editorial Credits
High Stakes Writing, LLC, Editorial oversight: Lawrence J. Goodrich
Department of the Air Force Editor: Linda Sackie

Production Credits
Chief Executive Officer: Dolly Oberoi
President: Curtis Cox
VP, Operations: James E. Threlfall
VP, Services: Jimmy Ruth
Program Manager: Gayla Thompson
Photo Researcher: Rodger Stuffel
Cover Design: Rodger Stuffel and Linda Sackie
Interior Design and Composition: Mia Saunders

Cover Images: © Monkey Business Images/ShutterStock, Inc.; © Goodluz/ShutterStock, Inc.; © Rawpixel.com/ShutterStock, Inc.; © Rafal Olechowski/ShutterStock, Inc.; © arka38/ShutterStock, Inc.; © xtock/ShutterStock, Inc.

Printing and Binding: Print Printers Inc / Citicap Channels Ltd

Some images in this book feature models. These models do not necessarily endorse, represent, or participate in the activities represented in the images.

Jeanne M. Holm Center for Officer Accessions and Citizen Development Credits
Director of Curriculum: Dr. Charles Nath III, EdD
Chief, AFJROTC Curriculum: Vickie Helms, MEd
Curriculum Instructional Systems Specialist: Linda Sackie, MACI

Library of Congress Cataloging-in-Publication Data on file
ISBN 978-0-692-54532-4

Printed by a United States of America–Based Company
15 14 13 12 11 10 9 8 7 6 5 4 3 2

We dedicate this to Dr. Charles Nath III, our Director of Curriculum. His exceptional leadership has enabled us to establish a tradition of providing "world-class" curriculum to teachers and students around the world.

Contents

Contents

Contents

Preface

Leadership Education 200: Communication, Awareness, and Leadership, Second Edition, is a customized course designed to improve communication, enhance awareness of self and others, and provide fundamentals of leadership and followership. The course focuses on the Air Force Junior Reserve Officer Training Corps (AFJROTC) mission to "develop citizens of character dedicated to serving their nation and community." Woven throughout is the underlying theme of developing personal integrity. The course also emphasizes leadership and values such as service and excellence. This update incorporates 21st century teaching, learning, and skills of critical thinking, communication, collaboration, and creativity.

Each lesson includes a "Quick Write" reading and writing activity related to the lesson; a "Learn About" that tells you what you'll learn from the lesson; a list of vocabulary words in the lesson; "Talking Points" that highlight specific and interesting facts; and many stories, biographies, and profiles. The lessons close with a "Checkpoints Lesson Review" that will allow you to review what you have learned. At the end of the "Checkpoints" is an "Applying Your Learning" section with a discussion question that will give you a chance to use what you have learned and provides another way to reinforce your understanding of the lesson's content. The text has eight chapters; each chapter contains three lessons.

"Chapter 1: Learning and Communication" explains the basics of the communication process, how to improve your listening skills, and how to think critically. "Chapter 2: Communicating Effectively" provides a basic checklist for constructing your communication, as well as ideas on how to write effectively and be a better public speaker.

"Chapter 3: Understanding Your Attitude" describes how you and others interpret the events and experiences around you. It discusses how to develop a positive attitude and what it takes to be a leader, and includes several examples of leaders who overcame serious difficulties in their own lives. "Chapter 4: Understanding Your Actions" focuses on integrity and character, your personality and how it affects your actions, and consequences and responsibilities.

"Chapter 5: Developing Vision and Teams" covers the essence of group and team dynamics, including how to build mutual respect and how to establish a common vision for a group or team. "Chapter 6: Solving Conflicts and Problems" examines how to identify levels of conflict, a series of steps for problem solving, and how to build consensus among team members.

"Chapter 7: A Leadership Model" presents an introduction to US Air Force leadership, including the basic elements of leadership, the Air Force leadership concept, and the Air Force Core Values. It also looks at the characteristics for effective leadership and the Air Force Leadership Principles. "Chapter 8: Adaptive Leadership" explores leadership styles and how to adapt them to the demands of the mission, the importance of good followership and its relationship to good leadership, and how to prepare yourself for the responsibilities of leadership.

This book was prepared especially for you—the AFJROTC cadet. Everyone involved in creating this course hopes it will help you prepare for different leadership roles in all aspects of your life—at school, in your unit, in the workplace, in private organizations, and in your family. The need for effective leaders has never been greater. This course will help you meet the challenge.

Lawrence J. Goodrich and Linda Sackie

Preface

Acknowledgments

Leadership Education 200: Communication, Awareness, and Leadership, Second Edition, is a collaborative effort by the Jeanne M. Holm Center for Officer Accessions and Citizen Development (Holm Center) Curriculum Directorate and AFJROTC teachers from around the world. The team involved in the creation of this course was under the leadership of Dr. Charles Nath III, EdD, Director of Curriculum for the Holm Center at Maxwell Air Force Base, Alabama, and Vickie Helms, MEd, Chief, AFJROTC Curriculum. Dr. Nath retired in July 2015 after serving as Director of Curriculum for 15 years. Throughout those years, he provided extraordinary guidance and support, enabling the transformation of our curriculum into the 21st century.

Special recognition goes to Linda Sackie, MACI, an instructional systems specialist for Holm Center Curriculum and the primary Air Force editor, reviewer, and significant contributor for this project. We commend Linda's continued dedication and perseverance in producing the best academic materials possible for AFJROTC units worldwide.

We are deeply indebted to our subject matter experts, academic consultants, and reviewers for their expertise and guidance. We want to commend the efforts of the teachers who provided invaluable input for the update of this course, to include SMSgt Corinne Smith (retired), BSBM, AFJROTC Unit NC-20066, Northwest Cabarrus HS, Concord, NC; MSgt Eric Yeager (retired), BSBM, AFJROTC Unit KS-961, Heights HS, Wichita, KS; and Maj Regina Harris (retired), MPA, AFJROTC Unit TX-948, Lake View HS, San Angelo, TX. Their comprehensive feedback and expertise on important topics helped make this course both engaging and up-to-date.

We would also like to express our gratitude to the C2 Technologies team for all its hard work in publishing this book. In addition to project manager Gayla Thompson, that team consisted of Lawrence J. Goodrich at High Stakes Writing, LLC, who provided editorial oversight, and Mia Saunders, the designer and compositor. Our thanks also to Erin Kelmereit, chief developer of the instructor guide.

All of the people involved with this project were committed to making this academic course another showcase for 21st century teaching and learning. Through their efforts, we believe this course will continue, once again, our tradition of providing "world-class" curriculum for our teachers and students around the world.

Monkey Business Images/Shutterstock

Learning and Communication

Communication skills are vitally important in any environment where teamwork is important. Simply put, communication enables us to come together to accomplish things better than we can accomplish as individuals.

AFH 33-337, *The Tongue and Quill*

Learning to Communicate

Quick Write

Have you ever been in a situation where you thought that someone just wasn't listening to you? How did you feel? Write a few sentences to describe your reaction.

Learn About

- how the communication process works
- barriers to effective communication
- the importance of feedback

How the Communication Process Works

Almost all living things communicate in some way. Whether it's male and female fireflies flirting with each other on the lawn on a summer evening or a pack of wolves working together in a hunt, creatures communicate as part of living. Humans, however, are nature's communication specialists.

Senders and Receivers

So what is communication? Communication is the creation and sending of information, thoughts, and feelings from one person to another. All communication takes at least two people: a sender and a receiver. The sender is *the person who originates and sends a message.* The receiver is *the person who receives the sender's message.* The best kind of communication is two-way: both people send and receive messages and give each other feedback. Feedback is *the receiver's response to the sender's message.* Feedback can indicate understanding or misunderstanding. It can show agreement or disagreement. Feedback can also be in the form of a question, such as a request for more information.

Communication requires two people: a sender and a receiver.
Monkey Business Images/Shutterstock

Based on the feedback you receive, you make decisions about your actions and about further communication. You decide, for example, whether the receiver interpreted your *meaning* correctly. Does this conversation sound familiar?

Did you do your homework?

—Not yet.

But you promised you'd do it. Why are you watching a video?

—I thought you meant to do it sometime tonight, not this minute.

Would both these communicators feel frustrated? Why?

Knowing Your Audience

Before you can communicate, you need to know some things about your receiver, or audience. In fact, the more you know about your receiver, the better your chances for successful communication. Is your receiver or audience a friend? A parent? A guardian? A teacher?

What are *the receiver's key characteristics— age, race, gender, education level, status, or role in the community*? Marketers, who are experts in communication, call these characteristics audience demographics. Understanding audience demographics is necessary for good communication. The more you know about your receiver, the better you can craft your message to hit the mark.

What's more, if you know your receiver, you'll be able to better anticipate his or her response. A teacher you are trying to communicate with might have a reputation for being stubborn. Or you know that an adult you are close to objects to a certain kind of music. These issues can be barriers

Vocabulary

- sender
- receiver
- feedback
- audience demographics
- encoding
- channeling
- decoding
- nonverbal communication
- communication cues
- noise
- external noise
- internal noise

Before you can communicate, you must know who your receiver is and some of your receiver's characteristics.
Monkey Business Images/Shutterstock

to communication if you're asking the teacher for an extension of a deadline or asking for money to download a new tune. Thinking about barriers in advance can help you decide how to communicate with your audience most effectively. That will increase the chance that you'll get the result you want.

Being Clear Is the Key

Being clear and specific when you communicate is one way of ensuring positive feedback from your receivers. Another method is not to wait for feedback. *Ask* the receiver if you've communicated clearly. Then use the feedback to fine-tune your next message.

Try to state your request for feedback in such a way that your receiver will have to show his or her understanding of your message.

> *You know that we're going to meet up at the basketball game Friday night, right?*
> *—This coming Friday, or next Friday?*
> *This Friday—the day after tomorrow.*
> *—OK, got it. See you then.*

Encoding and Decoding

How does the communication process work? People who study this subject say that communication among humans takes place through a process known as *encoding-channeling-decoding.*

Let's say a soccer coach is standing on the sideline and wants to tell the team on the field to execute a certain play. He quickly tells an assistant coach, "Execute Play Topeka." By putting his message into spoken words, he's encoded the message he wants to send. Encoding is *turning a message into symbols that will have meaning for the receiver.*

But how does the assistant coach get the message to the team? The players are on the other end of the field and can't hear her over the cheering crowd. So she touches her right elbow, then the top of her head, with her left hand. The coaches and team agreed on this signal before the game. This is called channeling. Channeling is *putting an encoded message into a medium of delivery.* In this case, the medium is the hand signal.

Down near the opponents' goal, the team captain sees the assistant coach's signal. He yells to the rest of the team, "Topeka!" The captain has decoded the message. Decoding is *turning the channeled, encoded message into meaning for you.* To anyone else watching the assistant coach, the signals are meaningless. They'll have to find out about the play when the team executes it.

When you text a friend on your cellphone, you're doing basically the same thing the coaches did. You type out your text—encoding it. You hit the Send button and the message is transmitted—channeled—through the data network to your friend. Your friend reads the message—decoding it.

Communication Cues

Communication isn't just about the messages that you encode and send. Poker players, police detectives, and psychologists all know about *the unconscious ways in which people communicate their true intentions and meaning, regardless of what they are actually saying.* These ways of nonverbal communication, or communication without words, are called "tells" or cues. Some receivers can interpret these cues very well. Other receivers have trouble understanding them. Depending on how well the receiver understands these cues, they can be helpful or harmful to the communication process.

Some people are experts at hiding their intentions. This can make communication harder. Maybe you've heard someone described as having a "poker face" or "game face" on. You can't tell what such people are really thinking. They are deliberately hiding or controlling their nonverbal signals or cues.

Cues Are Signals

Communication cues, then, *are the signals that a person sends in addition to the message that may affect how the receiver interprets your meaning.*

For example, suppose that Mr. Brown, a teacher, is trying to explain a math problem to Maria. Maria is fiddling with her hair, looking out the window, and sneaking peeks at her phone. What is she signaling to Mr. Brown about her interest in the class or her desire to do well in math? Or suppose a friend yawns when you tell him about your date last Friday night. Does that mean he's tired? Or completely not interested? And how would you feel if you joined a group of friends and one person kept his or her back to you while talking to the others? What's this cue telling you?

What are this student's cues telling the teacher?
wavebreakmedia/Shutterstock

Barriers to Effective Communication

In a perfect world, all communication would be instantly received and understood. But as the examples you've just read show, the process is full of opportunities for failure. One barrier to communication is noise. Noise is *anything that interferes with communication*. It can include the words the sender uses, receiver distractions, or even bad handwriting. Noise works against the clarity of communication. Cellphone users frequently have to cope with noise: A caller's voice might suddenly become garbled, or the call might be dropped.

Noise can interfere with face-to-face communication, too. Maria playing with her hair, your friend's yawning, and any of thousands of habits, intrusions, or filters are noise.

Communication experts divide noise into two forms: external and internal.

External noise *happens outside your own head. A siren, a phone ringing, a dog barking—* all are sources of external noise if you are trying to communicate.

Internal noise *is inside the receiver. Daydreaming, worrying, hunger, reminiscing, and strong emotions* are examples of internal noise.

Eliminating Noise

Internal noise is one of the human factors in the communication cycle. As a sender, you have no way to eliminate it, but you can take some steps to reduce it.

Here are some suggestions.

Know the Purpose of Your Message

Most messages fit into one of two categories:

Information-only messages. These messages simply tell the receiver something: "I've got a bad cold." "I lost my textbook yesterday." "I'm going home now."

Action-and-information messages. These messages may give information, but they also ask the receiver to do something: "Can you meet me at the mall tomorrow?" "Will you give me a ride to work this afternoon?" or "Can you help me with this homework tomorrow?

Many action-and-information messages fail because the receiver mistakes them for information-only messages. For example, if you need a ride home from the mall but you say, "I don't know how I'm going to get home from the mall," you are providing an information message. You have left out the action you require. Your receiver wonders what your message really means. Better to say "Can you give me a ride home from the mall around 4:30 today?" This message is direct, clear, and specific. It gives your receiver enough information *and* the action request to respond.

Before you communicate, decide whether your message is action-*and*-information or information-*only*. If you're communicating an action-*and*-information message, specify what your receiver must *do* and *know*. If you are communicating an information-*only* message, specify what your receiver needs to *know*.

In brief: You must focus your message so that your receiver understands what he or she is supposed to do and know.

Break Through the Noise

As the sender, you have the responsibility to communicate clearly. This requires *breaking through the noise*. To do this, think in terms of your receiver. Use your receiver's point of view. Walk a few minutes in his or her shoes. Then after communicating, ask for feedback. Use the feedback to adjust your message to the needs of your receiver.

Use Simple Words

All great communicators use this trick. Consider these examples:

"I came, I saw, I conquered." (Julius Caesar, Roman emperor)

"The only thing we have to fear is fear itself." (President Franklin D. Roosevelt)

"I have a dream." (Dr. Martin Luther King, Jr.)

"To jaw-jaw is always better than to war-war." (Sir Winston Churchill, British prime minister)

Look at these examples. The words are short. Most have only one syllable. No long words are used simply to impress the receiver. Whenever you have the choice between a simple word and a long word that has the same meaning, use the simple word. It'll help you be a great communicator, too.

Use Concrete Words

Constantly using words that are too abstract can be a sign of lazy writing and thinking. When you say "a plane flew over," you haven't really told the receiver what happened. Was the plane a Cessna? A Boeing 737? A B-2 bomber? When you use concrete words, you draw pictures in your receiver's mind. Suppose you're describing a concert. You might tell your friend, "The band was super awesome," which tells her that you liked the music, but doesn't tell her much else. On the other hand, if you say, "The band played a sweet mix of classic rock, jazz, and hip-hop from the 1980s and '90s, and the female lead singer had a range of four octaves," you've communicated a lot more information.

The Importance of Feedback

As a sender, you can control the quality of your messages. You can also control how you respond to your receiver's feedback. Remember that feedback is the receiver's response to the sender's message. This is sometimes called the feedback loop. It lets you know what happened on the other end of the conversation.

Feedback can be positive or negative. It can indicate that your receiver got the message and whether he or she understood it. It also indicates whether the receiver wants to respond to your message. Sounds like exchanging texts, doesn't it?

Never ignore the importance of feedback. It lets you—the sender—know that something happened: You got your message across loud and clear. Or maybe not so loud and clear, and you have to say or send it again.

Ask for Feedback

Feedback is important. So important, in fact, that if you don't get it, you should ask for it. But be sure to ask the right kinds of questions. If you ask simply, "Did you understand me?" nine times out of ten the listener will say "Yes." So don't use yes-or-no questions. Instead, ask questions that let you verify that the listener really does understand. For example, if you are trying to teach your little brother how to cross the street safely and have just explained traffic lights, don't ask, "Should you stop at a light?" Instead, ask, "What color on the traffic signal means you must stop?" You can also ask your listener to repeat what you just said or to say it in different words.

Feedback is so important that if you don't get it, you should ask for it.

Jacob Lund/Shutterstock

Revise your message as needed to be sure that your listeners understand it. Use listener feedback to learn what they didn't understand, and find a clearer way to explain it. Watch your listeners' cues or body language for signs of distraction, boredom, or lack of interest. Then adjust your message as needed.

Four Steps to Improve Communication

If you are the sender, it's your job to find ways to get through the noise that prevents communication. Following these four steps will help you do so:

- Focus your message
- Magnify the listener's attention
- Penetrate barriers
- Listen actively

Focus Your Message

Focusing your message requires planning before you speak or write. Think about what you want to say and how you want to say it. Decide what your goal is: It may be, for example, to inform, to persuade, or to direct. Understand who your audience is. Make your message specific and concise. Present it politely. Be as objective as you can. If the listener perceives that you are one-sided, you may be creating a barrier to communication.

Magnify the Listener's Attention

Think about your message from the receiver's point of view instead of your own.

Ask yourself: Why should my listener care about what I have to say? Try to create interest—make your message relevant to the listener. For example, if your teacher mentions that something will be on your next exam, you're more likely to pay attention.

Find something in your message that your listener can relate to and focus on that.

If you announce that what you're about to say will save your listeners time or money, they will probably pay attention. Or if you say, "What I'm about to say could save your life," before you discuss a safety issue, you'll grab the listener's interest.

A word of warning: Your ideas must really be important. Simply saying that they are won't do it. You have to persuade your receiver through the clarity and logic of your argument that your message is significant.

Penetrate Barriers

As noted earlier, vagueness is a serious barrier to good communication. If you say, "There was a fire downtown last night," you have communicated little. But if you say, "Twenty firefighters from three stations fought an inferno last night that nearly destroyed an entire city block, including the fireworks factory," you have provided detailed information. The listener now understands that you're talking about a major disaster, not a fire in a trashcan. Be as precise and concrete as you can.

Analogies and comparisons can help your message break communications barriers. "Like looking for a needle in a haystack" is a cliché, but it does give a concrete idea of how difficult a task is. Try to find an original way to say the same thing, such as "like trying to melt a glacier with a hair dryer" or "like trying to heat the moon." Note that analogies work only if both the sender and the receiver understand the things you are comparing.

Listen Actively

Listen carefully to what your receiver says. The difference between *hearing* and *listening* is as important as the difference between seeing and examining. You can *hear* background noise but not think anything of it. Or you can *listen* and realize that what sounded a minute ago like an owl is really a person trying to imitate an owl.

Hearing is automatic. It happens when sound waves bounce off your eardrums and cause them to vibrate, sending messages to your brain. Listening is the active, voluntary effort to receive, understand, and respond to a message.

A Valuable Life Skill

Communication skills are essential any time people must work together—in the family, at school, in groups and teams, and at the workplace. Communication allows people to do more together than they could alone.

Brevity Is the Soul of Wit

A publisher once sent a letter to the British humorist and writer Oscar Wilde saying he would pay Wilde a large sum of money for 40,000 words. Wilde wrote back, "Don't know 40,000 words." What kind of feedback was that?

If you look at job ads online, you'll see that many of them have the same requirement: *good communication skills*. Employers value workers who can communicate well for a simple reason: They save their organizations time and money. Good communication can prevent costly mistakes. The ability to communicate clearly—to get your intent and ideas across so that others understand your message and act on it—is also one of the primary qualities of a good student and a good leader.

Your ability to communicate—to write, speak, and listen—affects your ability to inform and influence those around you. And with a little effort, you can develop these essential skills, as you will see in the lessons to come.

✔CHECKPOINTS

Lesson 1 Review

Using complete sentences, answer the following questions on a sheet of paper.

1. What are the people in the communications process called?

2. What is one way of ensuring positive feedback?

3. What are the two types of noise as a barrier to effective communication?

4. What two categories do most messages fit into?

5. Why is feedback important to communication?

6. What are four steps to improve communication?

APPLYING YOUR LEARNING

7. Describe the responsibilities the receiver has in the communication process.

Learn About

- the listening process
- the four types of listening
- the importance of listening
- myths about listening
- bad listening habits
- effective listening techniques

The Listening Process

Hearing is one of the five senses. It's your long-range sense. For example, you can hear a jet airliner or a helicopter approaching long before you see it.

Hearing is also the sense that gives you the most information. Find that hard to believe? Think about this: Suppose you're sitting in your car. You're stopped at a traffic light. You don't have to look at the people in the car next to you to know what song they're listening to on their radio. You can tell if that car is an SUV or a sports car just by the sound of its engine. And you don't even need to keep an eye on the traffic light. You can tell when the cars start moving from the sound of tires on pavement. And maybe somebody honks—two quick and two long toots. You recognize that sound and wave to your friends in the car behind you.

You experience much of life through your sense of hearing. You continuously interpret what you hear by filtering out what's important from background noise.

You experience much of life through what you hear.
CristinaMuraca/Shutterstock

The Difference Between Listening and Hearing

Think about the last time you were standing on the corner waiting for a bus. You were listening for the sound it would make as it arrived. The sound would be an important cue. But if you were hanging out on that same corner with friends, you'd be focusing on your conversation with them. A bus might go by, but you wouldn't even notice it. The roar of the bus would just be background noise. You would filter out the engine noise to listen to what your friends were saying.

These examples show the difference between listening and hearing. Hearing is continuous, unfocused, and unconscious. Listening is *a focused, conscious, hearing activity.* Listening is doing something.

The Need for Better Listening

Listening is the neglected communication skill. Most people have had instruction in reading, writing, and speaking, but few have had any formal instruction in listening. This void in education and training is especially interesting in light of research showing that most people spend nearly 50 minutes of every waking hour in some form of communication. Of these 50 minutes, 15 minutes are spent reading or writing, 10 minutes talking, and 25 minutes listening.

Think of it—people spend half their communication time listening, but few make a concerted effort to be better listeners. For those who do, however, the effort pays great dividends: higher productivity, faster learning, better jobs, more promotions, and improved relationships.

In some cases, listening determines people's physical well-being—perhaps even whether they live or die.

Vocabulary

- listening
- passive listening
- competitive listening
- active listening
- reflective listening
- clarifying
- restating, paraphrasing, or mirroring
- acknowledging
- summarizing
- framing
- note taking

talking POINT

Each hour people are awake they spend 50 minutes communicating:

- 15 minutes reading or writing
- 10 minutes talking
- 25 minutes listening

The Four Types of Listening

You can become a better listener by understanding the four types of listening:

- Passive listening
- Competitive listening
- Active listening
- Reflective listening

Listening to your music downloads is passive, one-way communication.

Dragon Images/Shutterstock

Passive listening is *one-way communication in which the receiver does not provide feedback and may or may not understand the sender's message.* Listening to the TV, a radio, or a teacher who doesn't take questions is passive listening.

Competitive listening *takes place when the receiver is not listening closely.* You listen only long enough to get what you think is the necessary information. You're already thinking about how you're going to reply. You can hardly wait for a break in the conversation so that you can jump in. Competitive listening occurs when people "talk past" each other in an argument. Neither person is listening to the other.

Active listening is *genuine, two-way communication.* The receiver is paying full attention and thinking about the information. The receiver asks questions if he or she doesn't understand the sender.

Active listening requires you to use effective listening and feedback techniques, including restating, paraphrasing, and asking for clarification. You'll learn more about these techniques later in this lesson.

During reflective listening, *the receiver not only actively listens to the speaker but also tries to interpret the speaker's feelings.* It involves the sense of sight as well as of hearing. This is because speakers often express feelings through gestures and body language. Good friends engage in reflective listening.

As the speaker or sender, you should try to communicate as clearly as you can. This will help ensure that the receiver understands your message. As an active listener or receiver, you can help the sender by providing feedback and asking for clarification. Don't depend on the sender to do it all. Listen actively and confirm that you understand the message.

Speaking has some advantages over writing. When you speak, you have your audience members directly in front of you. You get immediate feedback from them. You can observe their *nonverbal cues*. These cues help you determine how they are receiving your message.

Positive nonverbal cues include leaning forward, nodding in agreement, smiling, and making eye contact with the speaker. Negative cues include leaning back, folding the arms, yawning, glancing at the clock, and looking around the room. If you see too many negative signs, you need to change your approach or your delivery. One way to do this is to pause and ask your listener for feedback. For example, ask, "What do you think?" or "Does that make sense?"

The Importance of Listening

Failing to listen can be dangerous in many ways. If you don't listen in class, your chances of getting a good grade are low. Failing to listen can affect your health, or even your life. Back at the traffic light mentioned earlier, you'd better start moving when the other cars do. And if the bus you were waiting for comes along, you'd better step out of its path. If you have a part-time job, you need to listen to the boss's instructions. If not, you could damage some equipment. You might also get hurt.

How important is active listening? Consider this example.

A military jet was preparing for landing. The following radio conversation took place just before radio contact was lost, and the plane crashed into the side of a mountain, killing the pilot and co-pilot.

CONTROL TOWER: *Turn right. Keep your heading 180 degrees. Descend and maintain 8,000 feet.*

PILOT: *Right. Maintaining heading of 180 degrees. Am leaving 15,000 and heading for 2,000…. Steady at 180 degrees. Am passing 10,000 for 2,000.*

CONTROL TOWER: *Roger. Your position is 12 miles southwest of airport. Maintain 8,000 feet.*

PILOT: *Roger. Passing nine for two (that is, 9,000 for 2,000).*

CONTROL TOWER: *Your position is 19 miles southwest of airport. Turn right 200 degrees for a slight pattern extension.*

Active listening is essential to safety in aviation and many other areas.
Maurizio Milanesio/Shutterstock

What happened? Who showed poor listening skills? Could this accident have been avoided with better listening?

Myths About Listening

People buy into a number of myths about listening. Below are some of the most common ones. How many of them have you heard before? What argument could you give to someone who believed them?

Myth #1: Listening Is Not My Problem

People generally overrate themselves as speakers. They assume that their listeners will understand. They need to realize that communication is a two-way street. Both speaker and listener need to work to make communication succeed.

Myth #2: Listening and Hearing Are the Same

Hearing is the reception of sound waves by your ears and your auditory nerves. Listening is the interpretation of those sound waves. Listening filters out noise and sounds that are not part of the message.

Myth #3: Good Readers Are Good Listeners

Both reading and listening depend on translating sounds into meaning. Because of this shared factor, many people think that good readers are always good listeners. This isn't true. Research shows that there is little relationship between the average person's scores for reading and listening. So even if you have trouble with reading, you can still be a good listener. And if you're a great reader, you still might have to polish your listening skills.

Myth #4: Smart People Are Better Listeners

Students who score high on intelligence tests don't always do well on listening tests. Smarter students do have the *capacity* to be better listeners than the average student. But a high intelligence may actually interfere with good listening.

Myth #5: Listening Improves with Age

The *ability* to listen and to understand does improve as people get older. For example, your younger brother or sister probably has a harder time understanding complicated things than you do. But although listening ability increases the older you get, listening *performance* declines. Several studies have shown that children are better listeners than adolescents. Young adolescents are better listeners than older ones. Most people become poorer listeners as they get older. You can tell your parents about that!

Myth #6: Listening Skills Are Hard to Learn

Good listening skills are not hard to learn. But applying those skills consistently does take practice.

Bad Listening Habits

You'll learn more about effective listening techniques later in this lesson. But first, take a moment to think about the bad listening habits you may have picked up without realizing it.

Here are eight typical bad listening habits. See how many of these you find yourself slipping into. How can you avoid them to become a more effective listener?

Bad Habit #1: Thinking About What to Say Rather Than Listening to the Speaker

Whenever you converse with someone, you're also carrying on an internal conversation—a conversation in your head. You're trying to figure out where the external conversation is going. This distracts you from listening and can detract from the quality of your responses.

Bad Habit #2: Talking When You Should Be Listening

You've probably heard the old saying, "The squeaky wheel gets the grease." Americans are reared to speak their minds. Unfortunately, you miss a lot by talking when you should be listening. Pay attention to what people say. Hold your response until they have finished.

Bad Habit #3: Interrupting

Interrupters speak up before someone else has finished. They do this accidentally or deliberately. They believe that what they have to say is more important than what others have to say.

If you've ever been interrupted, you know how annoying it is. Train yourself to be patient. Let the other person talk. Nod and smile if you understand or agree. Shake your head and furrow your brow if you disagree. But never break in before the other person has finished. It's not good manners to do that.

Bad Habit #4: Listening for What You Expect to Hear Rather Than What Is Actually Said

This bad habit is often more common in older people. It's partly the result of being more experienced. As people grow up, they begin to formalize their ideas and opinions. Taken too far, this can lead to stereotyping and prejudging.

Your background, experiences, preferences, emotions, and fears can create a barrier between you and what someone might be trying to tell you.

There's always something to distract you as a listener—keep your mind on the topic at hand.

bikeriderlondon/Shutterstock

Keep your mind open. Listen to what the other person is actually saying. Think about the subject from the other person's point of view. Don't filter it through your own experience. Ask questions.

Bad Habit #5: Being Preoccupied

The world is full of distractions. There's always something to take your attention away from the matter at hand. Plans, worries, daydreams, fantasies, and memories intrude on your thinking. Strive to keep your mind on the topic at hand. If you find yourself preoccupied about something else while someone is talking, "bookmark" the topic by politely saying, *"Oh, remind me to tell you about _____ later. You'll get a kick out of it."* And then let the person continue speaking.

Bad Habit #6: Falling Victim to Stereotyping

Human beings like to categorize people, events, and things. It makes their lives easier. Presidential campaigns are a perfect example of how stereotyping works. Members of each party listen to the exact same words, but their party loyalty colors their thinking and closes off their ability to truly listen to what the other side has to say.

Men and women communicate differently, and research has shown they listen differently—which may be part of the reason people talk about men and women being from completely different planets! For example, men typically put statements in the form of commands, such as, "Park your car over there on the grass." Women typically state things to create cooperation, as in "Let's keep the driveway clear.

Could you park over there on the grass?" As a result, men and women frequently misunderstand each other, stereotype the other gender, and never make an honest attempt to understand each other.

Bad Habit #7: Being Self-centered

Most people spend most of their time thinking about themselves rather than about others. This "me first" approach can interfere with listening. It's probably not surprising that this can lead to other bad listening habits.

Bad Habit #8: Not Paying Attention

All the other bad habits stem from this one. To be a good listener, *you must pay attention.* "First, seek to understand," the old advice goes. To understand, you must focus on the sender of the message. Watch for nonverbal cues as well. Give the other person assurances that you are listening.

Effective Listening Techniques

To be a good active listener, you must focus on what the speaker is saying. The following techniques can help you do this.

Clarifying

In clarifying, *you ask specific questions to ensure you have understood the message.*

> **Example:** *When you say the research paper is due on the 15th, do you mean in class or by the end of the day?*

Restating, Paraphrasing, or "Mirroring"

In restating, paraphrasing, or mirroring, *you use the speaker's words or your own and repeat what you think the speaker has said.* This will let the speaker verify that you have correctly understood.

> **Example:** *Did I understand you correctly? Did you say that classes would be canceled if the temperature falls below zero degrees Fahrenheit?*

Show You're Listening

- Nod if you agree, frown if you don't.
- Smile at your sender.
- Make eye contact.
- Don't fidget, rock, tap, bounce your leg, or look out the window.
- Ask questions.
- Give feedback, particularly if you don't understand the message.

To be a good listener, focus on what the speaker is saying.

Monkey Business Images/Shutterstock

Acknowledging

Acknowledging is *letting the speaker know that you have understood the message and that you appreciate the speaker's point of view.* It doesn't mean that you necessarily agree. Your acknowledgment can be neutral.

> **Example:** *I appreciate the fact that you can't attend every meeting. I realize that you live much farther from school than most students do.*

Summarizing

Like restating, summarizing is *a way to review progress in a conversation. You touch on the main ideas or conclusions, not on each individual point. You restate the main ideas briefly and set the tone for the next subject or conversation.* This can be useful when you are discussing several issues.

> **Example:** *OK. We've agreed that I'll work your shift on Thursday evening and you'll work mine on Friday morning, right?*

Framing

Framing *can let you see whether the speaker is open to hearing your ideas. It can also let you draw suggested solutions from the speaker.* Framing allows you to present information in a neutral way. You can then find areas of agreement on which to focus. Framing helps shape the conversation.

> **Example:** *I can see your point that we need new team equipment but that we won't get it soon. Do you think we can make better use of what we have?*

Note Taking

Nobody can remember everything a teacher or a speaker says. One solution is to take notes. Taking notes helps you listen actively and better remember what the speaker said.

In note taking, don't try to write down every word a speaker says. If you take too many notes, you can't listen. Just *jot down words, phrases, diagrams, or the occasional sentence that will remind you of the speaker's main points.* Draw arrows and use bullet points.

Often your teacher will give you clues that something's important. Here are some ways teachers do this:

- Reviewing at the beginning of class
- Writing something on the whiteboard
- Repeating information
- Using tone of voice and gestures to emphasize a point
- Giving word signals: "On one hand…, on the other hand"; "The first point is…, the second point is…, and the third point is…."
- Summarizing at the end of class

Suppose your teacher is talking about the Civil War and says, "Although it was a military stalemate with thousands of casualties, the Battle of Antietam or Sharpsburg was a victory for the Union. First, it turned back General Lee's invasion of the North and his attempt to encircle Washington, D.C. Second, it allowed President Lincoln to issue the Emancipation Proclamation freeing the slaves in the Confederate states. This turned the war into a fight to end slavery, not just a dispute over states' rights. Third, it helped persuade the British and French not to recognize the South as a separate country. This kept them from giving the Confederates any help."

Taking notes helps you listen actively and better remember what the speaker said.

antoniodiaz/Shutterstock

You might write down:

Antietam (Sharpsburg): military stalemate, victory for Union

1. Halted Lee's invasion of North
2. Lincoln issued Emancipation Proclamation, made war about ending slavery
3. British and French did not recognize South as country or give help

You can use your notes to help you apply the listening techniques above. Read over your notes soon after you take them, while the speaker's ideas are still fresh in your mind.

✔ CHECKPOINTS

Lesson 2 Review

Using complete sentences, answer the following questions on a sheet of paper.

1. What is the difference between hearing and listening?

2. How much time do most people spend each hour talking or listening?

3. What kind of listening occurs when you're watching TV?

4. What are some advantages of speaking over writing?

5. What are some ways failing to listen can be dangerous?

6. As people age, what happens to their listening ability and listening performance?

7. What are some of the things that can create a barrier between you and what someone might be trying to tell you?

8. What does it mean to "bookmark" a topic while someone else is talking?

9. What is *clarifying* in a conversation?

10. When you're taking notes, what should you jot down?

APPLYING YOUR LEARNING

11. Monitor yourself over the next few hours. How much of your listening is competitive listening? Active listening? Reflective listening?

LESSON 3

Learning to Think Critically

Quick Write

_____

_____

Think about the last movie you saw or book you read. Did you like it? Why or why not? What do you remember most about it? Would you recommend it to someone else? Write five sentences giving your thoughts about the book or film.

Learn About

- the importance of learning to think
- the standards of critical thinking
- asking good questions
- designing and evaluating your learning

The Importance of Learning to Think

Thinking is a basic human activity—you do it all the time. It happens when you take the information you see, read, and hear, and make sense of it. Thinking is *what happens when your mind tries to make sense of what is happening to you and leads you to conclusions and judgments*. Thinking involves reasoning, deciding, reflecting, judging, and remembering, among other things.

Information comes at you from all kinds of sources. Some you get just from your own observation. Other information comes from your family, your school, your religious upbringing, your friends, and the media.

Your mind is constantly vacuuming up this information. You may not even realize this is going on. For example, have you ever reacted to a situation by blurting out a statement that sounds just exactly like something an adult would say? When you hear a news story about someone from a different ethnic or racial group, do you immediately jump to conclusions about that person just because of his or her background?

Most people take in this constant stream of information without really thinking about or reflecting on it. Reflection is *the act of thinking seriously about the world around you*. You have to take time to reflect; when you do you begin to form thoughts and ideas. When you do this, you can begin to examine your own biases, prejudices, and ignorance and see how they hold up against the information you've received.

Reflection is an activity that requires focus and concentration. You do it best when you seek a quiet place with few or no distractions. This might be in your bedroom, in a library, or somewhere in nature.

The Parts of Thinking

People who study critical thinking have broken the thinking process down into eight parts. Analyzing these parts can help you understand better what critical thinking is.

- **Purpose**—This is the goal of your thinking, or what you're trying to accomplish. It's important to be clear about your purpose. It also helps to return to your purpose every now and then to make sure you haven't lost sight of it.

- **Question**—This is the problem or issue you are considering. Stating your question clearly helps focus your thought and guide the process. Some questions will have factual answers, others will be a matter of opinion.

- **Information**—The data, facts, and other evidence you gather are the information you need to consider. Sift through and toss out information that is not relevant to your question. Consider information that goes against your opinions as well as facts that support them.

- **Interpretation or inference**—Inferences are the interpretations or conclusions you come to in the thinking process. You want to make sure these interpretations fit the facts you have rounded up. Don't interpret beyond your data.

- **Concepts**—These include the ideas, principles, theories, and hypotheses you are using in your thinking. Be sure you understand which concepts you are using and that you're using the right concepts for the problem at hand.

- **Assumptions**—Examine your assumptions—your beliefs and biases. These often are floating in your subconscious mind, and you're not always aware that they're there. Not taking them into account can derail your thinking process.

Vocabulary

- thinking
- reflection
- intuition
- decision making
- problem solving
- critical thinking
- analysis
- critical reading
- logic
- bias
- premise

Reflection requires focus and concentration.
Africa Studio/Shutterstock

- **Implications and consequences**— Always think through the implications or truths that follow from other implications or truths. Then consider what the result of your actions will be before you take those actions.

- **Point of view**—Your point of view is the mental location from which you are looking at the problem or issue. It's important to understand the way in which your point of view determines how you see the problem. Take time to consider other viewpoints and ways of examining the situation.

Wanting something, hoping for something, and feeling emotions are not the same as thinking. Nor is thinking the same as intuition—*the feeling that you know something without any reasoning or proof.* When you're thinking or reflecting, you must separate what you think from these emotions and intuitions. Only in this way can you make good decisions and solve problems— two activities where clear thinking is very important.

Decision Making

Decision making is *the process of setting goals, considering your options, and choosing the one you think best, given what you know.* Your goal should be always to make the best decisions you can that are most beneficial to you and those around you. You can't do this if you don't think and reflect about what you're trying to do and how you're going to get there. When you think and reflect, you make *rational* decisions. Otherwise, you're just reacting or making *irrational* decisions—decisions based on fear, ignorance, or prejudice. Irrational decisions lead to harmful and bad choices. They can complicate your life and make things difficult for the people you care about and who care about you.

Many experts at universities, in business, and in the military have studied decision making. As a result, they've developed what they call the *decision-making process*. It involves a series of steps that have various names, depending on the field in question. But they usually involve the same kind of activity.

The process has six steps:

1. **Identify the situation**—determine the decision you need to make.

2. **List the options**—do research to gather the information you need to make the decision.

3. **Weigh the possible outcomes of each option**—evaluate the evidence you have to determine which choice is best.

4. **Consider your values**—use them to make a choice from the alternatives open to you.

5. **Make your decision and take action.**

6. **Evaluate the decision**—see if it solved the need you identified in Step 1.

Problem Solving

Closely linked to decision making is problem solving—*thinking through a problem or an issue to come up with a solution.*

Suppose, for example, that Antonio has to figure out the best way to get to school and back home every day. He also has a part-time job. He explores various possibilities—does research—and finds his choices are:

- **To walk**—but the school is far away, and the weather gets pretty cold in the winter

- **To take the bus**—but the bus schedule doesn't fit well with Antonio's school and work schedule

- **To get a ride with someone else**—again, his schedule makes this difficult and most of his friends live in another neighborhood

- **To buy a car**—but he can't afford this and would have to get help from his parents to make the payments and buy insurance

Antonio and his family have identified the problem and collected information on the various options. They consider the possible solutions and evaluate which will work best. They decide the best option under the circumstances is to buy another car. As part of the deal, Antonio agrees to help his grandmother run errands and take his sister to her Girl Scout meetings. He'll also pay part of the monthly payment with earnings from his job.

Now the family must decide what kind of car to buy. Antonio would love to have a snazzy red sports car to drive around in. But he knows it would cost too much to buy and insure. His parents point out that a car with better gas mileage would also help keep costs down. So the family settles on a used economy car—it's not flashy, but it will get them what they need at a reasonable price.

After a month, the family finds that the arrangement is working well. Antonio is able to get to school and his job on time. Helping his grandmother run errands for the family makes life easier for his mother, who doesn't have to do it after work. And his sister is happy she's not missing her scout meetings.

Critical Thinking

In solving Antonio's transportation problem, he and his family used critical thinking. Critical thinking is *making sure you are thinking, reflecting, and reasoning the best you can in any situation*. The word *critical* here does not mean to find fault or think negatively. It means to use careful analysis and your best judgment. Analysis is *breaking an issue or problem into parts and studying each one and how it relates to the others*. It's the ability to sift through the pieces of the puzzle and put them together to form a picture that makes sense.

Critical thinking is making sure you are reasoning the best you can, using careful analysis and your best judgment.

racorn/Shutterstock

If your history teacher asks you why President Lincoln waited until after the Battle of Antietam (Sharpsburg) to issue the Emancipation Proclamation, she's asking you to *analyze* what he did. This is deeper thinking than just *knowing* that he issued the proclamation. It's asking *why* he did it, why he did it *when* he did it, and *what were the consequences*—the results—of his doing it. It also demands that you think about *what might have happened* if he had *not* issued it.

Critical Reading

You take in much of the information you know through reading—whether on your mobile device, in a book, or in a newspaper. Part of critical thinking is the ability to be a critical reader. Critical reading means *not just passively accepting what you read, but thinking about what you are reading, asking questions about the material, and interpreting what the writer is saying*.

Perhaps you've read J. K. Rowling's *Harry Potter* books or seen the movies. Are they just adventure stories about witches and warlocks, or are they saying something more?

A critical reader might ask: Does the attitude of the magical world toward non-magical people—"Muggles"—say anything about racial and ethnic relations in real life? What does the series say about the love of parents for their children—or children for their parents? Why does the Ministry of Magic—the government—insist so strongly that Voldemort has not returned? What qualities do Harry, Ron, and Hermione represent? By asking such questions as a critical reader, you try to understand what Rowling was trying to say about loyalty, friendship, and sacrifice; about the conflict between good and evil; and about the choices people must make in difficult times.

That's not to say there are easy answers or even "right" answers to any of these questions. Good writing may be open to any number of interpretations. People have been arguing about the meaning of Shakespeare's plays for hundreds of years. But by critical reading you get below the surface into the real "meat" of the writer's message.

When you're reading critically, you're asking three basic questions:

* What does the text say?

* What does the text do? Is it an argument? Does it make you sympathetic? Does it exaggerate to make its point?

* What does the text mean? This is where you analyze and look for deeper meaning.

Critical reading gets you below the surface into the "meat" of the writer's message.

Pablo Calvog/Shutterstock

The Standards of Critical Thinking

The ancient Greek philosopher Aristotle believed that logic was a must for good learners and thinkers.

thelefty/Shutterstock

The ancient Greek philosopher Aristotle thought that logic was a must for good learners and thinkers. Logic is *a way of thinking that seeks to build on facts and the conclusions you can draw from them.* For example, if you know that 1 + 1 = 2, and 2 + 2 = 4, then it logically follows that 1 + 1 + 1 + 1 = 4. Or, if you know that water freezes at 32 degrees Fahrenheit, and you know that it's 30 degrees out, you can logically assume that the puddle in the driveway is frozen without even having to look outside at it.

Trying to think logically is a good way to overcome your own biases, which can prevent your reaching a good conclusion. Bias is *a belief, judgment, or prejudice that gets in the way of impartial thinking.*

A referee who called fouls on one team but did not call the same fouls on the other team would be demonstrating bias. A teacher who gave boys and girls different grades just because of their gender would be demonstrating bias. Bias interferes with logic. If you don't account for it, it can cause you a lot of trouble when you're trying to make decisions and solve problems.

Premises and Conclusions

For your thinking to be logical, you must base it on premises that are true. A premise is *the foundation on which you build a logical conclusion.* Your premise may be factual, or it may not be. If it isn't, your conclusion will be faulty.

For example, take the premise "All birds have feathers." Put that together with your observation that a robin has feathers. You can logically conclude that robins are birds.

But say you take the premise "If the street is wet, it has rained recently." Put that together with the factual premise "The street is wet." Can you then correctly declare, "It has rained recently?" No, because your first premise is false. There could be several other explanations for why the streets are wet. As a critical thinker, you must consider your premises carefully and make sure they agree with the facts.

Check out these premises and conclusion to see where the logic fails:

Premise A: All African-Americans are Democrats.

Premise B: Edward Brooke of Massachusetts was the first African-American elected by voters to the U.S. Senate.

Conclusion: Edward Brooke was a Democrat.

There's a problem with this conclusion: You do an online search for "Edward Brooke" and find out that he was a Republican. What happened? Premise A was faulty. While surveys show that most African-Americans support the Democratic Party, this does not mean all African-Americans are Democrats. That's an assumption or bias not based on facts. If you don't carefully check the premises you're building on, you're not thinking critically.

You can help guide yourself to good reasoning by following the *standards* of critical thinking. These standards give you a yardstick for measuring the thoughts and ideas in your decision making and problem solving.

- **Clarity**—Is the idea expressed in clear language? It is understandable? Can you illustrate it?

- **Accuracy**—Is it factual? Can you verify it? Are there any errors?

- **Precision**—Is it specific? Is there enough detail?

- **Relevance**—Does it relate to the question? Does it help solve the issue?

- **Depth**—Does it get into the factors that make the problem complex? Does it dig deep enough?

- **Breadth**—Does it consider the issue from different points of view and consider other ways of looking at the problem?

- **Logic**—Do all the parts fit together and make sense? Do any of them contradict each other?

- **Significance**—It is important and meaningful, or it is just trivia?

- **Fairness**—Is it free of bias and false assumptions? Does it accurately present all viewpoints?

You become a critical thinker by thinking about your thinking. You break your thinking into its parts and examine them. You try to think logically, examine your assumptions, and eliminate bias. You make sure your premises are factual, and you test your conclusions. Finally, you use the standards to measure your progress. The result is that you'll get better and better in your learning, your decision making, and your problem solving.

Asking Good Questions

Like a good journalist, you must keep asking questions to get the information you need.

lev radin/Shutterstock

An important part of learning and critical thinking is asking the right questions. The quality of your questions will determine whether you get the information you need. Like a reporter on a news story, you try to find out *what* happened, *when* it happened, *why* it happened, *who* was involved, and then *how* it happened. If you've ever watched a press conference on TV, you've seen that people don't always like to answer these questions. But good journalists don't give up easily—they keep asking questions.

You may not be a reporter, but your ability to think critically depends on getting the facts you need about the problem you're trying to solve. Learning how to ask the right questions is an important tool in your thinker's toolbox.

The Waste of Dead Questioning

Asking the wrong type of questions doesn't get you the information you need. It wastes your time. One kind of question you want to avoid is the "dead" question. That's a question that doesn't dig deeply and doesn't go anywhere.

A dead question gets you useless information or derails the discussion. For example, a high school student spent a semester on a foreign exchange program in Germany. The school asked her to appear before an assembly and tell her fellow students about her experiences. The time came for questions, and a student stood up and blurted out, "Did you drink beer?"

This was a dead question. The student asked it, not to gain information, but to show off for his friends. Had he wanted to ask a serious question about German attitudes towards alcohol, he might have asked, "I understand the legal drinking age in Germany is lower than in the United States. Do German high school students drink more than Americans? Do they have more problems with drunk driving, or fewer?" This could have led to a serious and perhaps educational discussion.

Other dead questions allow the person you're asking to avoid giving you information. Questions that can be answered simply by "Yes" or "No" fall into this category. If you ask someone, "Did you have a good day at school?" he or she can answer "Yes," and leave it at that. If you ask, however, "What happened at school today?" you're more likely to get some information.

Try to ask questions that invite people to share opinions, thoughts, and feelings. Ask your teachers questions that will go deeper into your lessons' content.

Three Types of Questions

In learning to ask good questions, it helps to understand that generally there are three types:

- **Factual questions**—These have a correct factual answer, but not necessarily a simple one. The answer to why an apple falls to the ground when it leaves the tree is "gravity," but the physics behind gravity are quite complicated. Another example of a factual question would be "In which direction does the sun rise?" The answer, of course, is "in the east," but behind that lies the whole discussion about whether the sun is actually "rising" or the earth is turning on its axis as it revolves around the sun.

- **Preference questions**—These have more than one answer, usually an opinion, choice, or preference. As long as it relates to the subject, you can't really say it's right or wrong. "What is your favorite color?" is a preference question. Other examples would be "Do you prefer baseball or football?" or "What is your favorite band?"

Asking intelligent questions transforms you from a passive observer into an active learner.

Lorraine Swanson/Shutterstock

- **Evaluation or judgment questions**—These questions require reasoning and have more than one answer. The answers require supporting evidence, and some answers can be better than others, depending on how well you reason or the quality of your proof. Examples of evaluation or judgment questions are:

> "Should there be more or less testing in schools?"

> "Should all parents be required to have their children vaccinated?"

> "What is the most effective thing the United States can do to fight terrorism?"

By asking intelligent questions, you transform yourself from a passive observer into a critical thinker and active learner. You'll get more out of your education and training—and become a more effective member of society.

Designing and Evaluating Your Learning

By practicing critical thinking, you begin to take charge of your experience. You find your decision-making and problem-solving skills increasing and you begin to make better choices. You can apply these skills right now to your high school experience. Asking good questions and thinking about your courses better prepares you to get the most out of them.

Designing Your Learning

Your classes are not just a set of requirements you have to fulfill to get a high school diploma. They are gateways to your life as an adult, preparing you for what lies ahead—college or the workplace.

Don't make the mistake of thinking that when you graduate, your learning days are behind you. A lifetime of learning lies ahead, and your high school courses are the next steps along the road.

Taking an active role in your learning now will pay big dividends later. The following are some tips to help you be a more active student, design your learning, and get the most out of your classes:

- Make sure you understand what each class requires, how the teacher will teach it, and what the teacher expects from you. If needed, ask the teacher for advice on how to prepare for class.

- Be a questioner. Participate with the teacher by asking good questions—this is a good way to discover what you don't know or didn't understand.

- Be aware of how what you are learning relates to what you already know. Consider how your different class subjects relate to each other.

- Think of your teacher as a coach in your subject—math, English, chemistry, history, business. Think of yourself as being on the "team" for that class. Just as you'd do your best to play football or volleyball the way the coach teaches, do your best in your class subject as a member of the "team."

- Use your classroom time to practice thinking about the class subject. Participate actively, don't just sit there and expect your brain to just soak up what you need to know.

- Practice explaining the subject to another student and answering his or her questions. This will also help you locate gaps in your learning.

- Try to relate what you are learning to issues and problems in your daily life. Look for ways to apply what you are learning.

- Think about how best to organize your time and effort so that you get the most out of the class.

Evaluating Your Learning

The next step in being a critical thinker and active learner is to evaluate how you are doing. The tests you take in class are one way of evaluating what you have learned and what you know. But there's more to it than that.

For one thing, evaluating your learning can help you prepare for those tests—it can help you know ahead of time whether you really understand the subject and what the teacher is talking about. If you realize there are gaps or weaknesses in your learning, you can work to correct them.

Evaluating your learning helps you identify gaps in your learning and prepare for tests.

antoniodiaz/Shutterstock

You can use the standards of critical thinking to develop questions to ask yourself to assess how you're doing:

- Do I express myself clearly on this subject?

- Do I strive for accuracy in my work?

- Are my ideas precise and specific, with a sufficient level of detail?

- Do I ask relevant questions in class or share related ideas?

- Does my study just skim the surface, or do I dig deeper to understand the subject?

- Do I consider different viewpoints, including those of my teachers and fellow students? Do I consider what I'm learning from different angles?

- Do I think logically, reasoning from factual premises?

- Do I focus on the most significant material and ask questions about important issues in class?

- Is my behavior fair to the teacher, the other students, and myself?

Find out at the beginning of your course how the teacher will grade it and what you must do to receive a specific grade. Your teacher will usually be happy to share this with you. Ask relevant questions about assignments to make sure you understand what you're supposed to do. If the teacher wants an assignment single-spaced in 12-point Times New Roman font, don't turn it in double-spaced in 10-point Arial font.

In addition, don't treat assignments as opportunities to see how far you can bend the rules. If the teacher says you'll be marked down for turning work in late, turn it in on time. Plan your time wisely so you can get your schoolwork done by the deadline.

Good study habits, critical thinking, and a willingness to be always learning will serve you well throughout your life. The time to develop this active approach is now. Then when the challenges of adulthood confront you—and they will—you'll be better prepared to take them on.

✔ CHECKPOINTS

Lesson 3 Review

Using complete sentences, answer the following questions on a sheet of paper.

1. What are some of the things thinking involves?

2. What are the eight parts of thinking?

3. What are the steps of the decision-making process?

4. What three basic questions are you asking when you read critically?

5. What happens if a premise is not factual?

6. What are the standards of critical thinking?

7. What do reporters on a news story try to find out when they ask questions?

8. What are the three types of questions?

9. What are three tips for designing your learning?

10. What are three questions to ask yourself to evaluate your learning?

APPLYING YOUR LEARNING

11. Describe a volunteer activity you've completed. Using good critical thinking skills, explain why you chose it from the options available, how it benefitted the community, and what you learned from it.

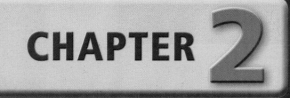

CHAPTER 2

Communicating Effectively

Chapter Outline

A document that looks hard to read is hard to read.

Diane Brewster-Norman, communications-skills expert

The Basic Checklist for Writing

Quick Write

Think about an article, short story, or graphic novel that you've really enjoyed reading. What was it that you liked? Write a paragraph or two explaining why you enjoyed it.

Learn About

- the basic checklist for writing
- analyzing your purpose and audience
- conducting research to support your ideas
- how to support your ideas
- getting organized
- drafting and editing
- fighting for feedback

The Basic Checklist for Writing

People who write for a living know that good writing is no accident. Journalists, technical writers, screenwriters, poets, advertising copywriters, speechwriters—even people who write textbooks—know that when it comes to good writing, you follow a *process*. Just as a chef follows the steps of a recipe for making a special dish, writers use set ingredients and processes to make their work turn out just right.

There's no secret process to good writing. The professional writers mentioned above probably all use a version of what's known as the basic checklist. The basic checklist is *a set of guidelines that can help you tackle any writing and speaking project with confidence and competence.* If you learn and use the six steps on this basic checklist, you'll almost always succeed in your writing and speaking. That means people will be able to understand your message and what you want them to do.

When it comes to good writing, you must follow a process.
leungchopan/Shutterstock

Imagine that you're ready to start planning to write several articles for the newsletter of an organization at your school. How do you proceed? Here's a version of the basic checklist you might use (Figure 2.1). Notice that all the items in the checklist are actions.

1. **Analyze your purpose and your audience**—Your purpose is your reason for writing. The audience is *the people to whom you are writing*. Who will be the main audiences of your newsletter? What are their interests? Their biases? Their hot buttons? How much do they know about your subject?

2. **Conduct research to support your ideas**—What types of articles will you need? How will you get material to back them up?

3. **Support your ideas**—Assemble and arrange your facts to support the logic and/or position.

4. **Get organized**—Create a story list. Newspaper editors call this the story "budget." Use the patterns of writing. Figure out how you will structure each article.

5. **Draft and edit**—Write the articles. Then read them carefully and make any needed changes.

6. **Fight for feedback**—Show a draft of the article to your classmates, friends, or teachers. Analyze their feedback. Make changes where necessary.

Vocabulary

- the basic checklist
- audience
- purpose
- tone
- research
- definition
- example
- testimony
- statistics
- explanation
- argument
- outline
- drafting
- editing
- topic sentence

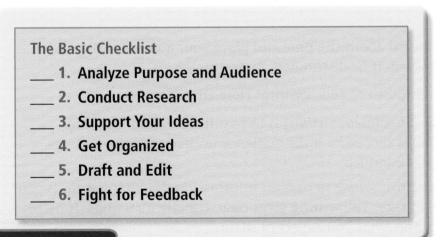

The Basic Checklist

___ 1. **Analyze Purpose and Audience**

___ 2. **Conduct Research**

___ 3. **Support Your Ideas**

___ 4. **Get Organized**

___ 5. **Draft and Edit**

___ 6. **Fight for Feedback**

FIGURE 2.1

The Basic Checklist

Remember that the basic checklist consists of *suggested* steps. Once you get used to using these steps, you'll find that you can adapt them to your own writing style. Sometimes you might use the steps in a different order. For longer assignments, such as a research paper, you might even find yourself moving back and forth between steps. That's OK. It's better to stray from the plan than to have no plan at all. The trick is to focus on writing *as a process, not a product.*

Finally, no matter how you rearrange the steps, don't leave any of them out. Completing each will increase your chances of success.

The only way to become a better writer is to work at it. There are no shortcuts. Your writing skills will become stronger the more you use them. The basic checklist is like a compass. It's a tool designed to help you on your journey to being a better writer.

Analyzing Your Purpose and Audience

Good writing is a lot like building a house—you need a good blueprint and a solid foundation. Don't launch into projects without a clear understanding of what you are trying to achieve. You're much more likely to hit the target if you know what and whom you're aiming at.

Know Your Purpose

Your purpose is *what you want your audience to think, do, say, or believe after they've read what you've written.*

Here are some questions to help you begin to analyze your purpose.

- What is the overall objective of the newsletter? Are you trying to change your audience's behavior? Are you writing mainly to share information?
- If you had one sentence (or 30 seconds) to explain your objective, what would you write or say?
- Which format will you use to communicate? How much time do you have to prepare?
- Is there anything unusual about the time and place your audience will receive your newsletter? How will it be distributed, for example?

What are some possible purposes of your writing? Here are a few:

- **To inform**—The goal of *informative writing* is to pass information on to the audience. This writing is successful if the audience understands the message in exactly the way you intended.
- **To direct**—You use *directive writing* to pass on information describing actions you want your audience to take. The writing gives clear, concise directions. It helps the audience understand what you expect of them.

- **To persuade**—You use *persuasive writing* when you are trying to "sell" your audience on an idea. Since the purpose is to guide your audience to a specific course of action, you shouldn't overlook tone and emotional delivery. But don't depend entirely on emotions. They are just one tool of persuasion. The best persuasive writers also use evidence that they put together in a logical way.
- **To inspire**—The emphasis in *inspirational writing* is dramatic delivery.

Regardless of your purpose, there are some principles that apply to almost all writing. These principles are all part of the basic checklist.

Purpose Statement

You don't want to waste your readers' time. Readers are often impatient. If they can't understand what you're saying, they'll toss your writing aside. You owe it to them to express yourself clearly and to let them know where your story is leading. One way to make sure you're clear on your objective is to write out a *purpose statement*. A purpose statement is a single sentence that sums up what you're trying to do— your "bottom line."

Possible purpose statements for your newsletter include the following:

- To inform students about the details of the organization publishing the newsletter
- To inspire teachers to support the organization
- To persuade local businesses to donate to the organization

You can update your purpose statement after you've researched your topic. Even if you revise it later, a written purpose statement will help guide your research and support your drafting efforts.

Know Your Audience

The better you know your audience, the more comfortable you'll feel writing for them. If you take the time to understand your audience and think about their backgrounds, interests, and motives, you'll be better able to write your message in a way that will accomplish your purpose.

The better you know your audience, the more comfortable you'll feel writing for them.

Rawpixel/Shutterstock

Here are some questions to help you begin to analyze your audience:

- Who will read this newsletter? Your peers? Teachers? Neighbors?
- What are your readers' education levels, career fields, and areas of expertise?
- Do you need to supply any background information, explain terms, or provide other information? Does your audience have experience with the ideas and concepts you are presenting?
- What does the audience think of you? Do they know and trust you?
- Is your audience motivated to read your communication?
- Are you making promises your organization will have to keep?

Audience Analysis: The Human Factor

How many times have you seen a friend get upset over an e-mail or text message that he or she misunderstood? Why does this happen? Partly it's because when you write, the nonverbal signals that are part of face-to-face communication are absent. You can't see the writer smile or frown. You have only written words to rely on. Because of this, when you are writing, you must think about the tone of your message.

In writing, tone is *the way you say something*. You know that people have a tone in their voices. Writers, however, have only words on paper. Pay close attention to how your writing *sounds*. Some words carry negative suggestions (*ignorant, opinionated*) or call up unpleasant thoughts (*goofy, unsuccessful*). They can defeat your purpose. Listen for your tone.

Conducting Research to Support Your Ideas

Regardless of your purpose in writing, you'll need more than words to succeed. You'll need content or substance as well as style. Once you're clear on your purpose and audience, you'll need to research your topic to uncover information that will support your purpose statement.

Research is *the process of digging up information that supports your purpose*. Think of it as doing your homework. Research can help you become an expert on your topic.

One good place to begin is a local library. And of course there's the Internet. In many ways, doing good research has never been easier—electronic databases and the Internet give you access to vast amounts of information.

If you know how to use these resources, you're off to a good start. But with so much information, how do you find the data you need to meet your purpose? How do you know you can trust a source? And what if you're dealing with a local problem or a sensitive topic, or feel uneasy with the research process or search tools? In that case, you might want to start by talking to another person—a peer, teacher, parent, or adviser.

By doing some planning, you'll be a more effective researcher. For simple projects, planning means spending a few quiet moments thinking about your purpose. For longer projects, you may want to write out a research shopping list.

Using the Library

The local library offers a number of terrific resources for your writing:

- Librarians who can help you find information and give basic research advice
- Free access to books and periodicals—many of which aren't available on the Internet
- Interlibrary loans that let you get at nearly any book in print— even at small libraries

The Internet is a convenient source of information, and most libraries today offer Internet access. But the information needed for serious research is not always on the Internet. You must find it in books, periodicals, or magazines. Libraries give you free access to these materials. Another advantage of libraries is that their information, unlike some information on the Internet, has been critically reviewed. It is more trustworthy.

Don't forget about your local college or university library. It usually has more in-depth research sources than your neighborhood public library does. Even if you can't borrow books there, many such libraries allow anyone from the community to visit and read their materials.

A good place to begin your research is in a local library.
bikeriderlondon/Shutterstock

Virtual libraries are another important resource. These are websites that give you access to resources in several libraries. Though you access these sites through an Internet browser, the information in them meets the same standards as the material in the library itself.

Using the Internet

How do you begin your Internet research? Most people use a search engine. Google is one of the best-known search engines; Yahoo!, Bing, and Ask.com are others. If you enter a keyword from your research topic into a search engine, it will supply a list of dozens, or even hundreds, of websites for you to review. To narrow your search, make your keywords as precise as possible.

When you start to review the sites, you want to make sure that the information they contain is as accurate as possible. Ask yourself questions such as the following:

- Who created the website?
- What are the authors' motives? Is the author part of a group whose goal is to influence public opinion or to sell something?
- What qualifies the authors to write about the subject?
- Are there things about the site that make you question its accuracy, objectivity, or currency?

Your adviser, teacher, or librarian can often help you evaluate the accuracy of a website.

Other Tips for Evaluating Research Sources

There are other ways to check the accuracy of your findings. For example, you can use multiple sources. If you can find the same piece of information at two or more sites, the chances of its accuracy are greater than if you find the information in only one place. Watch out, though, for sites that are just quoting each other, or when many sites are quoting the same single source.

When evaluating a source, one factor to consider is the distance between the writer and his or her subject. Since people and their research are often misquoted, it's better to refer to original material than to rely on someone else's interpretation of that material. This is true for research published in books and print journals as well as on Internet sites.

Research can be enjoyable and rewarding, but make sure you review your purpose, scope, and schedule before you begin. Doing so helps you stay focused and keeps you from getting lost in the data.

How to Support Your Ideas

Once you've researched your topic and collected information, you must figure out how to use what you've found to meet your writing goals. In this process, you'll sort out the information that provides the best support. For informative writing, you provide facts. For a controversial question or problem, you first assemble sound evidence as your foundation. Then you must arrange that evidence in a logical argument that can stand up to other people's questions.

In the writing process, after researching you sort out the information you've gathered and use the evidence that best supports your ideas.
Jacob Lund/Shutterstock

Using Good Evidence

During this phase of the writing process, you select individual pieces of the evidence you've collected to build your arguments. Here are some common types of evidence you might use to help explain your ideas to your audience.

A definition is *the precise meaning or significance of a word or phrase.* In writing an argument, it is often helpful to establish a common definition for important words. Defining things can avoid misunderstandings.

An example is *a specific instance chosen to represent a larger fact to clarify an idea or support a claim.* Good examples must be brief and attention getting.

Testimony is *the comments of authorities that you use to support a claim.* These comments can be direct quotations or paraphrases, but direct quotations are more convincing. When you're using testimony as evidence, make sure the individuals you quote are believable.

Statistics *provide a summary of data in a numerical format that allows your audience to interpret the information.* Statistics can be very persuasive. They provide excellent support for a claim if you handle them well. Keep them simple and easy to read. Round off your numbers whenever possible, and document their exact source. But be aware that leaning too much on statistics is risky. People who put all their trust in numbers can fall prey to people who spout numbers or questionable statistical "proof."

Definitions, examples, testimony, and statistics provide data that you can use to construct an argument. Another category of writing—explanation—can also be helpful. Explanation *makes a point plain or understandable or creates a relationship between cause and effect.* You can use it to clarify your position or provide more evidence to help make your case.

You can use the following techniques as part of an explanation:

- **Analysis**—The separation of a whole into smaller pieces for further study, analysis enables you to clarify a complex issue by examining one point at a time.

- **Comparison and contrast**—Comparisons highlight similarities between objects or situations. Contrasts emphasize differences.

- **Description**—A description provides details—it paints a picture with words. Descriptions are more personal and subjective than definitions are— they are more the writer's opinion, not necessarily accepted fact.

Why Are Logical Arguments Important?

When you write, you should use the evidence you gathered during the research process to create a logical argument. When used in this sense, the word argument does not mean a disagreement or a fight. It's just making a case. It's *a series of statements intended to persuade others.* It's giving your readers enough information to make decisions on your subject.

Building logical arguments is part of life. You build logical arguments every day— when you talk to your teachers about assignments, to your parents about curfew, or to your friends about making plans. If you build strong arguments, things are more likely to go your way.

Other people present you with their arguments all the time, too. By understanding how arguments work and where they go wrong, you're less likely to buy into somebody else's half-baked idea. You should try to recognize mistakes in others' arguments and avoid them in your own.

Logical arguments are instruments of power. You use them to make things happen.

Getting Organized

You know your purpose and audience. You've done your research and selected the evidence that you want to present. It's time to deliver your message, right? Not quite. You'll save time and frustration if you first take time to organize your thoughts and develop an outline of how you are going to present the information.

Successful writers organize their material in an order that leads their audience from one point to the next. Well-organized writing helps the audience understand your point. If you take the time to organize and outline your work before starting to write, you're halfway toward your goal. How you actually draft and edit paragraphs will take you the rest of the way.

Selecting a Pattern

The next step in writing a great paper, story, or article is to select a pattern that enables you and your readers to move smoothly through your ideas— from the beginning to the end. Six of the most common organizational patterns are listed below. The pattern you choose should depend on your purpose—whether you want to inform or persuade— the needs of your audience, and the nature of your material.

Patterns to Inform

Topical pattern. Use this format to present groups of ideas, objects, or events by categories. This is a commonly used pattern to present general statements followed by numbered listings of subtopics to support, explain, or expand the statements.

A topical pattern follows some logical order that reflects the nature of the material and the purpose of the writing. For example, if you were writing about the nutrition of the food served in the school cafeteria, you might categorize the material according to the United States Department of Agriculture's MyPlate icon, which emphasizes the fruit, vegetable, grains, protein foods, and dairy groups (see Figure 2.2).

If you take time to organize your work before you write, you're halfway toward your goal.

Ermolaev Alexander/Shutterstock

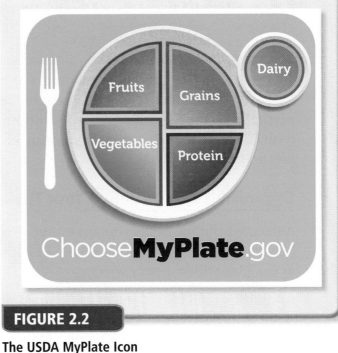

FIGURE 2.2

The USDA MyPlate Icon
www.ChooseMyPlate.gov

Chronological pattern. When you use this pattern, you discuss events, problems, or processes in the sequence of time in which they take place or should take place (past to present or present to future). Consider this pattern when writing histories or tracing the evolution of processes or situations. Biographers also use this pattern. For example, in profiling a student in the newsletter, you might tell, in chronological order, how he or she became involved with the issue you're writing about.

Spatial/geographical pattern. To use this pattern, start at some point in space and proceed in sequence to other points. The pattern is based on a directional strategy—north to south, clockwise or counterclockwise, bottom to top, right to left, and so on. You might use this pattern if you are writing about a guide to an exhibit, the layout of your school, a museum, or a geographical location.

Patterns to Persuade

Problem/solution pattern. This pattern comes in handy if you need to identify and describe a problem and one or more possible solutions. It's also helpful if you want to describe an issue and possible techniques for resolving it. When describing the proposed solution, include enough support to convince your readers that the solution is practical. A variation of this is Pro/Con. This popular format includes a discussion of the advantages (pros) and disadvantages (cons) of each solution.

Cause/effect pattern. Use this pattern to show how one or more ideas, actions, or conditions lead to other ideas, actions, or conditions. Two variations of this pattern are possible. You can begin with the effect, and then identify the causes. Or you can begin with the causes, and then identify the effects. For instance, an article in your newsletter might discuss the relationship between good nutrition and success at school.

Reasoning/logic pattern. In this pattern, you state a position and then provide support for it. Use this pattern when your purpose is to present research that will win over your audience to your point of view. For example, if you are trying to persuade teachers to support your solution, look at it through their eyes. Start out with the argument that they are most likely to accept, and then move into other, less popular arguments.

Organizing and Outlining Your Thoughts

A detailed outline helps you arrange your material logically and see relationships between ideas. It keeps you on target as you write your draft. Think of your outline as the blueprint for your writing.

An outline *contains your main points and supporting ideas arranged in a logical order* (see Figure 2.3). Every main point and supporting idea in your outline should relate to that purpose statement. Get rid of irrelevant facts or opinions.

You're more likely to stay on course during the outlining process if you refer to your purpose statement often. If you're writing for a class assignment, ask your teacher for advice before writing your purpose. The teacher may want a thesis statement. A *thesis statement* is a special form of purpose statement used in academic or persuasive writing. The thesis statement captures the author's point of view on a controversial topic, which he or she logically defends throughout the paper. The writer usually finalizes the thesis statement after completing the research. Whether you use a purpose statement or a thesis statement, you must determine your "bottom line"—your main point—and state it early in the message, in most cases.

talking POINT

Classical Outline Format

I. Section I. …
  A. First Subheading to Section I
    1. First subheading to I.A
      a. …
      b. …
    2. Second subheading to I.A
      a. …
      b. …
  B. Second Subheading to Section I
    1. First subheading to I.B
      a. …
      b. …
    2. Second subheading to I.B
      a. …
II. Section II. …

History of Aviation—The twentieth century saw incredible development in human flight.

  I. **Before the Wright brothers**
    A. Leonardo da Vinci
    B. hot-air balloons
    C. gliders
    D. failed attempts

  II. **Heavier-than-air flight before World War II**
    A. the Wright brothers
    B. World War I
    C. Airmail and the Ford Tri-motor
    D. Charles Lindbergh
    E. commercial air travel begins

FIGURE 2.3

A Rough Outline

Benefits of an Outline

To some people, preparing an outline looks like a lot of useless work. Good writers know, however, that though an outline does take some effort, it's a time*saver*, not a time waster. It allows you to test the flow of your ideas on paper without having to write out complete sentences and paragraphs. If some ideas don't flow naturally, you can easily rearrange them.

A well-planned outline can ease the pain of writing your first draft. The outline will help you remain focused on your purpose statement. It will help ensure your support is organized, relevant, and tailored to your purpose and audience. The outline will also help in the editing process.

Take a break after working on your outline. Then approach your draft with a fresh outlook.

Drafting and Editing

Drafting is *a quick first writing of a paper, focused on ideas and not style.* A draft is not the finished product, and each sentence does not have to be perfect. Your goal is simply to get your ideas on paper. Don't worry about grammar, punctuation, spelling, and word choice at this point. You can catch these later, during the editing process.

Keep an eye on your outline when drafting your article, especially when you're writing something longer than a page or two. You'll be less likely to lose focus and include unimportant information.

Editing is *the slow, careful examination of a piece of writing to correct and clarify ideas and to ensure the proper form.* When you draft, you are a creator. When you edit, you shift from creator to critic.

Spotting problems in your own writing is not easy. Once your words are on paper, you might resent the suggestion that something could be wrong. That's why you should get into the habit of editing your own writing before asking for feedback. Editing your own work develops your editing skills. You'll be better prepared for those times when you don't have access to a second opinion. When you edit your own work, you also show respect for the people you're seeking feedback from. Why should someone else invest time and effort to improve your writing if you aren't willing to do so yourself? Self-editing also saves face. You'll catch the worst mistakes yourself.

Get into the habit of editing your own writing before asking for feedback.
Pixsooz/Shutterstock

A Three-Step Approach to Editing

One way to make sure you edit well is to read your document at least three times. In the first pass, look at the big picture. In the second pass, look at paragraph construction. In the third pass, look at the details—sentences, phrases, and words.

The First Pass: The Big Picture

This is the time to pay attention to the arrangement and flow of ideas. Here are some areas to think about:

Check your purpose.

- What is my purpose? Check the wording one more time.
- What is my purpose statement? For short assignments, underline the statement in the draft. For longer assignments, write it down on a separate sheet of paper and refer to it as you edit.
- Does the purpose statement make sense or does it miss the point?

Check the introduction.

- Does the introduction contain the purpose statement?
- Is it an appropriate length? (One paragraph is sufficient for most short assignments.)
- Does my introduction give the readers a good idea of what they are about to read? Does it tempt them to keep reading?

Compare the introduction and conclusion.

- Read the introduction and then read the conclusion. Do they sound like they go together without being identical? Does the introduction state the purpose, and does the conclusion show readers that you've achieved it?
- Does the conclusion sum up your main points?

Check overall page count and length.

- What are the audience's expectations regarding length? Are you on target? Will you have to make the draft significantly longer or shorter?
- Check the scope and flow of paragraphs.

Check for relevance and completeness.

- Do the paragraphs clearly relate to the thesis statement?
- Are some paragraphs unnecessary?
- Have you missed any main points in this assignment?
- Are the paragraphs arranged in a consistent order?
- How does the draft compare with the outline?

Some writers can write powerful and clear sentences but have trouble keeping on target. Their main editing challenge isn't grammar—it's the big picture.

If this sounds like you or someone you know, try this simple editing check.

Read the following sections aloud:

- The complete introduction
- The first sentence of each paragraph in the body, in order of appearance
- The complete conclusion

Does it answer the question? Does it stay on message? Does it flow well? If so, you've got the big picture in place.

Now it's time to check your paragraph construction.

The Second Pass: Paragraph Structure and Clarity

After the first pass, you know that your article contains what it needs to do the job. In the second pass, you will check whether the main points and supporting ideas are appropriately organized.

Take a close look at individual paragraphs. For each paragraph, ask the following questions:

Unity of focus.

- Is there one, and only one, main point of the paragraph?
- Is all the information in the paragraph related enough to be in the same paragraph?
- Can you identify the central idea of each paragraph?

Topic sentence.

- Does the paragraph have a topic sentence—*one sentence that captures the central idea of the paragraph*?
- Is the topic sentence the first sentence of the paragraph? (Or, if you're starting with a transitional sentence, the second sentence?)

Supporting ideas.

- Do the sentences expand, clarify, illustrate, and explain points that each main idea mentions or suggests? The goal is to lead the reader in a smooth step-by-step process to each main idea.
- Are there enough details in the paragraph to support the central idea?
- Do any sentences seem to be irrelevant to the main point?
- Do all transitional words, phrases, and clauses improve the flow and show proper relationships?
- Do most paragraphs contain three to seven sentences, the best length for a paragraph?

The Third Pass

Now you're ready to look at details. Though you've probably corrected some minor errors in the first two passes, it's now time to check the small stuff that can make a big difference. This includes unclear language, wordiness, and errors in grammar and spelling.

Read your article out loud. This will help you catch errors because you slow down and use two senses—seeing and hearing. What one sense misses, the other may pick up.

Listen to the sound of words, phrases, and sentences. The quicker your audience can read and understand what you've written, the better. If you find yourself needing to read a sentence two or three times, chances are your audience will, too. Edit it.

Set aside time for editing— especially for assignments with tight deadlines. With practice, the process will seem second nature.

Editing isn't the final step, however. Someone else needs to look at your work. The final step to good writing is fighting for feedback.

Fighting for Feedback

After you've finished editing and done what you can to improve your article, it's time to get someone else's opinion. No one can judge his or her own work fairly. Too much ego is involved. You need a fresh pair of eyes.

Feedback is the response of another person to your writing. When you fight for feedback, you seek someone else's views on your writing. You then analyze the feedback and use it to improve your article.

Why is a second pair of eyes necessary? Even the best writers get so close to their projects that they can no longer see them objectively. They may omit vital information or fail to see a weakness in their argument. They may overlook the need for a transition between two points. They are just too close to the material. Pride of authorship can distort their opinion of their own work. If you seek out and listen to feedback, you are much more likely to produce an accurate, understandable article.

It's a good idea to show your writing to others and get their feedback.

Syda Productions/Shutterstock

Choose your feedback sources carefully. Ideally, they should be people who represent your audience. When you approach your feedback sources, let them know what kind of feedback you're looking for. Encourage them to be honest. Don't say, "I think this article is wonderful. I've worked so hard on it!" Unless you give them clear guidance, reviewers may focus only on details such as spelling, grammar, and margins. While these are important, make it clear that you want feedback on the big picture, too.

To make good use of feedback, you need an open mind. You also need to be able to accept criticism. Don't take comments personally. Accept feedback willingly and use it constructively—it's an important step in the writing process.

✔ CHECKPOINTS

Lesson 1 Review

Using complete sentences, answer the following questions on a sheet of paper.

1. What are the six steps of the basic checklist?

2. Which of the six steps can you leave out if necessary?

3. What are four possible purposes of your writing?

4. What are some questions you can ask to analyze your audience?

5. What are three resources you can find at your library?

6. List four search engines you can use to find information on the Internet.

7. What are four types of evidence you can use to support your ideas?

8. What are three techniques you can use as part of an explanation?

9. What are the six common organizational patterns for writing?

10. Why is writing an outline a timesaver?

11. Why should you get into the habit of editing your own writing?

12. In which pass do you focus on unclear language, wordiness, and errors in grammar and spelling?

13. Why is a second pair of eyes necessary to improve your writing?

14. Ideally, who should your feedback sources be?

APPLYING YOUR LEARNING

15. On the next writing assignment you receive for any class, try out the steps in the basic checklist and make them part of your overall writing strategy. Which come easiest to you? Why? Which seem hard? Why?

LESSON 2

Writing Effectively

Quick Write

_____

_____

Why is effective writing important in almost any field? Why would a pilot, a computer engineer, or a biologist need to be able to write effectively?

Learn About

- what makes writing effective
- tone and clarity
- continuity: the three-part structure
- writing effective sentences
- safe and responsible practices for communicating online

What Makes Writing Effective

Anyone who sits down at a computer keyboard can "write"— if you define writing as putting down words in sequential order. But writing is much more than this.

In Lesson 1, you learned that the main purpose of writing is to get your audience to think, do, or believe something. In other words, you want to *have an effect* on your audience. *Effective writing* is writing that provokes some response in the reader—a laugh, a gasp, a nod, a sob, a growl, a shrug— anything but a yawn!

Effective writing is powerful because it causes people to do things. Newspaper editors love it when people write letters to the editor because it tells them they're doing their jobs: getting people to think about issues and events and to *react*.

Effective writing is much more than typing out words—it must provoke an audience response.

A and N photography/Shutterstock

Patrick Henry before the Virginia House of Burgesses in Williamsburg.

Everett Historical/Shutterstock

- style
- synonym
- clarity
- jargon
- continuity
- transitions
- voice
- active voice
- passive voice
- subject-verb agreement
- pronoun
- antecedent
- e-mail
- text messaging (texting)
- social media

In March 1775, the patriot Patrick Henry read a speech before the Virginia House of Burgesses. He spoke about the outrage many of his fellow colonists felt over the way the British government was treating them. Henry ended his speech with a famous line: *"I know not what course others may take; but as for me, give me liberty or give me death!"* Those words helped inspire Virginians and other colonists to start a war of independence against Great Britain.

Patrick Henry motivated people to *act*. It's not as easy as it sounds, and it's no accident. Writing like that takes work.

Becoming an effective writer is one of the most important things you will accomplish in your education. Effective writing will help you become a successful student in high school and beyond, a successful employee, and a successful communicator throughout your life. So the work is well worth it.

But how do you make your writing as effective and powerful as Patrick Henry's speech was? Follow *the process* you learned in the previous lesson and work on your writing style. Style is *how you communicate in your own personal way, through the words you choose, the order in which you place them, and their level of formality.* As you practice your writing, you will get better at expressing yourself through your style. This lesson will help you do just that.

Tone and Clarity

You've learned that your writing has a tone, just as your voice does. What do you think was Patrick Henry's emotional state when he made his famous speech to the Virginia House of Burgesses? If you are happy, angry, sad, confused, or amused, it's usually easy for your friends to pick up on your state of mind by your tone of voice. And when you're with your friends, you're listening to *how* they sound as much as to *what* they are saying. Your tone of voice—its speed, pitch, and volume—goes along with the words to help add meaning. That's why you understand your friends on a level that goes deeper than mere words.

So how does the written word convey tone of voice and that deeper level of meaning? How do you express anger, enthusiasm, or joy in writing? When you write, you have fewer obvious ways to get your state of mind across to your readers, but you do have some important methods in your writer's toolbox. A few of them follow.

Tone: Choosing the Right Words

Think about how words affect people. Suppose your friend Amy texts you about a problem she's having. You don't have time to call her, and you can't write back in detail at that moment. Even in a short message, however, you can show your concern by your tone. There's a big difference between responding, "Let's talk later" and "No big deal—we've all got problems." The first response tells Amy that you understand the problem and are willing to help—but later. The other response communicates that you couldn't care less. In one case, your tone is concerned; in the other, it's insensitive.

Words are a lot like fruits and vegetables. Some are sweet like apple slices, and some are as hot as chili peppers. Some please, and some offend. And some can be neutral.

Think about how you use words to describe other people. What's the difference among the words *student, bookworm, egghead,* and *nerd*? Do they all mean the same thing?

Do some have more emotional weight than others? Is one fairly neutral? Which one describes *you*?

Or how about the way you might describe your best friend's car? You might use the term "wicked bad wheels," "a nice ride," "a tricked-out low rider" or "a sketchy junker." How would you describe the car your science teacher drives? Your grandparent's car?

To control the tone of your writing, be *precise* and *concrete*. Make your writing as descriptive as possible. Use words that relate to the senses. Write about what you can see, hear, taste, touch, and smell. Writing that is general and abstract doesn't evoke experiences in your reader's mind. Lazy writers overuse vague terms. People who write or say "whatever" or "awesome" aren't interested in letting you know what they're thinking. Maybe they're not thinking at all!

Think about words' shades of meaning. Just as a painter uses a palette of many colors to create detailed images, writers use different words to express various shades of meaning. The writer with a rich, well-chosen vocabulary writes about the *aroma* of a baking pie, the *fragrance* of a flower, the *scent* of a perfume, or the *odor* of chopped onion. They don't just write about the *smell* of all these things.

Using concrete, specific nouns and verbs makes your writing stronger. Instead of writing, "The pick-up truck came down the lane," why not experiment a little? What kind and color of pick-up? What did it sound like? Where was it going? After thinking about those questions, you might write, "Its engine roaring, a metallic-blue Dodge Ram ground its way along the muddy cow path." Include only the ideas your reader needs, and then express those ideas with specific words to help the reader understand your message.

Writing is storytelling—using concrete nouns and verbs tells your story better.

Monkey Business Images/Shutterstock

Where do you find such a variety of word choices? Try a good *thesaurus*—or synonym finder—in print or online. A synonym is *a word that has nearly the same meaning as another word does*. Once you start thinking about it, you'll be surprised at the range of choices for a word that you at first thought was exactly the one you wanted.

Clarity: Simple Is Best

In writing, clarity is *the quality of clearness that lets your reader understand your meaning quickly.* That's the goal of all effective writing. If your reader can't quickly grasp your meaning, it's less likely that he or she will do what you want.

What are the enemies of clarity? One is jargon. Jargon is *the overly specific or technical language used by people within a specialty or cultural area.* Jargon consists of "shorthand" words, phrases, or abbreviations that are particular to a relatively small group of people.

The aim of effective communication is to transmit meaning in the clearest possible way. And the simplest way to do that is to use familiar, everyday words. The use of some jargon among members of a specialty group is essential. How else would pilots communicate with their tower controllers? Or how would doctors, lawyers, accountants, or architects communicate about their professional duties? Jargon lets people with a common base of knowledge share information efficiently.

But using jargon simply to inflate your writing or to try to seem smart is unfair to readers. It can backfire on you by confusing them. When that happens, you've failed as a communicator. So before you use jargon, think about your audience. If you decide to use jargon, explain or define any such terms that you use.

Abbreviations, like jargon, can sometimes be helpful because they're timesavers. For example, suppose you're talking to a friend about downloading music onto your cell phone. Both of you know how to do this and you've done it before. So you might use jargon and abbreviations such as *download, MP3, gig, meg,* and *shuffle.*

But if you had to explain how to download music to a group of senior citizens who'd never used a smartphone, you'd have to recompose your message. You'd think about questions such as, "What do they understand?" and "How can I help them understand better?" To be an effective writer, you need to adapt your writing style to specific circumstances. If you use an abbreviation, spell out the entire word the first time it appears. If you know that you'll use the abbreviation only a few times, it may be better to spell the whole word out each time and avoid the abbreviation.

Continuity: The Three-Part Structure

Effective writing holds together in a natural way. It has continuity. In writing that has continuity, *every part works toward the goal of communicating meaning clearly and quickly.*

A key question to think about as you plan your writing is what your draft is going to look like. In most cases, you'll organize your draft in a three-part structure—an introduction, a body, and a conclusion.

- The *introduction* captures your audience's attention and states your purpose.
- The *body* is a sequence of ideas that flows logically in a series of paragraphs.
- The *conclusion* summarizes the main points in the body and brings the writing to a smooth close.

Drafting the Introduction

The introduction sets the stage and tone for your message. Although the content and length of your introduction will vary with the assignment, the introduction should at least clearly state your purpose and where you plan to take the audience.

Even though readers read the introduction first, you don't have to write it first. In fact, some good writers do the introduction last. Regardless of when you write your introduction, make sure that it captures your purpose. It should prepare your audience for what is to come.

Drafting the Body

The body of your paper is the heart of your message. It includes your main ideas about your subject and supporting details under each main idea. The length of the body will vary depending on your purpose and subject. As a general rule, each main idea should have its own paragraph. You might confuse your reader if you have two or more main ideas in a single paragraph. If you're writing a long paper, you may have to use more than one paragraph to cover one main point or idea.

Drafting the Conclusion

The conclusion is the last part of a well-arranged paper. Unfortunately, it's sometimes the most neglected. Writers occasionally stop as soon as they've finished discussing their last main idea. When they do, they miss a good opportunity. This is because the conclusion is your chance to summarize your paper and give your audience a sense of closure. An effective conclusion summarizes the theme and main points discussed in the body. If your paper has a simple purpose, you might want to emphasize it by restating it in the conclusion using slightly different words. If your paper is long, use the conclusion to reemphasize your main ideas.

Drafting Effective Paragraphs

Paragraphs are the tools that you use to develop ideas in your writing. They serve three purposes:

- To group related ideas into single units of thought
- To separate one unit of thought from another unit
- To alert your readers that you're shifting to another phase of your subject

A paragraph is a functional unit. It has clusters of ideas built around a single main idea and is linked with other clusters before and after it. It's not just a handy means of breaking up text. It performs a planned function—it presents a single major idea or point, describes an event, or creates an impression.

The flow of your paragraphs should follow the organizational pattern or format you have selected and set down in your outline. That is, you build your paragraphs to meet the overall structural requirements of your writing project.

The guiding principle is to cover one main idea or point in each paragraph. To help you do this, you'll need to rely on another tool, the topic sentence. A *topic sentence* announces your intent for a single paragraph. A topic sentence does the same job for a paragraph as the purpose statement does for the entire assignment. Topic sentences usually lead the paragraph (check Lesson 1 to review this).

Most readers are better able to understand how ideas relate to each other if they can anticipate what's coming. The way you structure your paragraphs and write your topic sentences helps your reader do this. If people have told you that they have trouble understanding the "flow" of your writing, check a sample of your recent writing. Read it through and highlight the topic sentences with a marker. Does each paragraph have one? Do they start the paragraph? Do they tie back to your purpose statement? Ideally, a reader should be able to understand the major points of your writing just by reading those highlighted topic sentences.

Creating Transitions Between Ideas

One way to make your paragraphs flow smoothly is to use transitions. Transitions are *words, phrases, or sentences that bridge gaps and help move the reader from one idea to another.* They help you link facts. There are two types of transitions: internal and external. *Internal transitions* improve the flow of sentences within a paragraph. *External transitions* create connections between the paragraphs of your paper.

Internal transitions are one or more related words that show the relationship between ideas *within a paragraph*. Woven skillfully into your writing, internal transitions help your reader follow your line of thought. Some internal transitions show a relationship between two ideas inside a single sentence. For example: "*First* go home, and *then* clean your room."

Other internal transitions show a relationship between two or more sentences within a single paragraph. For example: "Our plan for Saturday afternoon involves both business and pleasure. *First*, everyone in the family will come home at noon and we'll eat lunch. *Next*, we'll clean the house. *Finally*, as a reward, we'll all go out for ice cream and a movie."

Internal transitions, in the form of one or more related words, are key to a well-written paragraph because they guide the reader among related ideas. But how do you move from paragraph to paragraph? For that, you'll need external transitions, which knit together the main points.

External transitions are sentences or paragraphs that guide the reader between separate paragraphs and major sections of your communication. Transitional paragraphs are usually reserved for long papers, books, and reports that contain major sections or chapters. Use them to summarize one section and lead the reader to the next. You can also use them to introduce the next section and tie it to the preceding section.

You'll probably use transitional sentences more frequently than transitional paragraphs. Transitional sentences are often used to bridge main points in two separate paragraphs. Whether you use transitional sentences at the beginning or the end of a paragraph, they can make your writing smoother and your reader happier.

Suppose you're writing about why Copernicus, who popularized the theory that the Earth revolves around the Sun, doubted that the Sun revolves around the Earth. Your research provides you with the following facts:

- Copernicus was Polish and lived from 1473–1543. He was a devout Roman Catholic priest.
- Ptolemy was a Greek scientist who lived round 150 AD. His model that the Sun revolves around the Earth was conventional scientific wisdom for 1,300 years.
- Copernicus found that Ptolemy's predictions for the positions of the planets were significantly off from what Copernicus could observe.
- Copernicus believed that since the Sun was the source of light and life, the Creator would put it at the center of everything.
- Ptolemy's theory didn't do a good job of explaining the differences in the brightness of Mars over time.

Using proper transitions, you might weave these facts together like this:

The Greek scientist Ptolemy, who lived around 150 AD, thought that the Sun revolves around the Earth. Scientists believed his model for 1,300 years—until Copernicus, a Polish astronomer (1473–1543) popularized the theory that the Earth revolves around the Sun. Copernicus doubted Ptolemy's theory for three reasons. First, he found that Ptolemy's predictions for the positions of the planets were far off from Copernicus's own observations. Second, he believed that since the Sun was the source of light and life, God would have put it at the center of everything. Finally, Ptolemy's theory didn't explain well the differences in the brightness of the planet Mars over time.

LESSON 2 Writing Effectively

Writing Effective Sentences

Most writers, students, and professionals alike make errors in the basics of style and substance—and repeat those errors frequently. Below is some advice on common style errors and how to prevent or correct them.

Sentence Fragments

Most conventional sentences have a subject (the actor) and a predicate (the action). The subject is a noun or pronoun, and the predicate contains a verb. You're allowed to break this pattern if you have a good reason, such when you write "Ouch!" "No problem," or "Of course!" Skilled writers use sentence fragments, or pieces, effectively for special purposes, such as dialogue.

Most of the time, a sentence fragment is a piece of the sentence that comes before it or the sentence that follows it. Think about how a railroad train works. A single railroad car (a sentence fragment) goes nowhere without a locomotive (a complete sentence) to pull it. Sentence fragments are the same. They need a complete thought to pull them along. To do away with a fragment, connect it with the sentence that comes before or after it.

Example of a Sentence Fragment

We were ready to go but couldn't find James anywhere. Until we looked behind the bleachers. He was sitting there tying his shoes.

The fragment is *until we looked behind the bleachers.* That doesn't make any sense by itself, does it? But what if you connected that piece to the sentence before it? Then you have, *We were ready to go but couldn't find James anywhere until we looked behind the bleachers.* Or you could connect the fragment to the sentence that follows it: *We looked behind the bleachers, and James was sitting there tying his shoes.*

Run-on Sentences

Sometimes your ideas might run together to form a "run-on" sentence—two complete sentences combined into one or joined with a comma. Writers sometimes stick in commas to make these sentences easier to read. But unless the comma is grammatically correct, it can also cause problems.

Use logic to decide how to join the two parts of a run-on sentence. Is choosing a laptop difficult *because* there are many good ones on the market? Or do the number of laptops on the market and the difficulty of choosing one have nothing to do with each other? You make the meaning clear to the reader by using certain *transitional words* or *punctuation*.

Examples of Run-on Sentences

The choice of a laptop is difficult there are many good ones on the market.
(no comma)

The choice of a laptop is difficult, there are many good ones on the market.
(improper use of comma)

You can correct this problem in four ways, depending on what you are trying to say.

1. **Divide the sentence in two.**

   The choice of a laptop is difficult. There are many good ones on the market.

2. **Use a comma and a coordinating conjunction**—such as *and, but, or, nor, for, so,* or *yet.* (*Conjunctions* are connecting words.)

   The choice of a laptop is difficult, but there are many good ones on the market.

3. **Use a subordinating conjunction**—such as *after, although, as, because, how, if, since, than, unless, until,* or *while.* (Note: You may need a comma in some cases.)

   The choice of a laptop is difficult because there are many good ones on the market.

4. **Use a semicolon.**

   The choice of a laptop is difficult; there are many good ones on the market.

Avoid Clichés

Clichés are expressions that people use to add color to writing. But they've lost their impact because of overuse. Strive for originality in your choice of words and phrases.

Figure 2.4 shows some common clichés. Can you think of others?

Choosing the Correct Word

One of the characteristics of English is that many words look and sound similar but have completely different meanings. Careful writers and speakers pay attention to these "twins," and make sure they use the correct word. Figure 2.5 contains a list of some easily confused words. Be on the lookout for others.

Common Clichés

- benefit of the doubt
- better late than never
- beyond the shadow of a doubt
- bite the dust
- bright and early
- bull in a china shop
- burn one's bridges
- burn the midnight oil
- bury the hatchet
- busy as a bee
- calm before the storm
- clear the decks
- cool as a cucumber
- crack of dawn
- cutting edge
- dream come true
- drop in the bucket
- fame and fortune
- food for thought
- hard as a rock
- head over heels in love
- heart of gold
- hook, line, and sinker
- hungry as wolves
- last but not least
- leaps and bounds
- lend a helping hand

- light at the end of the tunnel
- lightning speed
- moment of truth
- more than meets the eye
- Mother Nature
- never a dull moment
- Old Man Winter
- posh resort
- powder keg
- round of applause
- selling like hotcakes
- sharp as a razor
- sings like a bird
- spreading like wildfire
- steaming jungle
- stick out like a sore thumb
- storm of protest
- sweep under the rug
- tempest in a teapot
- tip of the iceberg
- vanish in thin air
- walking encyclopedia
- wealth of information
- wave of the future
- whirlwind campaign
- wouldn't touch with a 10-foot pole

FIGURE 2.4

Common Clichés

Easily Confused Words

accept, verb—to receive
except, verb or preposition—omitting or leaving out

advice, noun—counsel given, an opinion
advise, verb—to give counsel or advice

affect, verb—to influence or feign
effect, noun—result
effect, verb—to bring about

all ready—everyone is prepared
already, adverb—by this time, previously

all together—collectively or in a group
altogether—wholly or entirely

allusion—indirect reference
illusion—a false impression

capital—city or money
capitol—a building

compliment, noun—an expression of praise
complement, verb—to supply a lack; to complete

compose—to constitute
comprise—to include or consist of

disinterested—impartial or objective
uninterested—indifferent

eligible—qualified to be chosen
illegible—unreadable, unable to be read

emigrate—to leave a country to settle in another
immigrate—to enter a country to settle there

eminent—noted or renowned
imminent—impending

ensure—to guarantee
insure—to obtain insurance for
assure—to make someone certain of something

farther—expresses distance
further—expresses degree

formally—in a formal manner
formerly—in the past

imply—to hint at or suggest
infer—to draw a conclusion based on evidence

later—after the usual time
latter—the second of two things mentioned

lay—to place (lay, laid, has laid)
lie—to recline; to stretch out (lie, lay, has lain)

persecute—to afflict or harass
prosecute—to pursue until finished or to bring legal action against a defendant

principal, adjective—foremost
principal, noun—main person
principle, noun—precept or idea

raise—to lift or cause to be lifted
rise—to move to a higher position

set—to put or to place
sit—to occupy a seat

stationary—in a fixed place
stationery—writing paper, envelopes

their—third-person plural pronoun, possessive
there—adverb or interjection
they're—contraction of "they are"

FIGURE 2.5

Easily Confused Words

Active and Passive Voice

You're out in a field playing ball with some friends. A huge dog that you've never seen before comes leaping toward you. It grabs your wrist and sinks its teeth in. You'd probably say, "Ouch!" But what might you say next?

That dog bit me!

or

I was bitten by that dog!

Chances are you'd use the first sentence. You would want to express yourself as clearly and quickly as possible in this situation. In that case, you would be using the *active voice*. The second sentence is in the *passive voice*.

Voice is *a property of a verb that shows whether the subject of a sentence is acting or being acted upon.* In active voice, *the subject is the actor, or doer, of the action.* In passive voice, *the subject receives the action or is acted upon.* In the examples above, the dog is the doer. The dog bit. You, unfortunately, received that bite.

Here are two more examples:

- **ACTIVE VOICE:** *The awards committee gave Holly the blue ribbon.*
- **PASSIVE VOICE:** *The blue ribbon was given by the awards committee to Holly.*

Effective writing uses the active voice. By using active voice, you will make your writing clearer and more direct. You will get to the point more quickly and with fewer words.

Passive voice doesn't just lengthen sentences; it also makes them less clear.

- **ACTIVE VOICE:** *The girl sang a song.*
- **PASSIVE VOICE:** *A song was sung by the girl.*

Recognizing the Passive Voice

How can you tell when you're using the passive voice? First, find the verb by asking yourself, "What's happening in this sentence?" Then find the actor by asking, "Who's doing it?" If the actor comes *after* the verb, the sentence is probably written in the passive voice. For example, in the second sentence of the "dog" examples, "dog," the actor, comes after "bitten," the verb.

Another way to spot passive voice is to look for the preposition *by* after the verb. ("A song was sung *by* the girl.") Also, watch for forms of the verb *to be* (*am, is, are, was, were, be, being, been*) and a main verb usually ending in *-ed* or *-en*.

Finally, use your ears. Many times, passive-voice sentences just sound clunky or "backwards."

Here are a few more examples:

- **PASSIVE VOICE:** *The mouse was eaten by the cat.*
- **ACTIVE VOICE:** *The cat ate the mouse.*

- **PASSIVE VOICE:** *Livelier sentences will be written by you.*
- **ACTIVE VOICE:** *You will write livelier sentences.*

- **PASSIVE VOICE:** *Water is drunk by everybody.*
- **ACTIVE VOICE:** *Everybody drinks water.*

Changing the Passive Voice to Active Voice

How do you change passive voice to active voice? Try one of these fixes:

1. **Put the actor (*doer*) before the verb.**

   PASSIVE VOICE: *The flagpole was broken by the <u>wind</u>.*
   ACTIVE VOICE: *The <u>wind</u> broke the flagpole.*

2. **Drop the part of the verb that ends in -*ed* or -*en*.**

   PASSIVE VOICE: *The exam results <u>are posted</u> on the board.*
   ACTIVE VOICE: *The exam results <u>are</u> on the board.*

3. **Choose a different verb.**

   PASSIVE VOICE: *The letter has not <u>been received</u>.*
   ACTIVE VOICE: *The letter has not <u>arrived</u>.*

Another sure-fire way to root out the passive is to do one of the following:

1. **Look for a form of the verb *to be*—**(Again, the examples include *is, am, are, was, were, be, being, been*).

2. **Find the verb after that *to be* verb—**The verb you're looking for will usually end in *-d, -ed,* or *-en*. Change that verb to an active form. Remove the *to be* verb form. Note: If there's no past tense verb after *to be*, it's not passive voice!

3. **Put the actor (subject) before the verb—**Actor—action—receiver.

Proper Uses for Passive Voice

Though most careful writers try to avoid the passive voice, sometimes it's appropriate. In diplomatic or political negotiations, for example, clear and forceful language might be inappropriate. The passive voice also softens bad news. You should also use the passive voice when the doer of the action is unknown, unimportant, obvious, or better left unnamed.

Here are a few examples where the passive voice is suitable:

The team uniforms were delivered Tuesday. (The *doer* is unimportant. What counts is that you got the uniforms.)

Presidents are elected every four years. (The *doer* is obvious.)

The day after Thanksgiving has been scheduled as a school day. (It might be better not to name the *doer.*)

In most cases, however, the passive voice leads to sentences that are wordy, indirect, and unclear. It reverses the natural order of English. The active voice is clear and concise. So "activate" your writing for clearer, more concise, and more-interesting sentences.

Subject-Verb Agreement

In addition to making sentences unclear by using passive voice, inexperienced writers may have problems with subject-verb agreement. Subject-verb agreement means that *the subject and verb are the same number.* In this context, the word number refers to singular or plural. A singular subject (one thing) has a singular verb. A plural subject (two or more things) has a plural verb.

In simple sentences, agreement is usually not a problem:

The boy eats the candy bars. (singular subject, singular verb form)

The boys eat the candy bars. (plural subject, plural verb form)

The key to avoiding problems in subject-verb agreement is to identify the subject, decide whether it's singular or plural, and then choose a verb in the same number. Generally, subjects that end in *s* are plural, while verbs that end in *s* are singular. (There are exceptions to this rule. For example, the words *mathematics* and *politics* are singular. So is *Mr. Jones.*)

But in long, complex sentences, finding the subject can be tricky. Here are a few tips on making sure your subjects and verbs agree.

1. **Phrases that come between the subject and the verb do not change the rule that the verb must agree in number with its subject.**

   EXAMPLE: *The soccer <u>team</u> of 24 members <u>is</u> traveling to the playoffs this week.*

   (The singular word *team* is the subject of this sentence, so it needs a singular verb.)

2. **A form of the verb *to be* agrees with its subject, not with the words that follow it.**

   EXAMPLE: *The club president's <u>problem</u> is too many absent members.*

   (*Problem* is the subject, so the verb is singular. It doesn't matter that *members* is plural.)

3. A *compound subject* consists of two or more nouns or pronouns joined by *and*, *but*, *or*, *for*, or *nor*—Some compound subjects are plural; others are not. Here are guidelines for subject-verb agreement when dealing with compound subjects:

   • If two nouns are joined by *and*, they usually take a plural verb.

     EXAMPLE: *The coach <u>and</u> the team captain <u>are</u> on the field right now.*

   • If two nouns are joined by *or*, *nor*, or *but*, the verb agrees in number with the subject nearest it.

     EXAMPLE: *The coaches <u>or</u> the team captain <u>decides</u> who will start in the game.*

   • Use a singular verb for a compound subject that is preceded by *each* or *every*.

     EXAMPLE: *<u>Each</u> coach and referee <u>needs</u> a whistle.*

   • Use a singular verb for a compound subject whose parts are considered a single unit.

     EXAMPLE: *Ice cream and cake <u>is</u> my favorite dessert.*

   • Use a singular verb with collective nouns (and noun phrases showing quantity) that are treated as a unit.

     EXAMPLE: *Sports <u>is</u> my favorite hobby.*

   • But—Use a plural verb when a collective noun refers to individual items.

     EXAMPLE: *The school's seven team sports <u>are</u> listed in the brochure alphabetically.*

4. **Use singular verbs with most indefinite pronouns**—*another, anybody, anything, each, everyone, everybody, everything, neither, nobody, nothing, one, no one, someone, somebody,* and *something*.

   EXAMPLES:

   Everyone <u>eats</u> in the cafeteria.

   The president said everybody <u>was</u> welcome to join.

   Everyone in the class <u>takes</u> a turn leading a service project.

5. **With *all*, *any*, *none*, and *some*, use a singular or plural verb, depending on the content.**

   EXAMPLES:

   All the money <u>is</u> reserved for emergencies.

   (singular—equivalent to *The money is reserved for emergencies.*)

   When the students <u>arrive</u>, all go straight to work.

   (plural—equivalent to *The students go straight to work.*)

6. **Try to avoid beginning sentences with *there is* and *there are*—**They require more effort to match subjects and verbs. So do longer sentences, where writers tend to match the verb with the closest noun—often incorrectly.

Develop the habit of analyzing sentences as you draft. Making your sentences shorter makes it easier on the reader. It also reduces the possibility of error.

TABLE 2.1 Personal Pronouns

Person	Singular	Plural
First Person	I, me, my, mine	we, us, our, ours
Second Person	you, your, yours	you, your, yours
Third Person	he, she, it, him, her, his, hers, its	they, them, theirs

Personal Pronouns

A pronoun is *a word that replaces a noun and refers to a specific noun. The noun a pronoun refers to or replaces* is called the antecedent.

All personal pronouns have a point of view. In other words, they can be first person, second person, or third person. Pronouns can also be singular or plural. Both properties of pronouns are shown in Table 2.1.

Pronouns must agree in person and number with their antecedents. A rule of thumb: If the noun is singular, the pronoun is singular, too. If the noun is plural, the pronoun should be plural.

Here are some rules for pronoun-antecedent agreement.

1. **With a compound subject joined by *and*, use a plural pronoun.**

   EXAMPLES:

   My adviser <u>and</u> I can't coordinate <u>our</u> schedules.

   John and Steve should have raised <u>their</u> hands.

2. **When parts of an antecedent are joined by *or* or *nor*, make the pronoun agree with the nearest noun.**

   EXAMPLE: *John <u>or</u> Steve should have raised <u>his</u> hand.*

3. **Avoid awkward phrasing by placing the plural noun second if one part of the antecedent is singular and one part is plural.**

   AWKWARD: *Neither my parents nor my sister <u>has</u> stayed on <u>her</u> diet.*

   BETTER: *Neither my sister nor my parents <u>have</u> stayed on <u>their</u> diet.*

4. **When correcting such a sentence, try for language that is gender neutral. Often the best approach is to make the subject plural.**

   CORRECT: *All <u>students</u> should bring <u>their</u> books to class.*

   CORRECT BUT AWKWARD: *<u>Everyone</u> should bring <u>his or her</u> books to class.* (His or her is acceptable, but it gets cumbersome if you have to repeat that form.)

Safe and Responsible Practices for Communicating Online

The Internet has made electronic communication quicker, more convenient, more powerful, more portable, and more widespread. Cell phones, text messaging, social media, and e-mail are all forms of electronic communication. They're part of the digital revolution. Even if you don't use a cell phone or have your own social media page, you know that people today are communicating in ways never before imagined.

It may surprise you to learn that effective writing is still an essential part of this technology. Your teachers and future employers will expect you to communicate electronically with the same skill and forethought people use when they communicate the old-fashioned way.

Effective writing is just as important in online writing as in paper documents.

Ermolaev Alexander/Shutterstock

E-Mail and Social Media

E-mail is *a message sent electronically over a computer network or the Internet.* **Text messaging (texting)** is *a message sent using the Short Message Service (SMS) protocol, usually on a cell phone or other mobile device.* These aspects of the digital revolution have probably caused the biggest change in how people communicate in the education and business worlds. Although communicating by e-mail and text is quick and convenient, it differs from communicating on paper in one very important respect: It's *not* private.

Many people think that when they send an e-mail or text, they're putting their words directly into the private mailbox or cell phone of their reader. But in reality, the words, symbols, attachments, and files you put into an e-mail or text go into a huge ocean of data flowing around the world at almost the speed of light. These electronic networks, like a telephone network, are subject to other people's—and the government's—monitoring. Every e-mail or text you send is saved on several servers in various places, and is not as secure or as private as you might think.

Social media refers to *websites and applications on which members of an online community share messages, photos, and other information.* Just as with e-mail, when you update your status or post a photo on a social media site such as Facebook, Twitter, Snapchat, or Instagram, your privacy is not guaranteed. Depending on how you have arranged your privacy settings on the site, anybody in the world might be able to see what you have posted. Potential employers, school officials, other family members, and law enforcement officers may be able to find your account and see every potentially embarrassing post or photo you've ever put up.

Ground Rules for Communicating Online

Just because you're communicating online doesn't mean the rules of what makes for good communication don't apply. You still have a sender and receiver, a feedback loop, and noise to contend with. You still want your reader to understand what you're trying to say.

Many years of experience have inspired the development of some ground rules for communicating online. If you abide by them, you'll be making efficient use of a powerful communication tool. These rules govern how you should format and transmit electronic information in a safe and responsible way.

Rule #1: Be Clear and Concise

Make the "Subject" line of your e-mail communicate your purpose. Be specific. Avoid titles like "Stuff on my mind," or "What I forgot to tell you." Some of your readers keep a lot of messages in their inboxes—a clear title will help them find your message quickly later.

Lead with your most important information. If your goal is to answer a question, paste the question in your e-mail to orient your reader. (Some e-mail programs will do this for you when you hit "Reply.") Use topic sentences if the e-mail has multiple paragraphs.

Be brief and stick to the point. Follow the basic rules you've learned for drafting clear and concise messages. They're even more important online because it's tougher to read from a screen. Use bold, italics, or color to emphasize key sentences. Choose readable fonts (such as Times Roman, Geneva, Arial, or Helvetica), use 12 point or larger font size, and save the fancy script fonts for your signature.

Rule #2: Watch Your Tone

Remember the golden rule of communication: Treat others as you want them to treat you. Be polite. Think of the message as a personal conversation. If you were face-to-face with your reader, would you use the same words? If not, rewrite the message with a more positive tone.

Be careful with humor, irony, and sarcasm. Readers often perceive electronic postings much more harshly than senders intend. This happens mainly because you cannot see body language, hear tone of voice, or perceive other nonverbal cues that make up 90 percent of interpersonal communications. Positive enthusiasm can be easily mistaken for angry defiance when you use capital letters, exclamation points, and strong adjectives and adverbs.

DON'T SHOUT! THAT'S HOW IT APPEARS TO THE READER WHEN YOU WRITE IN ALL CAPITALS! People consider this rude and amateurish. Watch your language, also. Receivers can easily forward e-mails, texts, and posts, so someone you never intended to might read your message or see your photo. If you wouldn't want everybody to overhear your thoughts or read them on the school bulletin board, they probably don't belong in an e-mail, text, or post.

Remember: Careless online communication can get you into trouble—its informality encourages impulsive responses (like a conversation), but your recipient can print out or forward your words. If you're really mad about an issue, don't send a message or post a response until you've calmed down and thought it over.

Rule #3: Be Selective About What You Send or Post

Don't discuss controversial, sensitive, or personal information in e-mail, text, or post. This endangers your privacy and is a gold mine for identity thieves. Don't create junk mail, forward it, or put it on a bulletin board. Don't create or send chain letters. They waste time and tie up the network.

Rule #4: Be Selective About Who Gets the Message

In e-mail, reply to specific addressees. Give those people who aren't really interested a break. Use "Reply All" sparingly. Get permission before sending messages to large mail groups. Double check addresses before sending, especially when you're selecting from a large list—your entire graduating class, for example—in which many people might have similar last names.

On social media, understand and use the privacy settings for each site. Divide your friends or followers into groups if possible, and think about whom you want to be able to see your post before you put it up. But don't rely on privacy settings alone to stay safe: If you'd be embarrassed to have your classmates, teachers, or parents see it, don't post it.

Rule #5: Check Your Attachments and Support Material

Provide all information in your e-mail the first time to keep from having to resend just one more fact or a "PS." Before sending, check your attachments; forgetting to attach them is the most common e-mail mistake. If you're forwarding a copy of information you've retrieved from an Internet research source, cite all quotes, references, and sources. Respect copyright and license agreements of information you don't own.

Rule #6: Keep Your E-Mail and Social Media Under Control

Close your browser or e-mail program, and sign off the computer when you leave your lab, school, or work computer. If you don't, the next person to come along might read your e-mail or send hostile messages using your e-mail address. If you don't sign out of your social media page on a public computer, anyone who comes along after you can read it, download information from it, or submit phony posts in your name.

Professional-Quality E-Mail

When it comes to being a good electronic communicator, remember one word above all: *professional*. Professional e-mail messages are like official business memos. This type of communication *can* affect you, your family, your standing in the community, your school, and your employer. Though professional e-mail is often less formal (and less carefully reviewed) than paper correspondence, here are some basic guidelines to help keep you on track to writing professional-quality e-mail.

- Use appropriate greetings and closings. Address people with their titles when appropriate. If you're sending an e-mail to a teacher, a coach, or an adviser, begin it with "Dear Mr. Smith" or "Coach Williams." At the end, type "Sincerely, (Your Name)."

- State your purpose at the beginning of the message—don't bury the most important information somewhere in the middle of the message. Write in brief, clear paragraphs. If you are forwarding a message or sending a copy to others, mention that fact in your message as a courtesy.

- Give your readers a clear "call to action." Tell them what you want them to *do*. Many busy people resent e-mails that leave them asking, "Well, what's the point?" Give the reader a specific date for completion of the action or for a response—and remember that business people and teachers *like* deadlines. Put your phone number at the end of your message and invite a phone call if the reader has any questions. *Always* thank the receiver.

- Avoid "cc-ing" (that is, sending a courtesy copy to) a large group of people. List "cc" recipients alphabetically to avoid hurt feelings or political issues.

Safety Online

You've probably heard about people who have gotten into trouble using the Internet, e-mail, texting, or social media, or who have put themselves in dangerous situations by corresponding with other people who weren't who they said they were. The absolute law of the Internet is, "Don't trust it." You can't know who is on the other keyboard, and there's no way for you to be completely safe when you're using the Internet, e-mail, texts, or social media. Online communication completely disguises the sender— who may want to hide his or her real identity.

Even if you think you are conversing with your good friend Brian, how do you know *for certain* that's it's not his younger brother or sister pretending to be Brian? Or someone who has hacked Brian's social media page? Online communication is a powerful tool. It can also be a dangerous weapon. When you open a connection online, you are basically talking to the whole world in bits of digital energy. An amazing ability, yes, but you need to protect yourself.

Here are some ways to keep safe:

- *Never give your password to anyone*, **even close friends**—If you suspect someone else has obtained your password, change it immediately.

- **Use good passwords, and change them often**—Use a different password for every site or account. Don't use a word that's in the dictionary, your birthday, Social Security number, phone number, street address, or name of your pet. Use a mix of capital and lower-case letters, numbers, and special characters.

- **Watch out for "phishing" messages and websites**—These are messages that appear to come from a well-known company or bank, but are really imitations trying to trick you into giving out sensitive information that the people behind the message or website can use for criminal or fraudulent purposes. Never click suspicious links in e-mail, games, or other online communications, and don't open attachments in questionable messages.

- **Don't open, download, or answer e-mails, texts, or posts from senders you don't recognize**—And *never give out personal information*—your legal name, address, picture, birthday, Social Security number, credit card number, or phone number— on the Internet unless a parent or guardian has supervised your communication.

You might have to give out such information if you are making an online purchase, applying for a scholarship, or sending for valid information from an accredited Internet source. A trustworthy and secure site will have "https" in the URL (website address) and show a padlock icon somewhere in the browser. But those alone don't guarantee that the site is safe. You can't let your conscience be your guide in this case—talk to an adult relative, teacher, or counselor before putting your identity out on the Web. Once it's out there, you can't control what people do with it.

Using complete sentences, answer the following questions on a sheet of paper.

1. What is effective writing?

2. What famous words did Patrick Henry say?

3. How do you control the tone of your writing?

4. What is the aim of effective communication?

5. What is the three-part structure of most writing?

6. What three purposes do paragraphs serve?

7. What is a sentence fragment?

8. How can you recognize the passive voice?

9. What is subject-verb agreement?

10. Why are e-mails and texts not private?

11. What are the ground rules for communicating online?

APPLYING YOUR LEARNING

12. Write an e-mail to your best friend describing a weekend event you attended. Now write an e-mail about that same event to your teacher. Compare the two messages. What do you notice? Why is audience awareness particularly important when you use e-mail?

Speaking Effectively

Quick Write

_____

_____

Think about someone you've heard who was a great speaker. What was it about that person that you admired? What impressed you most about the delivery of the speech?

Learn About

- what effective speaking is
- the importance of preparing to speak
- how to organize your presentation
- the effective use of visual support
- how to use presentation skills
- practicing and giving your presentation

What Effective Speaking Is

The politician speaks to gather votes. The lawyer presents her case to win a trial. The coach gives a pep talk to inspire his team. The student government president speaks to the student body to encourage recycling. The civil rights leader makes an emotional plea to win followers to the cause.

Speaking to an audience in public is one of the oldest forms of human communication. It's a valuable art. The ancient Greeks honored this activity by building beautiful structures where their orators could practice their art and compete with each other. An orator is _someone who is known for his or her skill and power as a public speaker_. And today, you still go to your school's auditorium—a word that comes from the Latin root for _listen_—to hear speeches by students, teachers, and visitors.

But as much as Western culture prizes the art of speaking, many people fear it. Studies have shown that speaking in front of a group is by far most people's greatest fear. It ranks ahead of the fear of dying, riding in an airplane, or failure in other areas of life.

Martin Luther King, Jr.'s "I Have a Dream" speech—on 28 August 1963—was one of the most effective speeches of modern times
©Bettmann/CORBIS

You may have that same fear—that churning feeling in your stomach when someone asks you to talk before a group. Don't worry; you're completely normal. Everyone—the politician, the lawyer, the coach, and the leader—has the same reaction to speaking in public. But some people learn how to manage their fear. They practice, speak, and gain control of their fear so that it becomes less noticeable.

Although the fear of speaking is common, studies also show that the ability to speak well in front of a group is one of the qualities people admire most. The person who can communicate ideas clearly—both in writing and speaking—has a greater chance of personal and professional success than someone who does not speak or write well.

If it hasn't happened already, chances are that someone will eventually ask you to speak before an audience. If you're still an inexperienced speaker, you'll probably have to confront your fear of speaking—including the knocking knees and sweaty palms. Learning the fundamentals of speaking can help you conquer your fear. That's the goal of this lesson: to help you become a better, more confident, more convincing speaker.

Like writing, speaking is a skill you can learn. Once you grasp the basics, the rest is practice, polish, and style. Your initial mistakes may embarrass you, but you'll survive. Learn all you can from your teachers and friends—some of them are already accomplished speakers. And once you've become more confident in your speaking skills, share with others your views, tips, and personal hang-ups about speaking. Help them learn what you've learned.

Similar to the ancient Greek orators, you'll find that the more often you accept opportunities to speak in front of a group, the more self-confident you will become. Confidence and knowledge of your subject are important preparations for speaking. Now you'll learn about some others.

Vocabulary

- orator
- impromptu
- extemporaneous presentation
- visual aids
- slide transitions
- gestures
- rate
- volume
- pitch
- pause
- articulation
- pronunciation
- stage fright

Pebble Practice Pays Off

Do you have something important to say but feel overwhelmed by the thought of sharing it with others? Consider the Greek statesman Demosthenes (Deh-MOSS-the-nees), who lived between 384 and 322 B.C. He wanted to be an orator and a leader, but he did not have a clear, strong, or pleasant voice. People had trouble understanding him. He decided to work at his speaking skills. He would walk down to the sea, put pebbles in his mouth, and shout to the crashing waves. (Warning: Don't try this at home!) His practice paid off, and he became one of the most famous orators in history. Demosthenes worked to overcome his limitations, and you can, too.

Demosthenes, Greek statesman and orator (384–322 B.C.), pictured here in seventeenth-century clothing on the city hall in Bremen, Germany.

Andrea Izzotti/Shutterstock

The Importance of Preparing to Speak

Good speaking involves the same fundamentals you learned for good writing. Good speaking, like good writing, is a result of the same type of *process*. Working through this process will help ease your fear of speaking. Do you remember the following six steps from the basic checklist? Keep them in mind as you read this section.

Six Steps for Effective Communication

1. Analyze your purpose and audience.
2. Research your topic.
3. Support your ideas.
4. Organize and outline.
5. Draft and edit.
6. Fight for feedback.

President Franklin D. Roosevelt used his speaking skills to rally Americans during the Great Depression of the 1930s in a series of radio talks he called "fireside chats."

Orhan Cam/Shutterstock

Purpose

Just as you do when you write, you should analyze your purpose when you prepare a talk. Speaking has three basic purposes: to inform, to persuade, or to entertain.

- The purpose of an *informative* presentation is to share your knowledge about a specific topic. Talks to clubs, orientation talks, and presentations at awards ceremonies are examples of speeches to inform.

- The *persuasive* presentation aims to move an audience to belief or action on an issue. Speeches at graduation and before class elections are meant to persuade.

- The goal of an *entertaining* presentation is to make the audience laugh. These rely on humor and colorful language. A speech at a roast, a talent show, or school follies is an example of entertaining.

Audience

Good writers aim the wording of a text at their readers. Likewise, good speakers tailor their remarks to their audiences. Analyze the listeners in your audience by asking yourself questions such as these:

- What are their listening traits, needs, desires, behaviors, and educational backgrounds?

- What do they expect?

- What do they already know about the topic?

- How can I gain and hold their attention?

President Ronald Reagan, a former actor who was a skilled communicator, stirred the world in 1987 when he stood before the wall built by the Soviet Union to divide the city of Berlin, Germany, and challenged Soviet leader Mikhail Gorbachev, "Tear down this wall!"

Joseph Sohm/Shutterstock

The better you know your audience, the more confident you'll be in facing them. Use simple, everyday language appropriate for your audience. Use contractions and keep sentences short. Use personal pronouns, if appropriate. Repeat key words and follow with specific examples.

Types of Speaking

Briefings, lectures, and speeches are often referred to by the generic titles *speech*, *talk*, or *presentation*; this lesson will refer to them interchangeably as talk or presentation. Differences exist among the three types of speaking. These differences will influence your organization, support, beginning, ending, and delivery. *Briefings* present information quickly and concisely. *Lectures* are used to teach new material. *Speeches* are given in a variety of situations.

Briefing

Briefings are the most common type of presentation in business and military settings. By definition, a briefing is brief, concise, and direct. Sometimes, a briefing's purpose is to inform—to tell about a mission, an operation, or a concept. At times briefings also direct—they enable listeners to perform a procedure or carry out instructions. At other times they persuade—they support a certain solution and lead listeners to accept that solution. Use the ABCs of briefing to help you remember that a briefing should always be *Accurate*, *Brief*, and *Clear*. Accuracy and clarity characterize all good speaking, but brevity distinguishes the briefing from other types of speaking.

Lecture

In a lecture, most of the speaking is directed toward teaching. The lecture is the most frequent method of instruction. As the name implies, the primary purpose of a teaching lecture is to teach or to inform students about a given subject. For convenience, you can divide teaching lectures into the following types:

1. Formal lectures, where the communication is generally one-sided, with no verbal participation by the students

2. Informal lectures, usually presented to smaller audiences—these allow for verbal interaction between instructor and students

Unlike during briefings, it is appropriate to use humor in the lecture.

Speech

Speeches to inform use the same kind of organization and support materials as lectures do. Entertaining speeches may rely heavily on humor and other attention-getting support. Persuasive speeches are characterized by more appeal to emotions or motives than any other kind of talk you will give. Appeal to such motives as fear, curiosity, loyalty, adventure, pride, and sympathy is common in persuasion.

Four Methods of Presentation

You can usually choose one of four common methods for your presentation:

1. Speaking from memory
2. Reading from a prepared manuscript
3. Speaking impromptu, with no specific preparation
4. Speaking extemporaneously, with preparation and a few notes

Memorizing

Speaking from memory is the least effective method of delivering a talk. You should avoid it when you can. While this method may seem appealing to people who can't think on their feet, the memorized talk is like a straitjacket. You can't adapt it to the immediate situation or to your audience's reaction. This method makes it nearly impossible to create a bond with your listeners. The memory method also requires a lot of preparation. Worst of all, you face the danger of forgetting your lines.

Manuscript Reading

Reading a presentation can be a good option in situations where every word must be perfect. To do this, you write a word-for-word script of what you are going to say. Such a script:

* Guarantees that you'll send the right message
* Ensures that you won't leave out key information
* Avoids trouble caused by ad-libbing or going off the message
* Gives exact definitions and precise phrasing, if these are important

Reading your presentation allows you to plan the exact words and phrases you will use. But the disadvantages of this method far outweigh the advantages. Many speakers use the manuscript as a crutch instead of thinking through the ideas in the talk.

If you must read from a manuscript, consider the following suggestions:

- Prepare your manuscript carefully.
- Make your words simpler, clearer, and more vivid than you would in a paper.
- Make your sentences shorter and your ideas simpler than in writing.
- Make clear transitions between your ideas.
- Use repetition to emphasize your main ideas and key points.

Prepare your paper so that it will be as readable as possible:

- Type the manuscript in large, easily readable type (at least 12 point).
- Number the pages.
- Double- or triple-space the manuscript.
- Never break words at the end of a line.
- Leave plenty of white space—fill no more than two-thirds of the page with text.
- Print on only one side of the paper to make the text easier to handle.
- Put a double slash (//) at places where you wish to pause during delivery.
- Underline words you want to emphasize.
- Mark places in the manuscript where you plan to use visual aids.

For more hints on how to read from a manuscript, see the section called "Handling Your Notes."

Impromptu Speaking

An off-the-cuff speech is an impromptu speech. Impromptu refers to *speaking without preparation*. It's what you do when you must speak without warning or on a few moments' notice. Making a good impromptu speech requires self-confidence, mastery of the subject, and the ability to think on your feet. Only people who know their subjects well and who can organize their thoughts as they speak should use this method.

If you have to make an impromptu speech, it's helpful to begin by stating the number of supporting points you will make. For example, "I support Germaine for class president for three reasons. She's honest, she's hardworking, and she has experience in student government." Then develop each point separately. By announcing your three points, you help structure your thoughts. You also help your audience know what to expect. It helps makes your talk brief, focused, and convincing.

Extemporaneous Speaking

The fourth method of speaking allows you the most freedom in adjusting to an audience as you speak. An extemporaneous presentation is *one that you carefully plan and outline in detail, and deliver with only minimal notes*. It is based on full preparation and adequate practice. The extemporaneous speaker's only guide is usually a well-constructed outline. You base all your remarks on that outline. You plan idea by idea rather than word by word. The presentation will sound natural, but it requires careful planning. It comes out a little differently each time, but the ideas are the same.

Speaking from a well-planned outline has many advantages. You've organized ideas and weighed materials in advance. You are free to adapt your talk to the occasion and to adjust to audience reaction. You can change what you plan to say right up until you step up to the podium. Finally, and most important, extemporaneous speaking tends to be the liveliest of the four types of speaking. Most effective speakers use this technique often. It is well suited for almost all the public speaking you will do.

And while you're at it, you may want to prepare two versions of your outline. Make one version complete—almost in manuscript form. You can return to it several weeks or months later if you are called upon to give a similar talk. Make the second version much briefer—perhaps only one page long. You could write it on cards so you can use it when you give your talk. Think of it as a keyword outline. Make sure it contains important words and phrases to remind you of main points, subpoints, support material you plan to use, and things to say in your introduction and conclusion.

How to Organize Your Presentation

Clear organization is vital to effective speaking. The most obvious weakness among speakers is their failure to organize their material for their audience. A speaker must lead listeners mentally from where they are at the beginning of a presentation to where they are supposed to be at the end. For that reason, you must organize your message with the audience in mind. Like a good written paper, every presentation needs an introduction, a body, and a conclusion. First, consider the introduction and the conclusion.

Organize your presentation so that each idea is in its proper place.
Digital Genetics/Shutterstock

The Introduction

Good speakers capture their audience's attention immediately. No matter how much you know about your subject or how willing audience members are to listen to you, you must motivate them to listen throughout your talk.

Introductions vary depending on the purpose, the audience, and the situation. For an informative briefing, it's helpful to begin with an overview. In such an introduction, you mention the main points you are about to discuss. Consider the audience, the occasion, and the objectives of your presentation, then decide what kind of introduction is appropriate. For a briefing, you might start with "Good morning, I'm (name) and I'm briefing on _____."

For lectures and speeches, you can use attention-getters and motivations. A *motivation* tells the audience why it's important to listen to the upcoming information. Here are some suggestions for gaining attention. You'll have to decide which one best applies to the talk you are giving.

- Ask an intriguing question.
- Read a stirring quotation.
- Describe a common interest.
- Tell a joke that is suitable to the occasion (more on this in the "Humor" section).
- Make a startling statement.
- Use a gimmick or prop.

Transitions are also part of good writing, as you may recall from Chapter 2, Lesson 2. You can apply some of the guidelines for transitions in writing to your presentations as well. For example, one good strategy is to use words such as *first, next,* or *finally.* They help the audience follow the development of your ideas. Another is to use words such as *however* or *on the other hand* (to indicate a change of direction in thought) or *in addition* or *moreover* (to indicate a related idea).

The Conclusion

As with the introduction, your speaking situation and audience will help determine what kind of conclusion is best. Most talks don't require a long conclusion. With informative presentations, you may want to summarize your main points. With persuasive presentations, your conclusion may be a motivational statement that emphasizes what you want your listeners to believe or how you want them to act. In an entertaining presentation, you might build to a brief, memorable punch line.

All talks need a conclusion. The conclusion brings the presentation to an effective close and satisfies your audience. The time you spend on your conclusion is important because it creates an impression that the audience will remember once you have finished. A good way to end a briefing is by saying, "Ladies and gentlemen, this concludes my briefing. Are there any questions?" For lectures and speeches, use a *remotivation* to remind the audience why it's important to know the information and how they can use it.

A key rule in verbal communication is to keep it short and sweet. You may have heard the time-tested advice, "Be clear, be quick, be gone." Few audiences will tolerate a speaker who wastes time. Get your act together before you speak. Know what you want to say, and then say it with your purpose and the audience in mind. Remember the old rule of public speaking: "Tell them what you're going to tell them; tell them; tell them what you told them."

The Effective Use of Visual Support

The *body* of your talk is where you discuss your main points, give information, construct your argument, persuade, or entertain using illustrations, examples, and clarification for support. Here's where you can really prove your point with testimony and statistics. You support this with visual aids.

Visual aids are *objects or displays that give emphasis to and illustrate your ideas.* Slides made with PowerPoint or other presentation software are the most common forms of visual aid for most talks. Other types of visual aids include whiteboards, flip charts, objects, models, photos, maps, charts, and drawings. They help you remember key points and keep the talk on target.

Use visual aids to help the audience "dig in" to what you have to say. Research shows that a week after people hear a presentation that has no visual aids, they retain only about 5 percent of the information. With visual aids, retention jumps to about 65 percent. The reason? The human brain processes visual images about 400,000 times as fast as text alone. In other words, "show and tell" is better and faster than just "tell."

Using visual aids such as whiteboards or flip charts helps you remember key points of your talk and helps the audience remember what you say.

Syda Productions/Shutterstock

When you deliver your talk, remember the following points:

- Don't put up a visual aid until it is relevant to your talk. The audience will focus on the visual aid instead of listening to you.
- Don't stand between your visual aid and the audience; make sure everyone can see.
- Talk to your audience, not to the visual aid.
- If necessary, use a pointer to draw the audience's attention to key items.
- Always point with your arm that is closest to the visual; otherwise, you might block the audience's view.

After you've covered the information in a visual aid, remove it or cover it up. One exception to this rule is when you use a visual aid as an outline. In this case, you can leave it up as long as it relates to what you're saying. But when it's no longer useful, remove it.

Using slide transitions can help you navigate through your presentation. In public speaking, slide transitions are *effects such as sound, animation, or movement that take you from one slide or part of the talk to the next.* They help your audience follow the flow of your ideas.

Here are some other tips on using visual aids.

Color

Color is an important communication tool. But don't overdo it. Limit your choices to four or five colors. Use colors to emphasize key elements, but avoid loud colors that might be distracting or hard to read.

To give your visuals a unified appearance, use the same background color on all images. Maintain good contrast between important information and background. Use light letters (for example, white or yellow) on a dark background or dark letters on a light background.

Text

Slides aim at the visual portion of the brain. If they are jam-packed with information, they'll confuse the audience. If you use slides, include lots of white space and keep words to a minimum using uppercase and lowercase letters. If your slides are self-explanatory, you probably have too much wording on them. Remember, this is a presentation, not a paper. You add value to your presentation with your eloquent speaking abilities, not by cramming words on a slide.

Equipment Operation

If you use a computer data projector, an overhead slide projector, or a 35-mm projector, it helps to ask a friend to operate the equipment. This person should be familiar with your presentation. Give the person an outline that indicates when to display and remove the visual aids.

If you don't have a friend to help, see if you can use a remote-control device to operate the equipment. This will allow you to move around a bit. Make sure you practice with the visual aids before the presentation.

Visual aids are tools that can help the audience remember and understand the content of your message. But don't overdo them: When you emphasize everything, nothing seems important.

How to Use Presentation Skills

While what you say is important, the image you project as a speaker is even more important. Numerous studies have shown that people remember less than 10 percent of what a speaker says. First impressions are largely based on nonverbal communication, such as how you dress, wear your hair, carry yourself, and use gestures and other body language. Other keys to a polished delivery include your voice, the appropriate use of humor, the way you handle your notes, and your ability to overcome stage fright.

talking POINT

If you look well groomed, professional, and are well prepared, you will be the most effective visual aid in your presentation. However, it doesn't matter how convincing your slides are—if you look sloppy and appear insecure and awkward, the audience probably won't take you or your message seriously.

Aspects of Physical Behavior

Your Appearance

Looking good boosts your self-confidence and builds your credibility with the audience. Do you need a haircut? Are your shoes shined? Are your clothes clean and freshly pressed? Are your buttons buttoned?

Your posture also creates a general impression of you as a speaker. Stand straight and alert, but relaxed. Don't lean on the podium, rock back and forth, or slouch on one leg and then the other.

Eye Contact

As soon as you're at the podium, establish eye contact with the audience. Let the audience know you are looking at them and talking to them. Effective eye contact is *direct* and *impartial*. Don't stare, but do look at the audience. Look slowly from one side of the room to the other. This is the best way to get audience feedback and hold listeners' attention. A speaker buried in his or her notes loses listeners. Effective eye contact is powerful and enhances your credibility.

Facial Expressions

Use facial expressions, but don't overdo them. Use them the same way you would if you were engaged in a casual conversation. You should not smile or frown continuously, but use these expressions as necessary to reinforce your ideas.

Body Movement

Everyone has quirks of movement. Usually they're not noticeable. But when you're standing in front of an audience for a long time, they may become a distraction. Be aware of your typical body movements. Keep yourself in check, and always seek feedback. In time, you will have speaking down to an art.

The following describe some of the types of speakers who have movement challenges:

- **The life-rafters**—These speakers cling to the podium or lectern.
- **The hand-washers**—These speakers store all their nervousness in their hands—while speaking, they wash and wash.
- **The caged tigers**—These speakers continually pace from one side of the room or stage to the other.
- **The rockers**—Rockers unconsciously move backward and forward, or side to side, or both.
- **Pocket maniacs**—These speakers jam their hands in their pockets.
- **Pen clickers**—These speakers have to be doing something with their hands—they are compelled to manipulate and click any pen in their possession.

Gestures

Gestures are *the purposeful use of your hands, arms, shoulders, and head to reinforce what you are saying.* Your gestures should appear natural and spontaneous. Used appropriately, they add life and vigor to your presentation. Inappropriately used, they can be a distraction to the audience. Make your gestures slowly and naturally, and watch your timing. Be sure they are consistent with what you're saying. Make them add meaning to your presentation. Practice your gestures in front of the mirror.

Your Voice

Using your voice is just like playing a musical instrument. You have control over the sounds that your voice makes—the rate of speaking, volume, pitch, and pause. You can learn to control your voice in each of these areas. Use your voice to create interest in your presentation and drive home your ideas and information.

Rate

Rate is *the speed at which you speak.* There's no single correct rate of delivery that works for every talk. You might consider this fact, however: People can listen four to five times as fast as the normal speaking rate of 120 words per minute. If you speak too fast, your talk will be impossible to understand. If you speak too slowly, your audience will find it harder to follow your meaning. And if you do not vary your speed, your voice will be monotonous and you may lose your audience's attention. A faster rate communicates excitement or sudden action, and a slower rate sounds calm or tired. Use the rate of speech that is most appropriate to the ideas you are expressing.

Volume

Volume is *how loudly or softly you speak.* It's another verbal technique that can give emphasis to your talk. Before you speak, survey the room where you will deliver your talk, if possible. Take time to practice talking in the room. Bring along a friend. Ask the friend to move to various parts of the room and tell you whether he or she can hear you. Know how loudly you must talk. Remember that when the room is filled with people, you will need to talk louder because their bodies will absorb the sound. If the audience members must strain to hear you, they will eventually tune you out.

Change your volume to emphasize a point. Using a softer level or lower volume is often a more effective way to achieve emphasis than shouting is.

Pitch

Pitch is *the highness or lowness of a sound.* To use pitch effectively, you need to practice as a singer does. Begin at a pitch that is comfortable for you, then move up or down your scale for emphasis. You can use pitch changes in individual letters, in words, or in entire sentences. You can use a downward (high to low) inflection in a sentence to indicate certainty and an upward (low to high) inflection for an air of uncertainty. (For example, think about how your voice naturally rises at the end of a question.) A varied pitch rivets the listener's attention.

A habit has developed over the past few years, especially among young people, in which speakers raise their inflection at the end of a statement just as they do for a question. This goes by several names: *high rising intonation, uptalk,* or *valleyspeak.* For many listeners, this creates a strange effect after several sentences—it makes the speakers sound as if they don't know whether what they are saying is correct.

People who "uptalk" when giving a presentation or telling a story sound to others as if they are asking a series of questions instead of making a series of statements. For example:

- *We went to the baseball game Sunday, because my dad won tickets at work?*
- *The Braves were playing the Cardinals?*
- *The weather was great, and we all had hot dogs, fries, and ice cream for lunch?*
- *The Braves first baseman hit the longest home run ever at Turner Field?*

Listen to yourself when you talk, see if you are doing this without realizing it, and try to avoid it.

Pause

A pause is *a brief halt in your presentation*. It gives you time to catch your breath and the audience time to collect your ideas. Never hurry a presentation; pause occasionally so your audience can digest your comments.

When it comes to pauses, the important questions are where to make them and how long they should be. Pauses serve the same function as punctuation in writing. Short pauses are like commas; they usually divide points within a sentence. Long pauses are like periods; they note the ends of sentences. You can also use even longer pauses for breaks from one main point to another—to separate the body from the conclusion of your presentation or to set off an important point worthy of short reflection. In this case, the pause has the role of a paragraph in writing.

A pause may seem long to you, but it's usually much shorter than you think—and your audience will appreciate it. Don't get pause-happy, however, and make your presentation sound choppy.

Articulation and Pronunciation

Two other aspects of your voice are articulation and pronunciation. The way you use them indicates your oral command of the English language. Articulation is *the art of expressing words distinctly.* Pronunciation is *the ability to say words correctly.* Listen to yourself and make your words distinct and understandable.

You can articulate a word correctly and still mispronounce it. If you are not sure of a word's pronunciation, consult a current dictionary—before you get up and give your presentation. You can even look up online dictionaries with audio links that will pronounce the word for you.

Vocalized Pauses

This is the name given to the syllables *a, uh, um,* and *ah* that often occur at the beginning of a speaker's sentence. While a few vocalized pauses are natural and don't distract, too many get in the way of effective communication. If you find yourself saying them, pause, collect your thoughts for a moment, then continue.

Humor

One way to capture and hold your audience is by using humor. But be careful! What one person thinks is funny may turn another person off completely. Always make sure your humor won't offend anyone.

The best sources for humor are the tried-and-true quotes from famous people who wrote humorous works. Quoting Mark Twain, Erma Bombeck, Will Rogers, and others can add zip to your talk and keep your audience stimulated. There's also a benefit for you: Hearing your audience laugh will give you a boost and build your confidence. There's almost no greater thrill in the world than making a roomful of people laugh.

Not sure whether a humorous line or joke will work? When practicing your talk in front of a test audience, pay attention to how your listeners react to the humor. If they don't laugh at a joke during the trial run or object to it, take it out.

Handling Your Notes

Unless you're an extremely talented speaker—or an actor—reading words aloud sounds dull. People who read presentations frequently lack spontaneity. They stand behind the lectern with their eyes glued to their script. How interesting is that?

You can use one of two methods for handling your notes:

1. Hold the manuscript in front of you with one hand high enough that you can see it without bending your head, but not high enough to hide your face. The other hand will be free to turn pages and gesture.

2. Place your notes on a speaker's stand or table so that both hands are free to gesture. Make sure, however, that the paper is high enough that you can read from it without bending over. Remember to let your eyes, not your head, drop to the paper.

It is important for you to rehearse your presentation so you can deliver it well while handling your notes so smoothly the audience won't notice them.

Overcoming Stage Fright

Before you actually speak, your biggest challenge will be to overcome (or at least control) stage fright. Stage fright is *the nervousness you feel when appearing in front of an audience—seen in misdirected energy, excitement, and anxiety displayed in your behavior.* Everybody experiences some degree of stage fright. Most people get a little nervous, and a few become physically ill. You may have witnessed a great presentation "gone bad" solely because the speaker's nervousness took over.

How do you banish stage fright? First, realize that your nervous energy is a tool you can use. Good actors know that, and they channel their nervousness into great performances.

Second, try taking a short walk right before you go on stage to help release some energy.

Third, know the first couple of sentences of your presentation cold. Usually, this includes the introduction and the transition into the first main point. This makes it much easier to get through the first minute, which is the most difficult.

Practicing and Giving Your Presentation

Read your presentation aloud several times, perhaps once a day for several days if you have time. Try to make your talk sound as if you are having a conversation. Act as if you were thinking the words for the first time as you read them. Edit words that are difficult to say. Make necessary changes on the manuscript. Practice looking at your make-believe audience most of the time as the manuscript becomes more familiar to you. Provide the punctuation through vocal inflection, variety, and pauses.

Another strategy is to record yourself on your computer or other recording device—listening to the playback will help you discover places where you may not be communicating effectively.

Even with this practice, you won't be able to judge the effect of your presentation on another person. Most people are poor judges of their own presentations' quality. That's why it's important to practice the presentation in front of a critical listener and ask for feedback. If you can find two people willing to listen, that's even better. If possible, hold the practice session in the room where you will make your presentation. Practice walking to and from the podium. Do your visual aids work? Are you hitting a smooth flow? Does the presentation sound natural? Practicing your presentation will help you polish your delivery.

Remember that your audience wants you to succeed.
wavebreakmedia/Shutterstock

The big moment has arrived. Walk to the podium. Take out your notes. Take a deep breath. Look slowly around the room. Survey the audience from left to right. Project confidence. Begin in a strong, self-assured voice. As you proceed, keep eye contact with the audience. Look for feedback (nods, puzzled looks, and so forth). Let members of the audience know you are looking at and talking to them. Smile!

Use natural gestures to relieve tension. Chances are your audience won't notice your nervousness if you don't telegraph it to them.

If you can capture and hold your audience during your introduction, you're halfway home. Keep moving forward, always paying attention to audience feedback. Once you've made your main points, you can close with confidence. After saying "In conclusion," end it. Smile and nod your head toward the audience while saying, "Thank you."

Although preparing a talk can be hard work, for many people the hardest part is presenting the talk. Questions speakers most often ask are: How many notes should I use? How can I overcome nervousness? What kind of physical behavior is appropriate for me when I speak? What if my voice isn't suited to speaking before a group? How can I project sincerity and enthusiasm?

The quickest way to find the answers to these questions is by speaking. The more you do it, the better you'll get, and the faster you'll work the kinks out of your delivery style. Continue to ask for feedback from people who've heard you speak. One of the most important things to remember: Your audience wants you to succeed.

talking POINT

Some Tips for Speakers

- "Tell them what you're going to tell them; tell them; tell them what you told them."
- "Be clear, be quick, be gone."
- Use visual aids to help the audience "dig in" to what you have to say.

Lesson 3 Review

Using complete sentences, answer the following questions on a sheet of paper.

1. Where does the word *auditorium* come from?

2. What two things are important preparations for speaking?

3. What are the three basic purposes of speaking?

4. What are the three types of speaking?

5. What three parts does every presentation need?

6. What is the "old rule" of public speaking?

7. What are five examples of visual aids?

8. What happens to audience retention when you use visual aids?

9. What are most first impressions based on?

10. What purposes do pauses serve in presentations?

11. What should you do when practicing your presentation?

12. What's the best way to judge the effect of your presentation on another person?

APPLYING YOUR LEARNING

13. Think about two different speakers you've heard recently. These could be politicians, religious leaders, sports announcers, teachers, actors, or musicians. Which one do you remember better? Why do you think that is? Compare the two, and explain why you think one was more effective than the other.

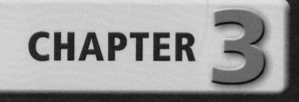

Understanding Your Attitude

Chapter Outline

LESSON 1

Interpreting Events and Experiences

LESSON 2

Developing a Positive Attitude

LESSON 3

What It Takes to Be a Leader

Patience and perseverance have a magical effect
before which difficulties disappear and obstacles vanish.

John Quincy Adams

Interpreting Events and Experiences

Learn About

- interpreting events and experiences
- the hierarchy of needs
- the importance of a positive outlook on life
- how perspective molds your understanding of life
- how perspective molds your purposes, passions, and practices
- how personality shapes your perspective and motivation
- how actions reveal your attitudes

Interpreting Events and Experiences

Learning how to interpret events and experiences is a big part of growing up. Your experience—what happens to you and what happens in the world around you—and how you interpret that experience have an enormous influence on your daily life and your future.

In history classes and elsewhere, you've read about how people like President Abraham Lincoln, pilot Lieutenant Colonel Jimmy Doolittle, and activist Rosa Parks made crucial decisions based on what they believed they were capable of doing. Their early life experiences helped them understand their potential. Potential is *your promise—what you are capable of doing or becoming*. Respected people such as retired Army General Colin Powell, US Senator John McCain, and actress Meryl Streep frequently speak about how experiences early in their lives helped them decide what they wanted to do as adults.

Your perspective and personality—your attitudes and behaviors—make you who you are.

Image Point Fr/Shutterstock

That's not to say people who achieve greatness never make mistakes—they'll admit they've made plenty! But they also say that their experiences molded them into the successful people they became. They accepted challenges and kept going. They persevered. *They became the result of their potential.* As one old saying puts it, "As the twig is bent, so grows the tree."

Growing up isn't just about getting older, even though at times you may think so. That's because for some things, such as getting a driver's license or being able to vote, age alone is an important requirement. But really growing up—reaching maturity—is much more. It means learning what's required to develop a positive attitude and then putting that attitude to use to meet life's challenges.

Maturity is *the state of being fully grown or developed.* Reaching maturity is the process of bringing your personality and experience to bear on your life in a positive, constructive way. Attaining maturity means becoming more aware of your abilities, your goals, and your place in the world. It also means understanding how your attitudes and behaviors affect you and influence others.

Experience shapes your personality. Personality is *what you are inside and what you show to others. It includes your actions, opinions, beliefs, biases, desires, and ambitions.* Personality is the foundation of your attitudes and behaviors. An attitude is *a thought, feeling, or belief.* A behavior is *an action that others can see you doing.* Attitudes are internal, and behaviors are external.

This lesson will help you become more aware of how your attitudes and behaviors make you who you are and who you are becoming as a result of your experience. Some people humorously define experience as "that thing you get just *after* you need it." That observation is true. Your experiences are a rudder as you navigate the course of your life. And just as skiers usually do better the *second* time they ski down a mountain course, you'll make better decisions as you mature. You will learn how to interpret events and experiences to make better decisions about where you want to go, what you want to do, and who you want to be.

Vocabulary

- potential
- maturity
- personality
- attitude
- behavior
- motivation
- hierarchy
- self-actualization
- perspective
- affiliation need
- belief
- desire
- goal
- intrinsic motivation
- extrinsic motivation
- achievement

The Hierarchy of Needs

Psychologists, who study people's mental processes, have always been interested in the ways personality, attitudes, and behaviors affect each other. Researchers have developed a number of theories to explain why people behave the way they do. These theories have two things in common. First, they all deal with both the inside and the outside of the person. Second, they all describe a series of steps, or levels, of human motivation.

Motivation is *the inner force that drives people to act.* The desire to get good grades is a source of motivation. It drives you to work hard, study for tests, and hand in your homework on time. The desire to be well liked and have friends is also a motivator. But motivations can also be physical: Consider that urgent feeling you get after school that moves you directly toward the refrigerator or snack bar! Some psychologists say it's possible to study, describe, and rank the factors that motivate people.

In the 1950s, psychologist Abraham Maslow proposed a "hierarchy of needs" to describe people's needs and motivations (Figure 3.1). A hierarchy is *a ranking, or series of steps, that follows a specific order*—for example, largest to smallest, oldest to newest, most important to least important, basic to complex. Maslow's hierarchy of needs includes five basic human needs:

FIGURE 3.1

Maslow's Hierarchy of Needs

microvector/Shutterstock

- **Physiological needs**—food, water, breathing, shelter, clothing
- **Safety needs**—personal and community security
- **Love and belonging needs**—family, friendship, affiliation, group acceptance
- **Esteem needs**—self-esteem, confidence, respect, recognition, achievement
- **Self-actualization needs**—realization of potential

As you can see, this hierarchy moves from the most basic needs, such as food and water and safety, to more-complex needs. Maslow believed people must satisfy each need in a particular order beginning with basic physiological needs. When the needs are satisfied at each current level, a person can progress on to the succeeding level.

After people fulfill their physiological and safety needs, they look to satisfy their needs for friendship, group acceptance, and love.

RyFlip/Shutterstock

According to this theory, as a person meets the needs at each level, he or she becomes more flexible and has more options. In other words, you can't make good decisions about your future if you're constantly hungry. Or, if your family is undergoing a crisis (belonging need), getting good grades (realization of potential) might not be one of your priorities.

Self-actualization, or personal fulfillment, is the highest need on Maslow's hierarchy. Self-actualization is *the process of becoming what you are capable of becoming*. It is realizing your potential. The drive for self-actualization is inborn in every human being. But again, other needs precede self-actualization. To become a major league baseball pitcher, for example, you first must have a place to live and regular meals. You must also belong to a team.

The Importance of a Positive Outlook on Life

Always look on the bright side of life.

Let a smile be your umbrella.

When life gives you lemons, make lemonade!

These everyday sayings emphasize the importance of a positive outlook on life. But you've also no doubt heard people say, "Colin has *such* an attitude," or "Sophie needs to chill." Those observations reflect negatively on Colin and Sophie. Why? How would their ongoing bad attitudes affect your friendship with them?

Your Attitude Is a Compass

Remember, your attitude is made up of your thoughts, feelings, and beliefs. It's your "slant" or "angle" on life. Your attitude determines your outlook and approach to life. It's like a compass—you go in the direction the needle points.

When you do positive things, you develop a more positive attitude.
michaeljung/Shutterstock

Fortunately, your attitude is largely under your control. It's essential to understand this. Attitude is not something you are born with. Some experts say that you can "program" your attitude like a computer, just by repeatedly thinking and saying positive things about yourself and others. You can change your attitude and mood simply by changing how you think and talk. Psychologists think that's how attitude works. It *follows* your behavior. If you *do* positive things, you'll slowly develop a more positive attitude.

I'm OK, You're OK

In 1969 psychologist Thomas Anthony Harris wrote a book called *I'm OK, You're OK*. It became one of the most successful self-help books ever published. For many readers, Harris's ideas clicked. The ideas were very simple, yet they reflected what millions of people have experienced in their lives. Harris and his colleagues, basing themselves on the work of Canadian psychologist Eric Berne, summarized personality as one of four life positions or attitudes. The four positions are:

1. **I'm not OK, you're OK**—disapproving of yourself, approving of others.
2. **I'm not OK, you're not OK**—disapproving of both yourself and others.
3. **I'm OK, you're not OK**—approving of yourself, disapproving of others.
4. **I'm OK, you're OK**—approving of yourself and others.

According to Harris, most people hold Attitude 1: "I'm not OK, you're OK." These people might lack self-esteem or self-confidence. They feel inferior to other people. Someone with Attitude 2, "I'm not OK, you're not OK," would tend not to look on the bright side. Such a person would need to do a lot of work to be happy. People with Attitude 3, "I'm OK, you're not OK," might have suffered from abuse or trauma as children, according to Harris, and the results of that abuse still affect their relationships with other people. Attitude 4, "I'm OK, you're OK" is the attitude of a healthy, well-adjusted individual.

Harris believed that no matter what your attitude is to start with, you can change it for the better. Anyone can move to Attitude 4.

The Value of a Positive Attitude

Why is a positive attitude important? One good reason is that it increases the chances that others will like you. People enjoy spending time with individuals who express positive attitudes. They tend to avoid individuals with an ongoing negative attitude. Psychologists use the term *toxic personalities* to refer to people who never have a nice thing to say about anyone or anything. That's not to say you can't occasionally have a bad day or a bad week: Ups and downs are a normal part of life. So if your friend Aaron is "down" from time to time, you try to cheer him up. And he does the same for you.

But it's not pleasant to spend time with someone whose attitude is always negative. What's more, this toxic, or poisonous, attitude can rub off on others without their even being aware of it. Hanging out with toxic people, in other words, can affect your own attitude. That's why it's so important to pick your friends wisely. There's an old saying from Latin, "If you lie down with dogs, you'll get up with fleas." This points to an important truth: Bad habits, poor behaviors, and negative attitudes are contagious.

A good attitude is essential for leaders. They know that a positive attitude has a powerful influence on others. Good leaders know that "throwing out positive vibes" is essential to gaining respect and encouraging others to follow them.

How Perspective Molds Your Understanding of Life

Like everyone, you look at things in your own individual way. That's what makes you unique—an individual. Your way of seeing things is special. This diversity is one of the things that make human beings so interesting. You can constantly compare your perspective with other peoples' perspectives—those of your friends, family, teachers, counselors, rivals, heroes, and villains.

Perspective is *your way of seeing the world*. It's your take on the world— your worldview. On a deeper level, perspective includes your insight into people, things, and events. Your perspective drives the way you interpret your life experiences. It helps form your attitudes and your personality. It guides your behaviors.

"But I'm still a student," you may be saying. "My perspective is really limited." That's not the case, if you really stop to think about it. Your current perspective as a student puts you in a lively and interesting world of discovery.

Is this glass half empty or half full? It depends on your perspective. Which perspective is correct?
Maglara / Shutterstock

You have many experiences and exciting things to look forward to in the near future: getting your driver's license, getting a part-time job, dating, graduating, voting. In the longer-term, you may look forward to going to college, getting a job, marrying, and raising a family. On the far, far horizon may be retiring to a home on the beach. As you mature, you'll enjoy a broadening perspective—just as when you ride an elevator to the top of a building or climb a mountain, you start to see farther.

As you mature and accumulate experience, you'll probably start thinking more and more about how you formed your unique perspective. Human beings have done this since the beginning of history.

In fact, the ancient Greek philosophers thought that the yearning for self-understanding was as essential to human life as food and water. They believed that everyone strives toward this knowledge. It's natural for you to want to understand *why* you are thinking and doing certain things at your age. In grasping the *purpose* behind your perspective, you'll gradually begin to see how a healthy, well rounded, fair-minded perspective can guide you in your studies, your job, your friendships, your family relationships, and your future.

Right now, your perspective may be based largely on the influence of your parents, guardians, friends, and teachers. This is a normal phase of your development. These influences give you a good foundation for growth. Feeling supported and loved is an important part of developing a sound perspective on life. In fact, you may even find yourself thinking or saying that your friends and family support your worldview. But questioning assumptions is also important. Both are signs of a growing, dynamic perspective.

How Perspective Molds Your Purposes, Passions, and Practices

Your perspective drives the purposes you strive toward; your passions, or the things you feel strongly about; and the practices you follow in your life. This means that your perspective will significantly affect your success—in school, at work, in friendships, and in family relationships.

By nature, human beings are social creatures. People want to belong to a group or an organization. They want to have friends—sometimes desperately so. The need to have friends and to belong is particularly strong among teenagers. But old and young people alike seek group acceptance. This natural human characteristic is called an affiliation need, *a desire to be and feel a part of a group*. It is that comfortable sense of belonging you feel when you are part of a group.

Human beings are social creatures who want to belong to a group or an organization.

Mark Herreid/Shutterstock

Especially when you're young, the desire for affiliation can sometimes lead to actions or behaviors that run counter to the influence of your family and teachers. Sometimes peer pressure to do the wrong, unwise, or inappropriate thing is almost irresistible. When you face a choice between going along with the group or sticking with values that your parents or teachers believe are best, you put your perspective to the test. The more you know yourself, and the better you understand what you believe and why, the better you'll be able to pass that test.

Cultivating a Healthy Perspective

People's beliefs and desires help shape their perspectives. A belief is *a strong and deeply held idea that forms the basis for much of your thinking.* It can be religious, social, political, or personal. A desire is *something you deeply want for yourself and those close to you.* Desires are frequently part of your emotional and psychological motivation.

Developing a healthy perspective requires keeping an open mind and seeing things as they really are. It also involves recognizing the short-term and long-term effects of mistakes or poor choices.

Everyone makes mistakes—the trick is to learn from them. That means adjusting your behavior after you make a mistake and committing yourself not to repeat it. This self-correcting ability is your ticket to success, and it's part of a healthy perspective.

Want to avoid mistakes as much as possible? Pay attention to the signs along the road. For example, a parent or guardian may have encouraged you to participate in school clubs, sports teams, or associations. Or they may have urged you to join a religious youth organization. As you've matured, your affiliation need may have led you to experiment with involvement in various kinds of groups.

When you're trying to decide which affiliations are appropriate, focus on the big picture, not the immediate situation. Some affiliations are dead-end streets. They might seem exciting for a moment, but in the long term they might also be counterproductive, or downright dangerous. Certain social media sites, cliques, gangs, or secret clubs aren't a good breeding ground for developing a mature, positive perspective. Similarly, focusing all your attention on violent movies, music, and video games can't be good for your developing worldview.

In the 1985 movie *Witness*, one character says, "What you take into your hands, you take into your heart." That simple statement points to the direct relationship between your experience—what you see, hear, touch, taste, say, and do—and your ever-widening perspective on life.

People who have made names for themselves in the world—some of whom you probably admire as heroes—expanded their worldview by concentrating on productive purposes, passions, and practices. They set goals, got excited about them, and then worked to achieve them. You can do it, too.

People and teams who are successful set goals, get excited about them, and work to achieve them.

Monkey Business Images/Shutterstock

How Personality Shapes Your Perspective and Motivation

As you might suspect, your personality has a big influence on your perspective and motivation. Personality influences what you think is important and unimportant. Those beliefs, in turn, influence what you strive for daily and what you aspire to in the future.

Since people are so different, it is not surprising that they are driven by different things. These things are their purposes or goals. A goal is *an external aim, or end, to which you direct effort.* Psychologists call goals "incentives."

The Cycle of Goal-Directed Activity

How do your goals relate to your motivation and behavior? Your motive helps you form a goal. You then choose a behavior that is directed toward that goal. If it all works, you meet your goal.

The process works for intangible goals as well as tangible ones. Suppose you're hungry—that's your motive. Your goal activity is to satisfy your appetite—to eat. In a behavior that will lead to accomplishing your goal, you go to the kitchen. In three goal-directed activities, you put two pieces of bread in the toaster, wait until the toast pops up, and butter it. Finally, you perform the goal activity: You eat it.

Goal-directed activity and goal activity form a cycle. You learn how to get better at fixing toast, you get used to how long it takes, and you satisfy your hunger whenever it hits you. One issue that may affect this cycle is competence. For example, if you never burn the toast, other family members may start asking you to make toast for them. On the other hand, if you start getting sloppy—leaving butter all over the counter—your family members might ask you to stop.

Two Types of Motivation

Researchers divide motivation into two main types: internal (intrinsic) and external (extrinsic).

The desire to get good grades is an example of intrinsic motivation. Intrinsic motivation is *a drive people feel that is based on internal factors such as the need for affiliation, achievement, power, wisdom, and security.* Intrinsic motivation originates from within. The things that motivate you from within are your goals, needs, desires, beliefs, and attitudes—in other words, your personality.

Your teacher's offer of an extra-credit project might be an example of an extrinsic motivation. Extrinsic motivation is *a force that drives people to act that is based on factors outside the individual.* Extrinsic motivations are beyond your control, but they still have an influence on you: In other words, it's the teacher's choice to suggest an extra-credit project, but it's up to you to decide to do it.

The difference between these types of motivation can get fuzzy. In fact, one motivation theory proposes that all motivation is intrinsic. Other theories hold that you can use external factors to motivate by linking them to people's intrinsic motivations.

For example, suppose that you really want a 10-speed bike. After some thought, you decide to get a job to earn money to buy one. Your intrinsic motivation to get a job is a desire for the independence and mobility that a new bike will provide. Your boss offers you an extrinsic motivation—pay—to keep you showing up for work. Together, the two motivating factors shape your perspective, or work ethic: "Working is good because it will enable me to earn money to buy a bike, which will help me get around faster."

How Actions Reveal Your Attitudes

You've probably heard the expression "Do as I say, not as I do." It points up the close—and at times contradictory—relationship between your attitudes (perspectives, purposes, beliefs) and your actions (practices, behaviors).

If you're like most people, you want your actions to be in harmony with your attitudes. "Walk the walk, and talk the talk," right? You'd seem hypocritical or two-faced if you expressed one attitude or belief and then did something that was completely contrary. A third familiar saying, "Actions speak louder than words," also comes to mind here.

Ultimately, it's what you do, not what you say, that counts. It's through your actions that you realize achievements—*the attainment of goals and accomplish of objectives that are in line with established standards of performance or behavior.* The desire to achieve shows itself in your efforts to make friends, earn good grades, be a part of your family, join the team or band, win awards, and produce results. All these things may be part of how you define success. You direct your actions to achieving these goals.

As a potter shapes her clay, your motivations shape your perspectives and work ethic.
Nenad Aksic/Shutterstock

You can't separate actions from attitudes. Your actions, for better or worse, reveal your attitudes. Showing up late for school, practice, or work, for example, sends a message about your attitude. Dressing in a deliberately provocative, sloppy, or outrageous manner might be one way of expressing your individuality, but it probably won't score points with your family, teachers, coaches, or employer.

See if you can tell what each of the following *actions* might say about the person's *attitude*:

- Chewing and snapping gum during a lecture
- Texting a friend during dinner
- Failing to use *Mr., Mrs., Ms., Sir,* or *Ma'am* in talking with adults
- Not using a turn signal when driving
- Never saying *Please* and *Thank you* in normal conversation
- Avoiding eye contact with others
- Putting your feet up on furniture
- Losing something that you've borrowed from a friend
- Ignoring personal hygiene with hair, teeth, bathing, and clothing

Ice hockey legend Wayne Gretzky once said, "You miss 100 percent of the shots you don't take." Think about your life as a sport for a minute. Are you a team player? Do you follow the rules? Take your shots? What's your attitude?

Intrinsic Motivation

Common intrinsic motivations include:

- **Affiliation**—wanting to belong to a group or to have friends
- **Achievement**—wanting to succeed
- **Power**—desiring to have control of your time, other people, situations, or things
- **Wisdom**—desiring to understand
- **Security**—wanting to be safe

Teachers, coaches, leaders, and managers know that winning breeds winning. In other words, an achievement-focused attitude can become a way of life and a positive, contagious habit. On the other hand, an attitude of negativity and "What's the use?" can create what coaches call a "culture of losing." Fostering an achievement-focused attitude leads to better results: The more you achieve, the more you're likely to achieve.

But you can't win if you sit out the game. You've got to throw yourself into it. Winning and success motivate those who value winning to push themselves even harder. On the other hand, repeatedly losing (or accepting repeated poor performance) will drain your enthusiasm and effectiveness. You'll develop a "What's the use?" attitude.

So, which team would you rather play for?

Extrinsic Motivation

Common extrinsic motivations include:

- Grades
- Money
- Food
- Threats or fears
- Status or promotion
- Awards and recognition

Lesson 1 Review

Using complete sentences, answer the following questions on a sheet of paper.

1. What do people who achieve greatness say about their mistakes and experiences?

2. What does "attaining maturity" mean?

3. What are some examples of Maslow's five basic human needs?

4. Where does the drive for self-actualization come from?

5. How can you "program" or change your attitude?

6. Which attitude did Thomas Anthony Harris believe most people hold, and which is the attitude of a healthy, well-adjusted individual?

7. What does your perspective do?

8. What did the ancient Greek philosophers think about the yearning for self-understanding?

9. What puts your perspective to the test?

10. How do you decide which affiliations are appropriate?

11. How do your goals relate to your motivation and behavior?

12. Which types do researchers divide motivation into?

13. What is the relationship between your actions and your attitudes?

14. What can an achievement-focused attitude become?

APPLYING YOUR LEARNING

15. Think about a decision you recently made. Describe the experiences that formed the basis for making that decision.

Developing a Positive Attitude

Quick Write

Why do you think it would be important to have a positive attitude? What effect might that have on others?

Learn About

- the significance of a positive attitude
- why people use defense mechanisms
- the importance of integrity and credibility
- the importance of humility and patience
- the importance of respect and appreciation
- the importance of focusing on task completion and people

The Significance of a Positive Attitude

As you learned in Chapter 3, Lesson 1, an attitude is a thought, feeling, or belief, while a behavior is an action that others can see you doing. Attitudes are internal, and behaviors are external. The attitudes and behaviors of a healthy, reasonable person are usually in harmony.

The previous lesson also discussed the difference between negative attitudes and positive attitudes. You learned that you can control your attitude. Will you have a positive attitude or a negative one? The choice is yours. This lesson will help you learn more about positive attitudes and how to develop your own.

Why do you need a positive attitude? For one thing, it will make you a happier and more successful family member, student, employee, and citizen. People are attracted to individuals with a positive attitude who can solve problems for themselves and others.

People with a positive attitude make things happen.
mangostock/Shutterstock

A positive attitude makes you a happier and more successful family member, student, employee, and citizen.

Monkey Business Images/Shutterstock

Vocabulary

- learning curve
- defense mechanisms
- displacement
- repression
- rationalization
- projection
- acting out
- denial
- integrity
- credibility
- role model
- mentor
- humility
- patience
- respect
- appreciation
- task completion
- black hole
- procrastination
- distraction

People with a positive attitude make things happen—or, as baseball executive Branch Rickey once noted, "Luck is the residue of design." He meant that if you plan things right and have the right attitude, you'll be prepared if things fall into place. It's not really luck at all. You made it happen.

Think about it. Do *you* want to hang around with people who are always saying things like, "I'm no good at anything," "I never get a break," or "I don't feel like doing anything"? That kind of thinking is not only depressing: It's contagious. If you want to be a winner (and who doesn't?), you need to think like a winner. And thinking like a winner starts with taking some concrete steps toward your goal.

Let's look at a few things you can do to develop a winning attitude.

Why People Use Defense Mechanisms

Everyone has faults and weaknesses. It's part of being human. So the first step to developing a positive attitude is to accept that you won't *always* succeed at *everything* you do. The second step is to realize that trial and error provide a wonderful opportunity to keep improving. In the business world, professionals set goals for themselves. Salespeople, for example, have sales targets. Their employers often reward them when they reach these targets. But failing to meet a goal—in business or anywhere else— doesn't mean that *you* are a failure. If a baseball player doesn't make every hit, or a lawyer loses a case, or a doctor can't cure every illness, we don't label them failures. People talk about the "practice" of law and medicine because those professionals are constantly improving their art.

Of course, some professions have a zero tolerance for failure—and it's a good thing they do. Take an architect designing a bridge, for example, or a pilot flying an airliner. You don't want them to make any big mistakes. But even the pilot isn't always on schedule. And even the best architect doesn't win every contract. Within reason, everyone is entitled to follow a learning curve—*the time necessary to get better at a task or to reach a goal.*

Why do some people handle their mistakes well, and even learn from them, while others don't? The difference often lies in a person's defense mechanisms. These are *behaviors and mental processes people use to deal with mental or emotional pain— with anxiety, shame, loss of self-esteem, conflict, or other negatives feelings and thoughts.* Defense mechanisms are normal. Everyone has anxieties, and defense mechanisms provide a way to deal with them. They can be healthy or unhealthy—it all depends on when and how much you use them.

If you're not careful, defense mechanisms can turn into excuses. People use them, often without even realizing it, to blame others or to divert responsibility from their own actions or inactions. They also use them when they've made a mistake or failed to meet expectations.

You probably don't respect the athlete, for example, who constantly makes excuses for his or her shortfalls—blaming the media, the coaches, the opposing team's noisy fans, and so on. Or how about the singer who throws a tantrum on stage and blames her band when the sound isn't just right? Constantly using defense mechanisms is a sign of an immature personality. It's the hallmark of someone who still has some growing up to do, no matter what his or her age may be.

Psychologists have identified and studied a number of defense mechanisms people use. Consider the situation of Tyler, Donna, and Tawana, as related on the next page under "How Defense Mechanisms Affect Relationships."

How Defense Mechanisms Affect Relationships

Tyler, Donna, and Tawana are all members of the high school cheerleading squad. They practice hard, but sometimes they make mistakes that embarrass them in front of the school or cost them points in state competition. The squad members often feel as though they are doing things right, but that their teammates aren't trying hard enough. They risk using one or more of the following defense mechanisms instead of addressing the real problems and improving the squad's performance.

- **Displacement**—*Transferring a feeling about a person or an object to another, less threatening object*

  Example: Tyler has a crush on Tawana, but he's upset that she sometimes misses practices or arrives late. So he yells at Donna instead.

- **Repression**—*Pushing disturbing thoughts, wishes, or experiences from one's conscious awareness while the feeling continues to operate on an unconscious level*

  Example: Donna doesn't think she's doing anything wrong, but she puts up with Tyler yelling at her. However, she's seething with resentment at both Tawana—who she thinks is the real problem—and Tyler.

- **Rationalization**—*Concealing the true motivations for one's thoughts, actions, or feelings by offering reassuring but incorrect explanations*

  Example: Tawana is doing her best to get to practice, but she sometimes loses track of the time. She doesn't think her mistakes are hurting the team, however, so she figures missing a practice here or there is no big deal.

- **Projection**—*Falsely attributing to others your own unacceptable feelings, impulses, or thoughts*

  Example: Tyler assumes that Donna feels the same way he does about Tawana's behavior, and accuses her of criticizing Tawana unfairly.

- **Acting out**—*Using actions rather than words to express the emotional conflict*

  Example: Tyler hides Tawana's knapsack, but makes it look like Donna did it.

- **Denial**—*Refusing to acknowledge some painful aspect of external reality or one's own experience that would be apparent to others*

  Example: Tyler doesn't realize that his inability to confront Tawana about her attendance is creating conflict within the squad and hurting its performance even more.

How many of these defense mechanisms do you recognize? Have you ever used any of them yourself? Because defense mechanisms can be unconscious, people sometimes use them without even knowing it. If the cheerleading squad is to work through its issues and improve its performance, Tyler needs to realize that he needs to talk to Tawana about showing up for practice; Tawana needs to understand that her absences are hurting the squad's performance; and Donna needs to talk to Tyler about his treatment of her.

A positive attitude can make it easier to handle life's troubles and work with others.
auremar/Shutterstock

Mature people don't fall back on defense mechanisms—mainly because they don't need them. They confront their problems directly and try to solve them. That doesn't mean they're always successful. Many times, you simply have to "grin and bear it." But growing up and developing a positive, productive attitude requires a willingness to keep working to solve an issue rather than dodge it.

Nobody comes into this world with a guaranteed perfect life. But the attitude you develop once you get here is under your control. A positive attitude can make it easier to handle life's troubles. As Norman Vincent Peale, who authored several books about positive thinking and attitudes, once wrote, "How you think about a problem is more important than the problem itself—so always think positively."

People with positive attitudes usually have other personality traits that help them meet life's challenges, frustrations, and disappointments. These people can call these traits into action to solve problems and to succeed. Some of the most important of these traits are integrity, credibility, humility, patience, respect, appreciation, and the ability to focus on task completion and on people.

The Importance of Integrity and Credibility

Who are your heroes? Whom do you admire most? What is it about those people that holds your attention and inspires you? Is it their good looks? Their wealth? The cars they drive? Their ability to make three-pointers on the basketball court? Or maybe it's something else. If you tend to admire people who always seem to say and do the right thing, you're admiring their winning attitude.

A person with a winning attitude sees the world as a whole rather than in bits and pieces. Such a person meets life's challenges in an orderly, calm, and unified way. He or she is an *integrated* person. There is harmony between the way that person feels, thinks, and acts. If you say that your friend Steve "has his act together," he is probably an integrated person.

An integrated person, in turn, expresses integrity. Integrity is *a commitment to a code of values or beliefs that results in a unified, positive attitude and approach to life*. For many people, their integrity is their most prized possession. They value honesty and a straightforward manner in dealing with others and events.

People with integrity are trustworthy. If you are trustworthy, people believe that what you say and do has value. In other words, you have credibility. Credibility is *a quality of character that inspires others to trust and have confidence in you—when you say or do something, people believe you.*

People learn integrity and credibility from role models. A positive role model is *a person with integrity and credibility on whom others base their own attitudes and actions.* A role model's values and behaviors, good or bad, rub off on others. Role models can be parents, guardians, grandparents, aunts, uncles, big brothers or sisters, neighbors, teachers, coaches, counselors, club advisers, community leaders, religious leaders— just about anyone. You usually pick your role models out privately. They may not even know you are holding them up as a model unless you tell them.

But when a role model knows you respect him or her, and when that person takes an active interest in your development, he or she becomes your mentor. A mentor is *a life coach who guides, advises, and advocates for you in your individual life path.* A mentor can be your guide in school, sports, work, and community service—in every aspect of your life. A mentor doesn't judge or criticize you, but provides positive feedback that helps you grow. A mentor is your custom-made role model. A mentor can also become a lifelong friend. Do you have positive role models? Do you have a mentor?

People learn positive values and behaviors from role models and mentors.

Monkey Business Images/Shutterstock

The Importance of Humility and Patience

Some people say that to learn anything, you have to be willing to admit that you don't know everything. They're demonstrating humility. Humility can be hard to define. You could say that humility is *not thinking you are superior to or better than other people.* It's the opposite of pride and arrogance. A humble person is willing to learn from others. People with humility don't think they have all the answers. This attitude puts them in a frame of mind where they can grasp new concepts and ideas.

But several mental states can block your ability to learn. These include fear, pride, and indifference.

Fear

Suppose you're taking an advanced math class. It's the first day of class. You page through the text and realize that you'll have many new concepts to master.

If you're not a math whiz, one result might be a fear of failure. Lots of people become "math phobic" because of this fear. Fear is an emotion that people may feel when they face something new or unknown. Fear can freeze your ability to respond. It cuts off the learning process.

If you're math phobic, a good teacher can help you overcome this fear. Such a teacher will help you realize that mastering any new subject takes time and patience. Overcoming other fears, such as fear of driving in heavy traffic or flying, also requires time and patience. Patience is *the ability to bear difficulty, delay, frustration, or pain calmly and without complaint.* A patient person calmly awaits the outcome or result. He or she is not hasty or impulsive. According to the old expression, "Patience is a virtue." But it's also a learning tool. If you don't understand something, you have to give it time to sink in.

Pride

Pride is an exaggerated feeling of self-worth. It can also be a barrier to learning. It can be both positive and negative. On the negative side, pride is the inner voice in some people that says, "I'm better than this. I know all about this. No one can tell me anything!" Pride can lead to negative attitudes about learning, about people, and about life in general. Self-esteem and confidence are fine, but pride goes a step further. A person who is proud ignores the needs and wants of others.

Indifference

The worst hurdle to learning is *indifference*—sometimes labeled the "whatever" mindset. Someone who is indifferent has no desire to get better at anything— whether it is playing an instrument, mastering a sports skill, meeting new people, completing a project, or being a good student or employee. The indifferent person is bored. He or she can't be bothered to pitch in or even to pretend to be interested in what's going on— in class, on the field, or at work.

Indifference has nothing to do with aptitude or intelligence. In fact, sometimes the people who exhibit this attitude are the smartest people in the group. They have the most to contribute in terms of helping others understand and learn. But they just don't want to.

Humility and patience are the keys to defeating fear, pride, and indifference. You can learn to be humbler and more patient if you want to. How does this benefit you? The answer to that question is complex but richly rewarding. When you show interest in other people, they will show interest in you. You will make connections with them.

Remember Maslow's hierarchy of needs? By being a participant, an interested party to the business of life, you move up in the hierarchy from the basic needs, such as food and sleep, to the higher levels of human functioning. You belong. You learn to love and to be loved.

The Importance of Respect and Appreciation

Unfortunately, there aren't many prestigious awards for being a nice person. You'll never win a Nobel Prize simply for being a decent human being. But you can earn intangible awards for your attitudes toward others. If you accept responsibility for yourself and show concern for others—in other words, if you do your duty to others—people will reward you with their respect and appreciation.

When you accept responsibility for yourself and show concern for others, you gain others' respect and appreciation.

Pressmaster/Shutterstock

Respect

Respect is *the esteem, regard, and consideration that you pay others and that you earn from them.* The way some people talk about respect, you'd think it was one of Maslow's first-level needs, right there with food and water.

"Graham dissed me yesterday about my jump shot." "Patti dissed her mother right out in public." You know the story: "dissing" someone means you pay him or her no respect—in fact, you insult the person by "*dis*respecting" him or her. Getting dissed hurts, doesn't it? It makes you angry and frustrated. Why? Because respect is like food and water. Every human being feels a deep-seated need for respect. It's in your nature to want it.

How do you get respect? The answer is simple: You *earn* it by respecting others. Here are some basic ways you show respect for others:

- **Listen**—People who listen in conversation are attractive to others—especially to people who like to talk.

- **Be polite**—Don't interrupt people when they're talking. Wait for a pause in the conversation before plunging ahead with what you think. Always say "please" and "thank you."

- **Keep your word**—When you say you're going to do something, have the integrity to do it.

- **Be on time**—When you agree to be somewhere at a set time, show up on time. Don't keep people waiting—their time is as valuable as yours.

- **Don't spread gossip, rumors, or loose talk about anyone—even if you have firsthand experience**—Your listeners will wonder what you're saying about *them* behind their backs.

- **Always give people the benefit of the doubt**—Before you judge people, consider how you'd feel if you were in their shoes. Realize they may be facing challenges you know nothing about.

- **Practice the "abundance theory"**—That way of thinking says there's enough of everything to go around—credit, glory, admiration, friendship, smiles, laughter, and compliments. Everybody needs them, and you can dispense them for free. Encourage other people and help them feel important.

- **Stick with what's important: people, their feelings, and their needs**—Pay particular attention to the person who's helpless or disadvantaged.

- **Don't take yourself too seriously**—Lighten up any situation with a joke about yourself. Help everyone in a conflict preserve his or her dignity.

- **Keep a flexible mindset**—You'll be better able to bend without breaking when life and other people draw on your time and energies.

Appreciation

A wise teacher once said, "It's hard to be grateful and unhappy at the same time." **Appreciation** is *the admiration, approval, or gratitude that you express to others and receive from them.* You show your respect for people when you express appreciation for what they do. They will be grateful, and show you their appreciation in return. This aspect of a positive attitude has a practical side, as illustrated by the anecdote that follows.

A young woman applied for a job and got an interview. The next day, she wrote a note of appreciation to the employer, thanking him for the interview and the chance to talk about the job. The employer interviewed five people that day. All were well qualified. But this young woman was the only interviewee to send a follow-up note. Guess who got the job? Showing your appreciation—especially by writing a note, letter, or e-mail—is not corny or old-fashioned. It is a wonderful way to demonstrate your maturity and positive outlook. And it may one day land you that position you want.

The Importance of Focusing on Task Completion and People

By now you've learned that teachers, parents, and employers value a positive attitude. You've also found out that a positive attitude includes personality traits such as integrity, credibility, humility, patience, respect, and appreciation. Two more things round out the picture: a focus on task completion and a focus on people.

Task completion is *the process of doing things expected of you in a timely, orderly, accurate, and honest manner.* To complete a task successfully you must set aside enough time for each of your classes, sports, and other activities. Doing this efficiently requires that you:

* Recognize things that waste your time
* Set goals that will reduce patterns of wasted time
* Adopt a system that will move you toward your personal, educational, and career goals

Keeping Calendars

To begin this process, you must first gain control of your greatest asset: time. Start by creating your own semester calendar that includes all classes, key assignments, fitness workouts, sports events, extracurricular activities, social events, and other important activities. In addition to keeping a daybook or calendar, make daily or weekly "to do" lists. Your computer, tablet, or smartphone may have calendar and other apps to help you do this.

Avoiding Black Holes

Once you start keeping a calendar, you may become aware of a strange entity: the black hole. Astronomers originated this term. For them, it's a point in outer space where a massive object pulls in all the light near it. In theory, nothing can escape the tug of the black hole. In your schedule, a black hole is *a period of time that eats into your productivity and prevents you from reaching your goals*. Black holes devour your productive time.

Being able to identify black holes is one of the most important aspects of task completion. To identify your black holes, make a list or diagram of how you use your time in a typical week. Within that week, chart a typical day. Most people are surprised at how much time disappears into a black hole. That time is unfocused and unstructured. It has no specific goal or purpose. It is wasted.

One main cause of black holes is procrastination—*the process of putting things off.* A second cause is distraction, or *anything that takes you away from your planned activities*. If you can overcome these two sources of black holes in your life, you'll be a lot closer to making better use of your time. And again, success breeds success. The better you get at doing things on time, the better you'll get at scheduling time for fun, such as hobbies, sports, social activities, and other things you enjoy.

Devoting Time to People

If you're able to stop wasting time, you'll have more time to devote to people. People you care about—your family, friends, relatives, classmates, and neighbors— know you best by the time you devote to them. The time you're willing to spend with others, more than any other single thing you say or do, shows your focus on people.

According to Maslow's hierarchy of needs, people begin their journey toward self-actualization by focusing on physical and safety needs. The middle stages in the journey focus on relationships with people and your place in society. Only when you move beyond these can you arrive at the fifth level, self-actualization.

So what does a positive attitude have to do with those middle stages, in which you form relationships with others? Having a positive attitude means trying to be on good terms with everyone. You must be able to work with other people in teams and focus on helping others. You need these skills to get along in high school and later in life— no matter what kind of a career you have. A team, group, or organization of any type can succeed only when its members can get along.

When you're talking with others, be a good listener: Ask about their families, interests, and hobbies. Don't hog the conversation. Stay away from controversial topics—such as politics and religion—and avoid off-color jokes.

When you're talking to others, be a good listener: Ask about their families, interests, and hobbies.

g-stockstudio/Shutterstock

At some point, you'll find yourself dealing with people of questionable character. It's best to distance yourself from such people and be careful about including them among your friends. Never do something that you know is wrong just because others are doing it. You always have the option of saying "No," and of going to a family member, teacher, counselor, clergy member, or neighbor and talking to him or her in confidence about how you're feeling.

Relationships with other people are often complicated. By following the suggestions in this lesson for getting along with and respecting others and yourself, you'll find that developing a positive attitude isn't as hard as you might have thought. And any work it does require will be worthwhile—the benefits are lifelong and enormous.

Lesson 2 Review

Using complete sentences, answer the following questions on a sheet of paper.

1. Why do you need a positive attitude?

2. What does thinking like a winner start with?

3. What are five common defense mechanisms?

4. What does growing up and developing a positive attitude require?

5. How does a person with a winning attitude see the world?

6. Who can be a role model?

7. What are the opposites of humility?

8. What mental states can block your ability to learn?

9. What are six ways you can show respect?

10. What will happen when you express appreciation to people for what they do?

11. What must you do to set aside enough time for each of your activities?

12. What, more than anything, shows your focus on people?

APPLYING YOUR LEARNING

13. Write a three-minute script for your first meeting with a potential mentor. What kinds of questions would you ask your mentor? What sorts of questions do you think the mentor would ask you? What would be your goals for the relationship?

What It Takes to Be a Leader

What Is a Good Leader?

A leader is _someone who can influence or guide other people toward a shared goal_. The goal might be to get a group job done, reach a mountaintop, or win a game. Leaders respond positively to adverse circumstances as well as to opportunities. They tap the qualities of their character, personality, and attitude to respond to challenges in a positive manner.

Good leaders lead by example. They don't sit on the sidelines; they're part of the action. They also realize that leadership is service to those whom they wish to influence.

You might have heard the statement, "Leaders are made, not born." In other words, becoming a leader takes work. No one hands you leadership on a silver platter. You must earn it. In this lesson you'll learn about three of the most important traits leaders share and how these traits help leaders overcome serious difficulties.

Good leaders lead by example—they're part of the action.
g-stockstudio/Shutterstock

Perseverance in a Leader

Vocabulary

- leader
- perseverance
- morale
- courage

Remember Aesop's fable about the tortoise and the hare? The slow-moving tortoise won the race because it never gave up. The fast-moving hare took too many breaks. The tortoise persevered. Perseverance is *the quality of being determined and steadfast, never giving up or straying from your goal*. If you persevere, you're not a quitter.

Leaders with perseverance set their minds on a task or an objective and then work until they've achieved it. People who persevere are tenacious, which means they hold on even after others let go.

Have you ever watched a tug-of-war, or been part of one? The size, strength, and number of the two teams' members might be evenly matched. But which side usually wins? It's the one that keeps pulling and holding on until the other side gives up. It's the same with a close basketball or soccer game. The winning team is relentless: It pushes just a little further than its opponent.

Perseverance is important for a leader because it has a positive effect on the morale of team members or followers. Morale is *a mental and emotional state of enthusiasm, confidence, and loyalty in team members and followers*. A team with high morale values perseverance.

You can spot people with perseverance by watching their actions. Some actions associated with it include the following:

- Setting clear, achievable goals
- Devising a plan to reach each goal
- Working with others steadily to reach the goal
- Never making excuses or dodging a task
- Never quitting before the team or individual reaches the goal
- Accepting the fact that the task will be difficult
- Encouraging others to keep going when morale falters
- Recognizing everyone's effort and accomplishment when the goal is achieved

Many famous leaders are known for their perseverance. In fact, their perseverance was key to their success. Some of these individuals went through times of tremendous personal and professional struggle—even temporary failure. But they kept going. They persevered.

American Biographies

General Daniel "Chappie" James, Jr.
Courtesy US Air Force

Born to Be the First

In September 1975, General Daniel "Chappie" James, Jr., became the first African-American officer in the history of the US military to attain four-star general rank. At that time, he was named commander of the North American Air Defense Command (NORAD), with responsibility for all aspects of the air defense of the United States and Canada.

Born to humble beginnings on 11 February 1920 in Pensacola, Florida, he learned to fly while attending the Tuskegee Institute. After graduation in 1942, he continued civilian flight training until he received an appointment as a cadet in the Army Air Corps in January 1943.

General James was commissioned in July 1943. Throughout the remainder of World War II, he trained pilots for the all-black 99th Pursuit Squadron and worked in other assignments. During the Korean War, he flew 101 missions in fighters. Later he flew 78 combat missions into North Vietnam, many in the Hanoi/Haiphong area, and led a flight in the Bolo MiG sweep, in which seven MiG 21s were destroyed—the highest total kill of any mission during the Vietnam War.

General James was widely known for his speeches on Americanism and patriotism, which were reported in numerous national and international publications. Excerpts from some of the speeches were read into the Congressional Record. He was also much sought after as a public speaker and devoted considerable time to addressing youth groups, particularly minority students.

General James was awarded the George Washington Freedom Foundation Medal in 1967 and again in 1968. He received the Arnold Air Society Eugene M. Zuckert Award in 1970 for outstanding contributions to Air Force professionalism. His citation read "… fighter pilot with a magnificent record, public speaker, and eloquent spokesman for the American Dream we so rarely achieve." His perseverance and dedication led him to be a monumental groundbreaker.

American Biographies

Major General LaRita Aragon
Courtesy Oklahoma National Guard

The Right Place at the Right Time

Major General LaRita (Rita) Aragon became the first female general officer of Native American ancestry. She was also the first woman commander in the Oklahoma Air National Guard in 1989. Then in 2003, she became the assistant adjutant general and the guard's first woman commander.

General Aragon entered the Air Force as an Airman Basic in 1979. At the time, she had a bachelor's degree in education and a master's in guidance and counseling but didn't apply for a commission. From there, she made steady progress. General Aragon rose to the top because of her perseverance and her determination to take every opportunity she could.

"I believe that the military is one of the greatest leveling fields for equality that there is," she said.

In her climb to success, General Aragon took on every mission possible. She volunteered to serve on boards and to do jobs no one else wanted to do.

"I built a reputation for getting the job done, and I had some great supporters in my squadron and in the wing," she said. "They gave me chances to train and be visible in mission assignments."

She also interviewed for every officer position that came open in her unit. General Aragon said, "I'd applied three times, but did not give up my hope of being an officer." She received her commission through the Academy of Military Science in Knoxville, Tennessee, in October 1981.

Of her military success, General Aragon said, "I was in the right place and the right time, and had great bosses that let me open some doors to 'diversity' in the Oklahoma Military Department."

American Biographies

Then-Lieutenant Louis Zamperini examines the damage from a Japanese shell to his B-24 Liberator bomber in 1943.

Courtesy National Archives, photo no. 16801972

An Unbroken Survivor

The son of Italian immigrants, Captain Louis Zamperini was often in trouble as a boy. A police officer suggested he devote his energy to running, and by the end of high school, he was good enough to make the US Olympic team. At the 1936 Olympics, he was the top American finisher in the 5,000-meter run. In the late 1930s, he competed for the University of Southern California.

When World War II broke out, Captain Zamperini joined the Army Air Corps. He was a bombardier in a B-24 Liberator that was flying a reconnaissance mission on 27 May 1943, when his plane malfunctioned and fell into the Pacific Ocean. He and surviving crew members drifted for 47 days on a raft—constantly fighting off hunger, thirst, heat, storms and shark attacks.

When he reached land, Captain Zamperini was captured by Japanese Navy forces. He spent nearly two years enduring torture as a prisoner of war (POW). He was declared missing at sea and later "killed in action," but he returned home to a hero's welcome in 1945. Captain Zamperini received the Purple Heart, the Distinguished Flying Cross, and the Prisoner of War medal.

Zamperini went on to become an inspirational speaker. His life was changed by a meeting with evangelist Billy Graham, and he became a Christian missionary to Japan. When he returned to the United States, he created a camp for troubled youths, teaching them the skills needed to succeed in life.

In 1998 at the age of 81, he ran a leg in the Olympic Torch relay for the Winter Olympics in Nagano, Japan, not far from the POW camp where he had been held. Zamperini is the subject of the bestselling book, *Unbroken: A World War II Story of Survival, Resilience, and Redemption* by Laura Hillenbrand. It was made into a hit movie directed by Angelina Jolie and released in December 2014.

Courage in a Leader

Courage is *the mental and moral strength to withstand danger, fear, or difficulty*. But you might say that every run-of-the-mill superhero has those qualities. Isn't courage more than that? Someone once said that courage isn't the lack of fear; it's being able to hang on a minute longer than everyone else. So you can see that courage and perseverance work hand in hand. Courageous people are afraid too, but they keep going. History is full of stories about people who became admired leaders because of their courage.

How can you identify a courageous leader? Look for actions such as these:

- Keeping your head while other people seem to be losing theirs
- Maintaining a steady eye on the goal or objective
- Being willing to sacrifice for the welfare of others
- Being able to withstand suffering or difficulty
- Standing up for what's right
- Leading by example
- Accepting challenges that build your self-confidence
- Keeping a positive attitude in the face of difficulties

In an emergency or a crisis, courageous people act. They do the right thing: rescuing, fighting back, protecting. That's *mental* courage. In the face of adverse situations and events, courageous people also step up and let others know what's right and what's wrong. That's *moral* courage.

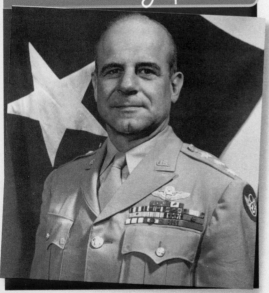

General James Doolittle
Courtesy US Air Force

Raid on Tokyo

Early 1942 was a gloomy time in America. The previous December, the Japanese had launched a surprise attack on the US Navy and Army at Pearl Harbor, Hawaii, killing more than 2,200 Sailors, Soldiers, Marines, and Airmen. In lightning fashion, the Japanese attacked and defeated American forces on Guam, Wake Island, and the Philippines, and seized Allied territory all over Southeast Asia.

President Franklin D. Roosevelt asked the US Army Air Corps to strike a blow to let the Japanese government know its territory was not safe from the war it had started, and to boost American morale. Since the Japanese had seized all the US land bases west of Hawaii and north of Australia, the Air Corps would have to launch the bombers from an aircraft carrier.

The planes had to fly over Japan and try to land in China, parts of which were also under Japanese control.

Lieutenant Colonel James "Jimmy" Doolittle volunteered to lead the mission. Colonel Doolittle was a well-known pilot who had won several aviation awards, including one for the first-ever flight completely by instruments. Doolittle led 16 B-25 medium bombers from the carrier USS *Hornet* in raids that hit targets in Tokyo, Kobe, Osaka, and Nagoya. He and his own crew had to bail out over China, but landed in a rice paddy and were rescued. Some of the other raiders lost their lives in the mission.

The exploits of the Doolittle raiders electrified the world, stunned the Japanese, and gave America's war hopes a terrific lift. President Roosevelt presented Doolittle the Medal of Honor for his courage. Doolittle's fellow raiders received the Distinguished Flying Cross. During the rest of the war, Doolittle commanded units of the Army Air Corps (later the US Air Force) in North Africa and Europe, ending the war with the rank of lieutenant general. He retired from the Air Force in 1959.

In April 2015 House and Senate leaders presented the Doolittle raiders with the Congressional Gold Medal, the highest civilian honor Congress can give.

American Biographies

Colonel Eileen Marie Collins
Courtesy National Aeronautics and Space Administration

Courage on Earth and in Orbit

As a US Air Force officer and a NASA astronaut, Colonel Eileen Marie Collins has shown uncommon courage throughout her career. She was a C-141 aircraft commander and instructor pilot and participated in Operation Urgent Fury in Grenada in October 1983. Later on as an astronaut, she became the first woman pilot of a space shuttle in 1995 and then the first woman shuttle commander in 1999.

Collins graduated in 1979 from Air Force Undergraduate Pilot Training at Vance AFB, Oklahoma, where she was a T-38 instructor pilot until 1982. She logged more than 6,751 hours in 30 different types of aircraft.

Selected by NASA in January 1990, Collins became an astronaut in July 1991. Collins served on the astronaut support team; worked in Mission Control as a spacecraft communicator; and served as the Astronaut Office Spacecraft Systems Branch Chief, Chief Information Officer, Shuttle Branch Chief, and Astronaut Safety Branch Chief. A veteran of four space shuttle flights, Collins logged more than 872 hours in space between 1995 and 2005. She piloted the first two of these flights and was commander on the other two.

In January 2005, Collins retired from the Air Force. She retired from NASA in 2006. A decorated pilot and astronaut, she was a role model in Air Force service. Her courage and determination were her keys to success.

American Biographies

Rosa Parks at a presidential award ceremony in 1999

Courtesy, William J. Clinton Presidential Library

A Seat on the Bus

In the American South before the Civil Rights Act of 1965, African-Americans had to sit in the back of public city buses. They also had to give their seats to white passengers if asked to do so. In December 1955 in Montgomery, Alabama, black seamstress Rosa Parks refused to give her seat to a white passenger. She didn't argue, but she didn't move. The police arrived and arrested her.

Parks wasn't the first African-American to be arrested for disobeying this law. But her courageous act drew attention. One reason was that she was already well known in the city's African-American community: She'd been secretary to the president of the National Association for the Advancement of Colored People (NAACP).

Parks's arrest led Martin Luther King, Jr., and other African-American leaders in Montgomery to organize a form of protest known as a boycott. Many citizens of Montgomery—whites and blacks alike—refused to ride the buses until the city changed its laws requiring segregation, the separation of people by race.

But other members of the white community fought back. The police arrested drivers who picked up people hitchhiking to work. They also arrested African-Americans waiting on street corners for rides. On 30 January 1956, angry segregationists bombed Dr. King's home.

Rosa Parks's case finally went to the US Supreme Court. On 13 November 1956, the court declared that Alabama's state and local laws requiring segregation on buses were illegal. The bus boycott had lasted 381 days.

Rosa Parks died on 24 October 2005. She was 92 years old. By the time of her death, she had earned national recognition and received many honors for her role in the civil rights movement. She left a legacy of steadfast courage in the face of racial discrimination.

Patience in a Leader

A third characteristic of a good leader is patience. Patience, as you have learned, is the ability to bear difficulty, delay, frustration, or pain without complaint. Patience does not mean you ignore your problems or just hope they'll go away. Patient leaders aren't passive, slow-witted, or "out to lunch." Patience is an active trait. A patient person keeps trying, despite the frustration. Patience means calmly and quietly bearing up under challenging circumstances.

Some actions associated with patience include the following:

- Putting the needs of others before your own
- Encouraging others to remain calm and focused in a crisis
- Choosing to do the right thing, even when the wrong thing is easier
- Accepting people's flaws and faults
- Accepting criticism with grace and confidence
- Continuing calmly and quietly to do your job
- Keeping your eye on the goal at all times
- Remaining steadfast in the face of adversity
- Being willing to wait for as long as it takes to succeed

American Biographies

Senator Daniel Inouye
Courtesy Department of Defense, photo by R. D. Ward

Patience With America

Daniel Inouye was a patient man who never gave up on America. He was born to a working class Japanese-American family in Honolulu, Hawaii, in 1924. When he was 17 years old in December 1941, the Japanese Navy attacked US forces at nearby Pearl Harbor.

Many Americans mistakenly thought that Japanese Americans had helped Japan prepare for the surprise attack. Soon after, the US declared Japanese Americans "enemy agents," and more than 100,000 were sent to internment camps in the Western United States.

In 1943, however, wiser heads allowed American children of Japanese immigrants to join the US armed forces. Inouye dropped out of the University of Hawaii and enlisted in the 442nd Regimental Combat Team, whose soldiers were all Japanese Americans. It became one of the most decorated units in US history.

Fighting in Italy, Second Lieutenant Inouye suffered severe injury to his right arm while leading his platoon in an attack on a German artillery and mortar post. The arm was later amputated in a hospital. But the platoon's victory allowed the Army to capture a ridge guarding an important rail junction. For his bravery, Inouye was awarded the Distinguished Service Cross, the Bronze Star, and the Purple Heart. When he returned to the United States, he went into a barbershop in San Francisco wearing his uniform. "We don't serve Japs here," the barber told him.

Back in Hawaii, Inouye became a lawyer and got involved in territorial politics. When Hawaii became a state in 1959, he was elected to the US House of Representatives, becoming the first Japanese American in Congress. Soon after, in 1962, he was elected to the US Senate and came to be regarded as the most powerful politician in Hawaii. He became nationally famous as a member of the Senate Watergate Committee that investigated wrongdoing in the Nixon Administration, leading to President Nixon's resignation in 1974.

Senator Inouye eventually became the longest-serving senator and thus the third person in line to the presidency after the vice president and Speaker of the House. In 2000, he received the Congressional Medal of Honor along with 21 other Asian Americans after a review of their military records.

Senator Inouye served Hawaii and the United States in the Senate until he died in 2012. The following year, he was awarded the Presidential Medal of Freedom, the nation's highest civilian honor. He was the first senator to win both the Medal of Honor and the Medal of Freedom.

American Biographies

Senator John McCain
Alan Freed/Shutterstock

Putting Others First

As a young man, John McCain fought as a Navy pilot in the Vietnam War. The North Vietnamese captured him in 1967 after shooting down his plane, and he spent more than five years as a POW in North Vietnam. Life as a POW was harsh. But because McCain was the son and grandson of high-ranking US naval officers, he received better treatment than other American POWs did.

McCain thought this was unfair. So when the North Vietnamese decided to release him and some other POWs, McCain refused to go. He thought that the POWs who had been held the longest should be freed first. As a result, his captors treated him much more severely. But that just strengthened his resolve and helped him survive.

John McCain's patience paid off. When the war ended, he returned to the United States and became one of the nation's most-respected US senators. In 2008 he was the Republican Party's candidate for president of the United States.

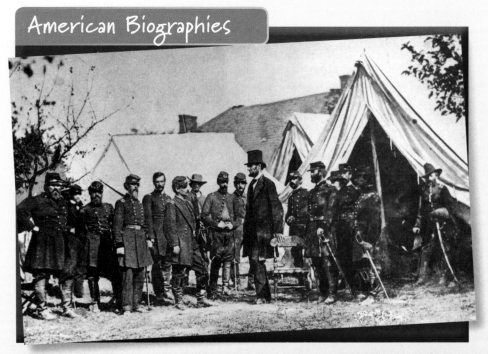

President Abraham Lincoln meeting with General George McClellan and his staff after the Battle of Antietam (Sharpsburg) in Maryland in 1862

Everett Historical/Shutterstock

Lincoln's Shrewd Patience

President Abraham Lincoln faced tremendous challenges from members of his own political party as well as from his enemies. Lincoln knew it would be better to have these influential men as allies rather than as enemies. So he decided to invite several of his rivals to become members of his presidential Cabinet. By surrounding himself with powerful men who did not always agree with him, Lincoln could get a reality check on how he was doing as president. He also could keep an eye on people who might otherwise have plotted against him.

By shrewdly making his rivals part of his team, Lincoln demonstrated his ability to trust others. He knew instinctively that this process of building trust could not be hurried. He was patient.

Lincoln led the United States during its most difficult conflict, the Civil War. As president, he was commander in chief of the Union Army. The generals whom he'd appointed to lead the fight to restore the Union tried his patience time and again. Many of these leaders became very good at camping and drilling, but they either refused to test themselves in battle or made poor decisions in combat.

Lincoln wrote letters to his generals urging them to attack the Confederate armies so that the war would end more quickly. He used reason, emotion—even humor—to convince them to move. But they either did not act, or when they did, commanded so badly that the Confederates won battle after battle. Finally, Lincoln appointed new generals—men such as Ulysses S. Grant and William Tecumseh Sherman. These men had a record of solid command in combat, and they knew that for the Union to win the war, they'd have to fight.

Lincoln's patience may have helped win the war and end slavery. He helped ensure that government "of the people, by the people, and for the people" did not "perish from the earth."

✔ CHECKPOINTS

Lesson 3 Review

Using complete sentences, answer the following questions on a sheet of paper.

1. What do leaders tap to respond positively to adverse circumstances?

2. What do leaders realize?

3. Why is perseverance important in a leader?

4. What was General Daniel "Chappie" James, Jr., the first African-American officer to do?

5. What is moral courage?

6. What award did President Franklin Roosevelt present to Lieutenant Colonel James Doolittle for his courage?

7. What are four actions associated with patience?

8. Why did President Abraham Lincoln surround himself with powerful men who did not always agree with him?

APPLYING YOUR LEARNING

9. Explain the relationship, as you see it, between perseverance, courage, and patience.

Understanding Your Actions

Parents can only give good advice or put them on the right paths, but the final forming of a person's character lies in their own hands.

Anne Frank

Integrity and Character

The Traits of Integrity

Your behaviors, beliefs, and values form your character. Character is *the inner strength you show through your actions.* A trait is *a distinguishing feature of your character.* Good citizenship involves the character traits you've learned about in previous lessons, such as courage, perseverance, and integrity. Expressing traits such as these in your daily life leads to good citizenship and personal credibility. That credibility earns people's trust and confidence, which are essential for a leader.

Having integrity means being whole: Your thoughts, actions, and words are in sync. You don't say one thing and then turn around and do another. As a result, people can trust you.

You can trust a person with integrity because you know where he or she stands. You know that such people will do what they say they'll do. Without integrity and trust, society could not function. It might eventually fall apart.

Statue of Abraham Lincoln in the Lincoln Memorial, Washington, D.C.
Tupungato/Shutterstock

Business, education, sports, entertainment, military service, politics, and government all depend on people's cooperation. You can't cooperate with people if you don't know where people stand—if you don't trust their integrity.

Of course plenty of people in government, business, and elsewhere have lied, cheated, and stolen. They've acted without integrity. While that's true, they are the exceptions to the rule. Society does not approve of such behaviors. When these people's actions are revealed and their lack of integrity has been proved, society punishes them.

Everyone values integrity. No permanent society has succeeded without it. The traits of a person with integrity include:

- Confidence
- Courtesy
- Honesty
- Trustworthiness
- Selflessness
- Service
- Credibility
- Humanity
- Justice
- Reverence
- Optimism
- Perseverance
- Patience
- Courage
- Responsibility

Which of these traits do you find hardest to express? How might you start practicing them more consistently in your daily life? Can you think of other traits to add to the list?

- character
- trait
- principles
- loyalty
- commitment
- accountable

Integrity in Action

What does integrity look like? Here are some examples:

- A girl finds a wallet on the seat of a city bus. She looks inside and finds five $20 bills. It's tempting to keep them. But she doesn't pocket the money. She gives the wallet to the driver and asks him to turn it over to the lost-and-found office. Honesty is part of integrity.

- A group of college students volunteers every week at a community center. They teach senior citizens crafts and help them learn basic computer skills. Helping people who are not as strong as you are is part of integrity.

- A boy gets a call from his friend about a homework assignment. The friend was out late at a concert and didn't do the work. "Can I see your worksheet before school tomorrow?" he asks. The boy gently tells the friend no, and asks him how the concert went. Doing the right thing, even when it's hard, is part of integrity.

People who find ways to be of service to their families, friends, classmates, teachers, and community are citizens of integrity. They don't think about themselves first. They show concern for others. "The supreme quality of leadership is integrity," said five-star General Dwight David "Ike" Eisenhower, who commanded Allied forces in Europe during World War II and became the 34th president of the United States.

AMERICANS *in action*

United Flight 93

By showing integrity, everyday people can become heroes. On 11 September 2001, terrorists hijacked four US airliners. Their goal was to crash them into highly visible targets in the United States. In three cases, the terrorists succeeded. Two planes crashed into and destroyed the World Trade Center in New York City. One plane hit and seriously damaged the Pentagon in Washington, D.C. Almost 3,000 people died.

A fourth plane, United Flight 93, didn't hit its target. It crashed in a field in Pennsylvania instead. When the plane was hijacked, passengers and crew called relatives and friends, who told them what was happening in New York and Washington. The passengers and surviving crew banded together and attacked the pilot's cabin, where the terrorists were flying the plane. These heroes lost their lives, but they probably saved many more.

"We are sure that the nation owes a debt to the passengers of United 93," wrote the 9/11 Commission that investigated the attacks. "Their actions saved the lives of countless others, and may have saved either the Capitol or the White House from destruction."

The heroism of the people on Flight 93 is an example to the world that everyday citizens have the power to influence what happens to them. The willingness of these brave passengers to act—even to sacrifice their own lives—honors and preserves the American spirit and way of life.

Being a Positive Role Model

Many people believe the crew and passengers of Flight 93 were role models for all Americans. The people you call role models sometimes aren't aware that you admire them and want to be like them. One reason for this is that role models are usually busy doing whatever it is people admire about them. They don't waste time trying to create personal fan clubs. You respect them because of their actions.

You've heard the saying "Actions speak louder than words." That's true of role models—their actions define who they are. The Greek philosopher Aristotle believed that if you're good at what you do—whether you're a carpenter, a police officer, a banker, a cook—you are worthy of other people's respect and admiration. For Aristotle, excellence in action was the most important indication of a person's character.

Are you anyone's role model? Do friends or younger siblings look up to you? It's a big responsibility to be a role model. But society greatly needs them. Who are your role models? How can you be a role model for others?

Here are some of the actions that characterize a role model:

- Approaching tasks with confidence
- Being courteous
- Being honest
- Gaining people's trust
- Thinking of others first
- Serving your family, school, and community
- Keeping a positive outlook on life
- Persevering and showing courage through challenging situations
- Being patient
- Acting responsibly
- Reserving judgment on others
- Helping people in need

These are actions everyone can take. They don't cost a thing. And you don't need a body suit, a funny mask, or a cape to be a good role model. It's just a matter of deciding that's the kind of person you want to be and the way you want to act. It's about having the right attitude. It's about letting others see your true character.

Former President Gerald R. Ford with his wife, Betty Ford

Featureflash/Shutterstock

Gerald R. Ford, the Appointed President

"Gerald R. Ford became president not because he was popular with the American public, not because he campaigned for the job, but because of his character," writes his biographer, James Cannon. "More than any other president of this century, Ford was chosen for his integrity and trustworthiness; his peers in Congress put him in the White House because he told the truth and kept his word."

President Richard Nixon nominated Ford, a congressman from Michigan, for vice president after Spiro Agnew was forced to resign in 1973 for taking bribes. At the time, Nixon was facing indictment for crimes connected with the Watergate scandal—he tried to cover up his involvement in a break-in at Democratic Party headquarters. When the House and Senate confirmed Ford, the members knew they might be choosing the next president of the United States.

"Ford personified what Nixon was not," Cannon writes. "Ford was honest. He could be trusted. Throughout twenty-five years in the House of Representatives, Ford had proved himself to be a man of integrity."

Within a few months, Nixon understood he would have to resign the presidency. He sent his chief of staff to try to make a deal: He would resign if Ford would promise to pardon him. Ford's character was severely tested—he wasn't sure what was best for the country. Finally, he rejected any deal.

A month after becoming president in 1974, however, President Ford issued Nixon a pardon. Watergate had badly divided the country, and Ford wanted to heal the divisions. Instead, many Americans were outraged. Ford was stunned—he thought the American people would agree that giving up the presidency was punishment enough for Nixon.

Many in Congress wondered if Ford and Nixon had made a deal. Ford knew he'd have to disclose that Nixon's chief of staff had asked for a pardon. He went to Capitol Hill and become the first president ever to testify before Congress. He explained what had happened: "There was no deal. Period. Under no circumstances," he said.

In 1976 Ford narrowly lost the election to Jimmy Carter. Many blamed the loss on his pardon of Nixon. But Ford never changed his view that a two-year trial of Nixon would be far more damaging to the country than the pardon.

Still, Americans understood the important role that Ford had played in shepherding the United States through a serious constitutional crisis. As President Carter expressed it in his inauguration speech, "For myself and for our Nation, I want to thank my predecessor for all he has done to heal our land."

How Character Affects Behavior

Character is the quality that people sometimes call *backbone*. Character is inside you, and it holds you up. It's standing firm for your principles, *your moral and ethical standards*. If you stand up for what you believe is right, if you protect the weak, if you work for justice, you are exhibiting character. Letting your character shine through is not always easy, but it can produce tremendous results and leave a lasting legacy.

Consider the example of an Army Roman Catholic chaplain, Captain Emil Kapaun, during the Korean War in early November 1950. When his unit was about to be overrun by Communist forces, he ignored an evacuation order and stayed behind to care for the wounded. He saved many by convincing a wounded Chinese officer to order a cease-fire.

Kapaun and wounded members of his battalion were captured and led on a death march to a POW camp. Some who were too wounded to march were shot. When Kapaun saw an enemy solider about to execute an Army sergeant, he pushed the soldier aside, saved the sergeant's life, and helped carry him the rest of the way.

During his six months as a POW, Kapaun often risked his life to steal and sneak food and hot water to his fellow prisoners. He gave his rations and extra clothing to others and provided spiritual care and guidance, despite threats from his captors. Sadly, he fell ill from numerous serious diseases and died in captivity.

Kapaun received numerous awards for heroism, and Kapaun Air Station in Germany is named for him. On 13 April 2013, his grand niece, Air Force 1st Lieutenant Kristina Roberts, attended a White House ceremony in which President Barak Obama awarded Kapaun the Congressional Medal of Honor. The men the chaplain had served had worked for decades for his recognition. The sergeant whose life he saved, Herbert Miller, was at the ceremony.

1st Lieutenant Kristina Roberts with a portrait of her great uncle, Captain Emil Kapaun
US Air Force photo illustration/Staff Sgt. Michael Means

Lieutenant Roberts, an Air National Guard officer who works at the local YMCA in civilian life, says her great uncle's legacy has shaped her life. "There hasn't been a day that I have not thought of my great uncle, especially when I was going through all my military training," she says.

"Just like my great uncle, I've always had a calling to help those around me; from adults faced with certain challenges to children who need someone to look out for them."

"He was a man who never gave up, and through it all, always maintained his integrity, faith, courage and his sense of humor. Helping others is not just a calling for me, but is a way to continue his legacy."

The Vatican is now considering Kapaun for sainthood.

Character and Loyalty

History has many examples of people of character who have served others and earned their loyalty—their *allegiance or faithfulness*. These people were old and young; they've lived everywhere in the world. Emil Kapaun, Presidents George Washington and Abraham Lincoln, civil rights leader Martin Luther King, Jr., missionary Mother Teresa of Calcutta—all knew that the secret to winning people's loyalty comes not from trying to dominate them but from serving them with respect and justice. They earned loyalty by expressing loyalty themselves to a cause, ideal, or duty. People knew what they stood for.

When you are loyal to others, others are loyal to you. Loyalty to a family member means helping him or her see the right thing to do when facing trouble. Loyalty to friends means standing up for them when others ridicule or make fun of them. Loyalty to your favorite sports team means supporting it even when it's in last place. Loyalty to your principles means sticking with them even if they are unpopular. Loyalty to the Constitution of the United States means upholding *all* its provisions— such as freedom of religion, freedom of speech, freedom of the press, trial by jury, and the submission of the military to civilian authority. It means respecting election results and the authority of all three branches of government—the administration, Congress, and the courts— regardless of who's in office.

Commitment and Responsibility

People follow leaders who have the qualities of good role models: strong character, integrity, and a willingness to serve.

Good leaders also show their followers that they are committed to achieving results. Commitment is *the dedicated focus on an idea, cause, issue, plan, or task to the exclusion of any interruption, distraction, or compromise.* A commitment to achieve results, or goals, is a major source of a leader's power.

Once they achieve their goals, leaders remain committed. They take responsibility for the results they achieve. When leaders have planned well, their results lead to improvements and progress. But that's not always the case. That's why leaders need to be responsible, or accountable—*answerable for the outcomes of their words and actions*. While many leaders in history have been irresponsible—and dodged the results of their efforts—true leaders seek out responsibility. They see it not as a burden but as a means to success.

What challenges or responsibilities have you taken on lately?

American Biographies

Former Secretary of State Colin Powell
stocklight/Shutterstock

From the Streets of New York to Secretary of State

Colin Powell was born in New York City in 1937 to Jamaican immigrants. He attended New York City public schools and then enrolled at City College of New York (CCNY). He joined Army ROTC at CCNY and received his commission as an Army second lieutenant upon graduation.

Powell served his country with distinction in Vietnam, Korea, and Europe. He became a general, served as President Ronald Reagan's national security adviser, and was named chairman of the Joint Chiefs of Staff, serving in this post under Presidents George H. W. Bush, a Republican, and Bill Clinton, a Democrat. Powell took a leadership role in planning and executing Operation Desert Storm in Iraq and Kuwait in early 1991.

Powell played a key role in expanding JROTC, which evolved from a program begun in 1916. He is credited with advancing JROTC in its current form, in part by influencing then-President George H.W. Bush in 1992 to more than double the size of the program, from 1,500 JROTC units to 3,500.

In his book, *My American Journey*, Powell wrote: "Inner-city kids, many from broken homes, found stability and role models in Junior ROTC. They got a taste of discipline, the work ethic, and they experienced pride of membership in something healthier than a gang.... Junior ROTC is a social bargain."

In 2001, President George W. Bush appointed Powell to be his secretary of state. Powell was the first African-American to serve as national security adviser, the first as Joint Chiefs chairman, and the first as secretary of state.

Powell served as secretary for four years. He later founded the Colin Powell Center to inspire young people with a sense of purpose and responsibility. In 2013, it was incorporated into the Colin L. Powell School for Civic and Global Leadership at CCNY.

Powell is a role model for many people because of his character, dedication, and unwavering loyalty to the Army, to his superiors, and to his country.

Lesson 1 Review

Using complete sentences, answer the following questions on a sheet of paper.

1. Why can you trust a person with integrity?

2. What are 10 traits of a person with integrity?

3. Why are role models sometimes not aware that you admire them and want to be like them?

4. What are 10 actions that characterize a role model?

5. What are some ways you exhibit character?

6. What does loyalty to the Constitution mean?

APPLYING YOUR LEARNING

7. What qualities did President Gerald Ford, Captain Emil Kapaun, and Secretary of State Colin Powell all share?

Personality and Actions

Quick Write

Draw a big circle on a blank sheet of paper. Label the circle "Me." Inside the circle, write five words that describe your personality. Are you outgoing or shy? Do you like to make plans or just hang loose? Do you try to analyze other people and events, or are you a "live-and-let-live" kind of person?

Learn About

- personality types and traits
- how personality influences actions
- the value of different kinds of personalities

Personality Types and Traits

As you've grown, you've no doubt become more aware that personality is a big part of who you are. Personality includes your actions, opinions, beliefs, biases, desires, and ambitions. It is the foundation of your attitudes and behaviors. It's what you are and what you show to others.

Personality determines what you like to do in school as well as in your spare time. It determines what you want to do in life. Your personality is a set of distinctive traits and behaviors that make you the person you are. Just as no two people have the same fingerprints, no two people have exactly the same personality. You are different from every other human being who has ever existed.

Some parts of your personality may change over time, but basically your personality stays pretty much the same throughout your life. Similar situations and challenges tend to cause you to react in similar ways.

Your personality is unique—you are different from every other human being who has ever existed.

Monkey Business Images/Shutterstock

The Theory of Personality Types

Psychologists, who study the mind and behavior, have long known that each person is unique. But these experts also know that people are similar in certain ways. Swiss psychologist Carl Jung, a pioneer in the field, believed that experts could categorize people's personalities based on certain personality types and on the ways in which people describe their own motivations. A personality type is *a recognizable set of functions that some psychologists believe can help you understand who you are.* You could think of it as a model that people tend to follow in their thoughts and behaviors.

Jung believed that people divide into two basic attitudes: they are either extraverted or introverted. An extravert is *a person who draws energy from people, things, activities, or the world outside themselves.* An introvert is *a person who draws energy from ideas, information, explanations, imagination, or their inner world.* Further, Jung thought that the mind has four functions: sensation, intuition, thinking, and feeling.

In the 1940s, Isabel Briggs Myers and her mother, Katherine Cook Briggs, developed the Myers-Briggs Type Indicator®, or MBTI®. They based the MBTI on Jung's work. They developed a series of 16 four-letter codes to describe people's personality types. Everybody, they believed, fits into one of these 16 types.

Your personality type is determined by your responses to four key questions, or *dimensions*:

1. **Where do you direct your energy?** You are either *extraverted* (E) or *introverted* (I) as described earlier.

2. **How do you process information?** If you prefer facts and direct evidence, you prefer *sensing* (S). If you prefer thinking deeply and trusting your inner voice you prefer *intuition* (N).

Vocabulary

- personality type
- extravert
- introvert
- personality trait
- interaction

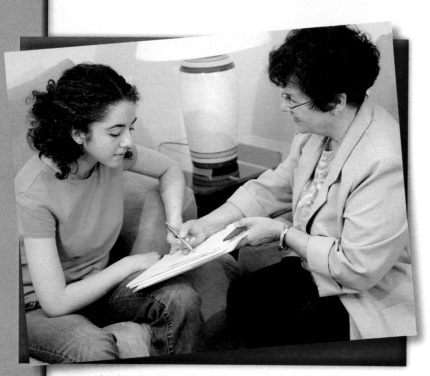

Your high-school guidance counselor might give you an opportunity to take a personality assessment.

Lisa F. Young/Shutterstock

3. **How do you make decisions?**
   If you base your decisions on logic and analysis, you prefer *thinking* (T). If you prefer to decide based on values and personal beliefs, you prefer *feeling* (F).

4. **How do you organize your life?**
   If you like things well planned, you prefer *judgment* (J). If you like to stay flexible and take things as they come, you prefer *perception* (P).

For example, if you preferred introversion (I), intuition (N), thinking (T), and judging (J), your personality would be described with the letter code *INTJ*. If you preferred extraversion (E), sensing (S), feeling (F) and perceiving (P), you'd be an *ESFP*.

The Myers-Briggs personality assessment, or test, is quite popular. Tens of millions of Americans have taken it. Many businesses use the MBTI when they're hiring. They believe it helps them know if there's a good fit between a job applicant and their workplace. Many schools and universities use the MBTI for career counseling and to help students decide what to major in at college.

Remember, however, that a personality "test" is not something you pass or fail. There are no right or wrong answers. It's just an instrument to help you understand who you are.

The Theory of Personality Traits

After more research, many psychologists today have adopted a different approach to personality: the theory of personality traits. A personality trait is *a characteristic that causes an individual to behave in certain ways*. This theory holds that people express personality traits along a spectrum of behavior instead of expressing specific personality *types*. Different people are located at different points on the spectrum for each trait between the two extremes. These theories wouldn't label a person an extravert. They would place that person somewhere in a range between extraversion on one end and introversion on the other.

Researchers have put the number of traits at anywhere from 3 to 4,000. But many psychologists now believe that the evidence shows there are five categories.

This approach is often referred to as the *Big Five* or the *Five-Factor Model*. The usual labels for the categories are:

1. **Openness to Experience**—This trait includes your degree of imagination and insight. It involves whether you have a broad or narrow range of interests.

2. **Conscientiousness**—This trait includes how thoughtful you are, how much attention you pay to details, and your ability to control your impulses. It involves how organized you are and how oriented you are to achieving goals.

3. **Extraversion**—This trait includes characteristics such as how excited you get, how social you are, and how much you like to talk. This involves how much you assert yourself and how you express your emotions.

4. **Agreeableness**—This trait includes characteristics such as how much you trust others and how much kindness you express. It also involves your affection for others and how concerned you are for others' welfare.

5. **Neuroticism**—This trait includes your degree of emotional stability and whether you are anxious, moody, irritable, or sad.

Note that in this order, the first letters of the traits spell *OCEAN*.

Not all researchers agree on the five trait categories. Some have different names for them. Current research supports the idea that these traits are universal across different cultures.

Personality trait theory is gaining increasing acceptance. Many personality tests based on it are available on the Web and elsewhere. A sample result of a test using the Big Five model might show a score like this:

- High on the openness scale
- High on conscientiousness
- High on extraversion
- Moderately high on agreeableness
- Moderately low on neuroticism

Again, the point of any personality test, using any model, is not to put you into a box. It's to help you understand yourself better. The study of personality is an ongoing process. There are theories other than those mentioned here. Further research may lead to new understanding.

Understanding your personality can be a useful tool for understanding what kind of teammate you are.

bikeriderlondon/Shutterstock

How Personality Influences Actions

Understanding your personality isn't like reading a crystal ball. It doesn't predict the future. It doesn't guarantee success or failure. It certainly shouldn't dictate how to live your life. Nevertheless, personality models can be useful tools. They can help you figure out why you react to events, situations, and other people the way you do, and which areas you might really like or do well in. For this reason, personality testing can help you with important decisions.

For example, if you are extraverted, you might prefer a job where you can be with other people. A job where you are alone most of the time might get you down. If you are introverted, on the other hand, a job with lots of alone time might very well appeal to you. An extraverted person might prefer team sports and big crowds, while an introverted person might prefer artistic activity in a quiet solo setting.

How Personality Affects Interactions

Put another way, your personality has a big influence on how you behave in interactions. An interaction is *a situation that involves you with other people in school, at work, at home, and in social life.*

Think about how your personality might influence how you behave in some typical interactions. For example, you've probably had occasion to say to yourself, "I just don't fit in here." Understanding your personality may help you understand better why you felt uncomfortable.

Understanding your personality can give you insight into your own and other people's motivation, feedings, and needs.

Monkey Business Images/Shutterstock

Now think about some interactions in which you've noticed other people's behaviors. How might those behaviors reflect their personalities? For example, you've probably seen instances where someone's behavior seems inappropriate for the situation. Perhaps you've asked yourself, "Why does Jonathan seem so out of touch with the other guys on the team?" But in other cases, you've noticed that a person's interactions seem just right: "Dave seems like a natural-born club president," you might say. What is it about Jonathan's and Dave's personalities that affected their interactions? If the two boys traded places, do you think that your reactions to their behaviors would have been the same? Why or why not?

As you observed Jonathan and David, you were taking note—without even realizing it—of personality in action. In their interactions, people continuously respond to others and others respond to them. You may feel totally comfortable in an environment where someone else is ill at ease, and vice versa. The reasons for these differences lie in your personality.

How Personality Affects Career Choices

Understanding your personality can help you make career choices. Say you like clothes—you enjoy everything about them. For the time being, your personality might make you a trendsetter. Your friends might turn to you for fashion advice. So it might be natural for you to think about working as a salesperson or manager in a clothing store, as a clothing designer, a fashion model, or as a buyer for a retail clothing chain. Or if you enjoy sports, you might want to choose a career that would put you close to sports. You could, of course, aim for a career as an NBA pro. But other, more-realistic choices include coaching, owning a sporting-goods store, or being the pro at the local golf course.

You feel comfortable doing what you like. That's why understanding your personality is useful in choosing a career path. It helps you identify your preferences.

Job counselors have divided careers into several categories to help people understand the interest areas different careers include. One version of these categories is the following:

- Realistic occupations
- Investigative occupations
- Artistic occupations
- Social occupations
- Enterprising occupations
- Conventional occupations

Pairing these with your understanding of your personality and work values— what you want most out of your career—can help you find work that is satisfying and rewarding.

The Value of Different Kinds of Personalities

Once you're aware of how personality works, you can be aware of how you react to things and how others interact with you—and why. Understanding your personality can help you get along with family and friends. It can give you insight into your relationships with people and help you understand their motivations, desires, needs, feelings, and ideas. That understanding can make you more tolerant of others' differences and can help you be a better team player—in the classroom as well as on the field.

Because your personality affects the way you process and organize information, it has a direct effect on your learning style. For example, some people learn better by doing hands-on assignments—actually getting their fingers into the work. But other people are more theory oriented and like to think things out in their heads. Some people like to learn on their own; others learn best in groups. Knowing your own personality and how it affects your learning style can help you be a more successful student or employee.

Because it makes you aware of your decision-making and organizational styles, a personality model can also help you understand what kind of leader you would be. It might even help you realize you don't want to lead at all. Some people are better suited—and more comfortable—working within an organization rather than leading it. The world offers plenty of opportunities for both.

Your personality affects your learning style. Some people like to learn on their own...

bikeriderlondon/Shutterstock

…while others learn best in groups.

Nonwarit/Shutterstock

If you recognize the variety of personalities and their powerful effect on everyone's life, you can understand why some people choose to become artists, writers, or singers while others become doctors, engineers, and scientists; why some choose to teach while others choose to run businesses; why some design and some build; and why some want to make laws and some yearn to defend their country.

What's the moral of the personality story? Each individual interacts with the world and with other people in a different way. These differences are important. They should be valued and understood, not hidden or brushed aside.

Once you recognize the importance of personality, it's easy to see why leaders in business, government, and education often use models such as the MBTI or the Big Five. The self-knowledge you can gain and the awareness of "what makes others tick" can give you a deeper appreciation of the wisdom of the old saying, "It takes all kinds to make a world."

✔ CHECKPOINTS

Lesson 2 Review

Using complete sentences, answer the following questions on a sheet of paper.

1. What is personality?

2. Who was Carl Jung, and what did he believe about personality?

3. How many personality traits do many researchers believe there are, and what are they?

4. What is the point of any personality test?

5. If you're an extravert, what kind of job might you prefer? What kind of job might an introvert prefer?

6. Why is understanding your personality useful in choosing a career path?

7. If personality gives you insight into your relationships with people, how does this help you?

8. Why does your personality have a direct effect on your learning style?

APPLYING YOUR LEARNING

9. Do you think you are an extravert or an introvert? Why?

Consequences and Responsibilities

Quick Write

In two or three sentences, describe a person you think has true leadership ability. The person can be a friend, an adult you admire, or a well-recognized leader. List some examples of this leader making a tough decision—even if it was wrong—and taking responsibility for his or her actions.

Learn About

- the consequences of taking or avoiding responsibility
- how defense mechanisms affect your actions and decisions
- learning to take responsibility for your actions and decisions

The Consequences of Taking or Avoiding Responsibility

Leadership is about taking responsibility for your actions and decisions. As you have learned, responsibility is the quality of being trustworthy, reliable, and accountable. It requires accepting the consequences of your actions and decisions. Consequences are *the outcomes, or results, of your actions and decisions.* They can be good or bad. To be an effective leader, you need to make sure that you understand the consequences of failing to take responsibility for what you say and do.

Taking responsibility isn't always easy. It requires maturity and patience. When things don't go well, or when responsibilities seem overwhelming, it can be natural to make excuses. But good leaders don't make excuses. They accept responsibility for their actions and decisions. They take quiet pride in their good decisions and they learn from their bad ones.

In this lesson you'll learn about the value of being responsible. You'll learn how to overcome the natural human tendency to make excuses. You'll learn how making excuses holds you back from realizing your potential as a mature person and as a leader. You'll also learn how to accept responsibility for your actions and decisions.

The Advantages of Personal Accountability

You can't lead if you can't make decisions. Sometimes it's difficult to know which decision is the right one— especially when you don't have enough time or information. At that point, you must make the best decision you can, based on the information you have. In a later lesson, you'll learn more about making decisions and solving problems.

But nobody's perfect: Sometimes you'll make a bad decision. When that happens, you must explain why you decided what you did and admit your mistake. "This is how I saw the situation at the time," a good leader says, "and that's why I decided to do what I did." Poor leaders, on the other hand, offer excuses. They look for any way they can to shift the blame to someone or something else. They seek a scapegoat—*someone who is made to take the blame for others*. They refuse to take responsibility for what they've done.

Vocabulary

- consequences
- scapegoat
- subordinate

A First Officer Steps In

The captain of an international flight arrived for the preflight check-in. He'd had a few drinks in the lounge while waiting for the flight. His speech was slurred and his movements were not coordinated. He was in no condition to pilot an aircraft. The ground staff realized he was drunk but said nothing.

When the first officer arrived at the check-in post, he knew that the passengers and crew would not be safe if the captain took charge of the cockpit. Even though the captain was older than he and had a higher rank, the flight officer decided to intervene.

Drawing the captain aside, the flight officer said, "Captain, it's evident that you've been drinking. We will need to find a different pilot for this flight. Will you turn yourself in, or will I have to turn you in?"

The captain went to the chief pilot's office and voluntarily grounded himself. Getting control of his drinking problem took the captain six months, but he eventually returned to flying. He had no further alcohol-related problems.

The first officer took personal responsibility for the safety of this flight. His behavior demonstrated professional competence and concern for the airline. He did not hesitate to take responsibility, even though the captain was his superior.

After the captain got control of his alcohol problem, the two men developed a positive, respectful relationship that lasted for years. The first officer's sense of personal accountability had long-term benefits for the captain and the airline, as well as for himself.

Personal accountability is everybody's business, whether you're the top leader or a subordinate—*a lower-ranking leader or individual*. Accountability is a form of honesty. It gives you several advantages:

- **You show that you are reliable**—you do what you say you are going to do.
- **You show people they can trust you with responsibility and authority**—if you make a mistake, you'll learn from it and do better next time.
- **You reassure others that you care about them**—you are concerned about their interest and welfare, not just your own.
- **You show that you are consistent**—people know what to expect of you.
- **You demonstrate that you are a careful and thoughtful decision maker**—you won't go and do something foolish.
- **You increase your ability to achieve your goals**.

The story "A First Officer Steps In" illustrates the advantages of personal accountability. Had the flight officer not intervened, the pilot would have put his passengers, crew, and aircraft at risk. At the same time, the ground crew, who knew the captain was drunk, did nothing about it. They failed to take responsibility for the flight's safety. If you had been the first officer, what would you have done? Would you have spoken up when others didn't?

The Consequences of Irresponsibility

The story that follows has a different set of characters, but they're playing similar roles. Gabe engages in a number of irresponsible acts. When he fails to listen to Elena's advice, he must pay the consequences. How do Elena and Gabe differ as far as personal accountability is concerned?

Whether you drive a car or pilot an aircraft, you are responsible for your passengers' safety.

William Perugini/Shutterstock

Gabe and the Broken Seatbelt

Elena and Gabe started dating a month after Gabe got his driver's license. He was proud of his "new-old" car, a 12-year-old SUV his uncle had sold him. Gabe waxed and polished it and lovingly took care of the engine.

Elena worried about Gabe's driving because, like lots of younger drivers, he went too fast. Elena would always buckle her seatbelt, but Gabe didn't like to wear his. He'd kid her about buckling up, but Elena didn't care.

One day, the passenger seatbelt in Gabe's SUV broke. Elena asked Gabe to fix the belt. He said he would, but he never seemed to get around to it.

A week or so later, Gabe and Elena were on their way to a movie. Gabe took a turn too sharply. The SUV skidded and ran into a telephone pole. Gabe wasn't hurt because he had the steering wheel to brace him, but Elena received cuts and bruises when she was thrown against the passenger door. Gabe claimed the accident wasn't his fault and took it all lightly, saying that Elena would soon be as good as new.

But the police officer who came to the crash site didn't agree. He gave Gabe a ticket and fines for speeding, reckless driving, and failing to wear a seatbelt. Elena had some ugly bruises, but she never said anything further to Gabe about the incident. A short time later, however, she broke up with him.

Everyone knows someone like Gabe. He acts without thinking through his decisions. He always wants things his way and ignores the needs and wants of others. His selfishness blinds him to his responsibility for the consequences of his actions and decisions.

People like Gabe often learn the hard way about the consequences of avoiding responsibility. Elena broke up with Gabe because she could tell he was immature and irresponsible. In the case of the accident, he endangered himself and almost injured her seriously. Although Elena liked Gabe a lot, she knew that he had to grow up.

How could Gabe have acted more maturely? How could he have accepted his responsibility, avoided an encounter with the police, and kept his girlfriend?

He might have:

- Made sure the seatbelts in his car worked
- Made certain he and Elena were wearing them at all times
- Driven more slowly and carefully
- Taken responsibility for the accident, admitted his fault, and apologized to Elena
- Talked to his parents or guardian, a teacher, or a counselor about the accident

Gabe's decision making was flawed. He acted without considering the possible outcomes of his actions. And once his action had a negative consequence, he refused to take responsibility for it. Gabe was old enough to obtain a driver's license but not mature enough to make careful decisions or to accept responsibility for his decisions to disobey the law.

If you've made a series of bad and irresponsible decisions and suffered the consequences, you may gradually lose self-esteem and self-confidence. That makes it even harder to make good decisions in the future.

How Defense Mechanisms Affect Your Actions and Decisions

Why do some people handle their mistakes well, and even learn from them, while others don't? The difference often lies in a person's defense mechanisms. In order to learn from a mistake, you have to admit that it was a mistake. People who hide behind defense mechanisms have a hard time doing this. Gabe's defense mechanisms were as well tuned as his car.

Do you remember the story about Tyler, Donna, and Tawana in Chapter 3, Lesson 2? It described how the cheerleading squad's defense mechanisms hurt its performance. Reflect on what you know about the defense mechanisms people use when they feel anxiety, stress, or pressure. As you may recall, these take a variety of forms. They include *displacement*, *repression*, *rationalization*, *projection*, *acting out*, and *denial*.

In the story of the drunken pilot, when the first officer confronted him, the pilot did not resort to defense mechanisms. He took responsibility for his condition and reported himself to the chief pilot, voluntarily grounding himself until he had his drinking problem under control. But Gabe was different. He employed a variety of defense mechanisms to avoid taking responsibility for what he had done. Think for a minute about which of those defense mechanisms he used.

One problem is that many people are unaware that they are using defense mechanisms. They employ them over and over in the same way when confronted with similar situations. Their patterns of behavior become predictable—you almost know what they are going to do before they do it.

If it seems as if the same thing happens to you repeatedly, you might be caught in such a pattern. To break out of it, you must understand yourself enough to know when you are resorting to the same defense mechanism in response to certain kinds of problems. That way you can analyze your reactions and escape the cycle. Often a teacher, counselor, or coach can help you identify these harmful patterns.

talking POINT

Some Consequences of Irresponsible Decisions

- You hurt other people's feelings.
- You harm or endanger others.
- You harm yourself.
- You lose people's trust.
- You hurt your ability to achieve your goals.
- You can cause damage to property.
- You can get into trouble with the law.

You might think of defense mechanisms as people's natural efforts to "save their own skin." But again, growing up and developing a positive, productive attitude about your life requires accepting responsibility for your actions and decisions. It means being willing to stand up and take the consequences, good or bad.

People with positive attitudes accept life's challenges. They set a good example. Because they do, other people look to them for leadership.

Learning to Take Responsibility for Your Actions and Decisions

How can you learn to take responsibility for your actions and decisions? It begins with thinking before you act. Here are a few guidelines:

First, try to anticipate the outcome of each decision you make. If you're trying to decide between two options, think of the outcome of each one in the long term. Will it solve your problem or provide only a temporary fix? Will the result be the one you want? That others want? How will the decision affect other people—your loved ones, your friends, your classmates, and your team?

Second, listen to what some people call "the little voice inside" or your "gut feeling." If you feel uneasy about a decision in any way, review the facts and your feelings regarding it.

Third, don't be afraid to ask someone for help. Get advice: Ask a friend, family member, teacher, or counselor to discuss the decision with you. In certain cases, you might want to talk to the school nurse or your family doctor. They may not have all the answers, and they can't make your decisions. But encourage them to ask you questions. This can help you think through your options. These people can serve as sounding boards. They can give you insight and, especially in the case of an older person, the benefit of their experience. And if you need more help, they can help you get it.

Finally, don't expect that you will always make the right decision. In other words, don't be afraid of failure. Failure is one of the best teachers. Everyone learns from their mistakes—the key is to try not to repeat them.

Responsibility and Leadership

There are few leader challenges like those in military combat. Victory in battle makes leaders into heroes, but the effects of defeat can be devastating. Whether a battle is lost or won, the true leader takes responsibility for the consequences of his or her strategic and tactical decisions.

American Biographies

General Robert E. Lee
Everett Historical/Shutterstock

General Robert E. Lee Accepts His Failure at Gettysburg

The three-day Battle of Gettysburg, Pennsylvania was one of the bloodiest that this nation has known. Some 51,000 men were killed, wounded, captured, or reported missing. After the battle ended, General Robert E. Lee, commander of the Confederate forces, led his troops back to Virginia in a sad retreat.

While General Lee lost the Battle of Gettysburg, he was still a great general. One reason for his greatness was his bravery and military skill. But equally important was his willingness to accept responsibility for the consequences of his decisions and his concern for his soldiers' morale.

On 3 July 1863, the final day of the battle, the Confederate forces mounted a major attack, now known as Pickett's Charge. Lee had miscalculated, and the result was disastrous: The Confederates broke through the Union line, only to be thrown back with heavy losses. When Lee saw that the assault was failing, he rode out among his men to rally them. He also visited the wounded. "All will come right in the end—we'll talk it over afterwards— we want all good and true men just now," he told them.

As that bloody afternoon ended, Major General George Pickett reported the sad truth: "General Lee, I have no division now." His top three generals had been killed or seriously wounded.

"Come, General Pickett," said Lee. "This has been my fight, and upon my shoulders rests the blame. The men and officers of your command have written the name of Virginia as high today as it has ever been written before."

As the survivors gathered around, Lee reassured Pickett once more: "Your men have done all that men could do; the fault is entirely my own." To show that he held himself accountable, Lee wrote to Confederate President Jefferson Davis and offered to resign. Davis, who recognized Lee's talents, told him to stay on.

In the story on the opposite page, notice how Confederate Civil War General Robert E. Lee demonstrated the characteristics of a true leader when he took full responsibility for his decision to send more than 12,000 of his soldiers against entrenched Union forces on the third day of the battle at Gettysburg. What do you notice about Lee's behavior, words, and attitudes? Why were so many men ready to lay down their lives for him? How did Lee deal with defeat and the frustration that followed?

Someone once asked Air Force General Curtis E. LeMay to provide a one-word definition of leadership. After some thought, LeMay replied, "If I had to come up with one word to define leadership, I would say responsibility."

A leader should reward a job well done and try to correct substandard performance. In this respect, a good sports coach is an example of a good leader. Think of a good coach. Does he or she accept the responsibility for the team's performance, discipline, and improvement? A good coach is like General Lee. A good coach doesn't single out individual players and blame them for a loss. The coach knows that winning (or losing) is a team effort.

What are some of the advantages of taking responsibility? When you take responsibility you:

- Gain the admiration of your peers and those you lead
- Earn the respect of your parents, teachers, coaches, and other leaders
- Build confidence in your own abilities
- Prepare yourself for future challenges
- Learn to trust your instincts and judgment

When you show that you can handle the responsibility others have given you, they will trust you enough to give you more.

Thunderbirds' First Female Pilot

The Air Force Air Demonstration Squadron made history in June 2005, when it announced the selection of then-Captain Nicole Malachowski as the team's No. 3 right wing pilot. The 1996 Air Force Academy graduate became the first female demonstration pilot in the Thunderbirds' 52-year history. In fact, she's the first female demonstration pilot on any US military high-performance jet team.

"It's a great privilege to be given the opportunity to be a part of the Thunderbird team, an organization that represents the finest traditions of our Air Force," the Las Vegas native said. "Women have been an integral part of the Thunderbird team for decades. The women of yesterday and today's Air Force maintain a tradition of excellence, and it is that heritage that has given me this exciting responsibility of being the first female Thunderbird pilot."

In 2008, then-Major Malachowski was inducted into the Women in Aviation International's Pioneer Hall of Fame. In 2010, as a lieutenant colonel, she played a key role in pushing for awarding of the Congressional Gold Medal to the Women Airforce Service Pilots (WASPs), who served as military pilots during World War II. From 2011 to 2012, she commanded the 333rd Fighter Squadron at Seymour Johnson Air Force Base, North Carolina.

Then-Major Nicole Malachowski
Courtesy US Air Force

✔ CHECKPOINTS

Lesson 3 Review

Using complete sentences, answer the following questions on a sheet of paper.

1. What do good leaders do?

2. What advantages does personal accountability give you?

3. What must you do to learn from a mistake?

4. How do you break out of a pattern of using the same defense mechanisms over and over?

5. How do you learn to take responsibility for your actions and decisions?

6. What are some of the advantages of taking responsibility?

APPLYING YOUR LEARNING

7. Several high school students are riding together in a car on a busy highway. What are the driver's responsibilities? What are the responsibilities of the passenger in the front seat? Of the passengers in the back seat? List as many as you can think of.

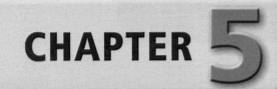

CHAPTER 5

Jacob Lund/Shutterstock

Developing Vision and Teams

Chapter Outline

What everyone in the astronaut corps shares in common is not gender or ethnic background, but motivation, perseverance, and desire—the desire to participate in a voyage of discovery.

Astronaut Ellen Ochoa

Group and Team Dynamics

Quick Write

_____

_____

Think of a time when you've been a member of a team or group. What were the group's goals? Write down the steps the team or group went through to accomplish its goals. What obstacles did the group need to overcome to be effective?

Learn About

- the importance of working as a team
- the characteristics of effective teams
- four stages of team development
- running an effective meeting

The Importance of Working as a Team

You probably know of a sports team with really good players at every position. But the team still doesn't win every game. In fact, it sometimes loses when up against a team that's ranked much lower. Why is that? Are the players constantly feuding with each other and disagreeing with the coach? Is every member out for his or her own share of the glory? You might know of another team that has no stars. But that team wins game after game. Why? One reason is that the players and coaches work together harmoniously. The players put the _team_ first. They put aside their own egos and work toward a shared goal: winning.

You may be a member of several teams or groups—in sports, in school, or in your community. And at some point, someone might ask you to lead a team. Perhaps it's happened already.

To win, team players must work together harmoniously.
Monkey Business Images/Shutterstock

In this lesson, you'll learn about how teams form and develop and the leader's role in that development.

But first, what exactly is a team? It's *a collection of individuals who are identified by others and by themselves as a group and who work together to accomplish a common goal.*

Individuals on a team depend on each other and on their coach or leader to achieve something. Each member's conduct affects the actions of all the other team members. Team members share responsibility for the outcome of their work.

Teams are composed of individuals with different talents and areas of expertise. Team dynamics, or *interactions*, are complex because each member must direct his or her unique talents toward achieving a shared goal. A team's leader or coach has a major influence on team dynamics. Because every team leader has a different leadership style, teams can work in different ways.

One of the team leader's most important tasks is preventing distractions from interfering with the team's work. This means paying attention to team members' concerns about:

- Whether they will fit in
- Who's in charge and who has the most influence
- Whether they will get along with, and be able to depend on, the other team members

If these concerns begin to cause problems between team members—someone is being left out, members are fighting for control, members don't get along with or trust each other—the team leader must address them, or they will prevent the team from achieving its goals. A team that is arguing with itself is a team that isn't getting much done.

Vocabulary

- team
- dynamics
- rule
- role
- trust
- forming
- storming
- norming
- performing

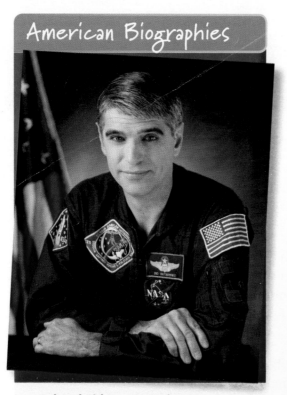

Colonel Sidney M. Gutierrez

Courtesy National Aeronautics and Space Administration

Colonel Sidney Gutierrez, Shuttle Commander

A space shuttle mission was incredibly complicated. It took a crew of several astronauts and mission specialists to perform all the work and research during the flight—not to mention the ground support staff. An effective shuttle commander— a good team leader—was essential.

One such commander was US Air Force Colonel Sidney M. Gutierrez. Colonel Gutierrez's lifelong dream to become an astronaut became a reality in June 1985. As an astronaut, he became the first Hispanic to both pilot and command the space shuttle on missions STS-40 and STS-59.

Colonel Gutierrez was born 27 June 1951, in Albuquerque, New Mexico, and graduated from Valley High School there in 1969. He began his Air Force career at the US Air Force Academy. While there, he was a member of the National Collegiate Championship Air Force Academy Parachute Team, with more than 550 jumps and a Master Parachutist rating. Colonel Gutierrez earned his bachelor of science degree in aeronautical engineering from the Academy in 1973 and a master of arts degree in management from Webster College in 1977.

Gutierrez attended the USAF Test Pilot School in 1981 and was assigned to the F-16 Falcon Combined Test Force after graduation. While there, he flew approximately 30 different aircraft, including the T-38, F-15, F-16, sailplanes, balloons, and rockets. In total, he logged more than 4,500 hours of flying time.

As the pilot on STS-40, NASA's Spacelab Life Sciences (SLS-1) mission, Gutierrez helped perform experiments that explored how humans, animals, and cells responded to microgravity in space and readapted to Earth's gravity on return. On STS-59, Colonel Gutierrez commanded a crew of five whose mission was to participate in the Space Radar Laboratory, part of the Mission to Planet Earth. The crew completed more than 400 precise maneuvers (a Shuttle record) to properly point the radar, imaged more than 400 selected sites with approximately 14,000 photographs (also a Shuttle record), and recorded enough data to fill 26,000 encyclopedias. Gutierrez spent more than 20 days in space.

In 1994, Gutierrez retired from the Air Force and NASA and returned to Albuquerque. He spent the next 20 years as a director of Sandia National Laboratories and in February 2015 became chairman of the board of Rocket Crafters, Inc. He serves on the board of directors of Goodwill Industries of New Mexico and the Roadrunner Food Bank.

The Characteristics of Effective Teams

Every successful team or group—whether involved in a long-term effort such as landing a man on the moon or a short-term project such as planning a class outing—has five common characteristics. These are goals, rules, roles, communication, and participation.

1. Goals

A *goal* is a team's target or objective. It gives team members a sense of purpose or focus. When you know your target, you have a much better chance of hitting it.

If you're a member of a team, you and your fellow team members must understand your goal. Each of you must have certain skills that will contribute to reaching the goal. The goal should be *specific* and *measurable*. This will make it easier to assess your progress and to demonstrate the outcomes of your work.

Experts know that it helps to express a goal in writing. This helps ensure that everyone understands it. For instance, your team's goal might be stated this way: *We will better our record of 8 wins and 4 losses from last season by at least two wins.* That means everyone on the team should understand that the team is shooting for a season record of 10 wins and 2 losses or better. It's a specific, measurable goal. If you win every game, that's great. But your goal is more modest: two more wins than last year.

2. Rules

Teams frequently rely on structure and rules. A rule is *a guideline for membership, conduct, or performance.* Rules can cover individual matters, such as team eligibility.

For example, an individual must have certain skills or knowledge in order to be named to a team. Teams have rules of conduct and performance that apply to each member.

In some cases, a group makes its own rules. In other cases, the group must follow external rules that govern it and other competing teams. For example, a team might decide on its own that it will hold practices every afternoon from 3 o'clock until 4:30. Its rule would be that every team member must show up for these practices. Team members must also, however, follow externally established rules. For example, they must show up for a tournament game at a scheduled time. If your team isn't on the court at game time, you will probably forfeit the game.

3. Roles

One of the advantages of teamwork is specialization. Not every member of the football team must be able to fill in for the quarterback. Team members have different roles. A role is *the specific job or task assigned to a team member.*

For example, you might know how to make French toast better than anyone else in your family. So when it's time to make French toast, you get the job. It's your role on the family "team." Examples of other specialized roles include the guard in basketball, the graphic designer on a project, or the trauma specialist on an emergency medical response team.

Roles can shift; they need not be permanent. But at any given time, each team member must know what his or her role is.

4. Communication

When you're on a team, you need to know what's happening. For that reason, good communication is critical to effective team performance. When communication is objective, honest, and focused on the team goal, rather than on personal matters, a team is better able to go out there and do its job.

Team leaders have particularly important roles in communication. For example, good leaders know the value of positive feedback. Everyone likes to receive approval for good performance, especially when it comes from a respected source. But a good leader also knows how to offer constructive criticism in a way that encourages performance improvement.

talking POINT

Effective teams...
- Work together to reach team goals
- Execute tasks thoroughly
- Meet or exceed the standard
- Thrive on challenges
- Learn from experiences
- Take pride in individual and shared accomplishments
- Strive for continued improvement

5. Participation

Team members typically focus on performance and collective improvement. To do this, members need to interact, not only with their leader but with each other. Although each member has a chance to shine at one point or another, it's the work of the team as a whole that comes first. In other words, participation is balanced—each member has an assigned role in achieving the group's shared goal. Each member's actions complement, or round out, those of the other members. Members build on each other's strengths and make up for any weaknesses.

Four Stages of Team Development

In the 1960s, Bruce W. Tuckman, an expert in organizational development, proposed a model of team development. Tuckman's model identifies four stages that teams typically go through—forming, storming, norming, and performing. It also describes the *behaviors* members exhibit and the *feelings* they experience as they move through each stage.

This model acknowledges the fact that it takes work to mold a good team— it doesn't just happen naturally. Conflict and resistance are natural during the early phases of a team's development. Strong leadership at each stage can help minimize conflict and reduce resistance. This will bring a team to its top performance more quickly.

Tuckman's team-development stages recognize the importance of other factors. Among the most important of these are trust and commitment.

Trust is *the degree of confidence and belief you have in others and they have in you.* Trust doesn't come in a can, an e-mail, or an express mail package. You have to earn it, and you have to build it. As Tuckman's model shows, building trust is a part of each of the four stages of team development. Trust becomes stronger as the group moves through each of these phases.

Commitment is the level of motivation and willingness—or level of intensity— that team members put into being team members and achieving a shared goal. When team members have commitment, they develop a sense of ownership or buy-in. They don't feel as if they're sacrificing their own interest—instead, they see the mutual benefits of collaboration.

Forming

Have you ever been a member of a newly created group or team? How did you feel? If you didn't know any of the other members, you probably felt a little awkward. That's because in this early stage of team formation, members have little shared history or background.

Forming is *the period when team members meet and begin to create relationships among themselves and with their leader.* At this stage, team members defer decisions to their leader. Members have limited commitment to the team. They are uncertain and tend to have only limited conversations. Members are concerned about what's going to happen in the future. They have not yet developed a high degree of trust.

At this stage, the team tends to focus on tasks and on getting behind its goal. But members are only thinking short term. The goal at this point is simply, "Let's get through this project." Members focus on the task at hand rather than on long-term goals or results.

If you are the leader, how can you move your team through this stage quickly and successfully? First, give members an exercise or activity that will enable them to get to know one another. Make introductions, and share each individual's personal talents. Clarify the team's goals, rules and expectations. Be as specific as possible. Give lots of direction and feedback. Review the purpose of the group and explain specific objectives. Show each member how he or she benefits from being part of the team.

Storming

The second phase of team development is well named. Storming is *a period during which personalities begin to clash as members try to overcome their natural tendency to focus on their own needs.*

talking POINT

Tuckman's Stages of Team Development

- **Forming**—Members become oriented to their roles. They test boundaries.
- **Storming**—Members confront conflicts stemming from interpersonal issues and resistance to task requirements.
- **Norming**—Team members develop cohesion and become comfortable with the group's standards, or norms, and their assigned roles.
- **Performing**—Members maintain team structure while ensuring enough flexibility to do the job well when conditions change.

The team may find it hard to focus on the task because individuals are still putting their own needs first. During this phase, communication may be unproductive, or even damaging. Some members may be unwilling to accept group rules or norms. Some may confront each other or the leader. Others may feel they cannot express their views, which leads to frustration. They are still unwilling to fully trust one another.

If you are leading a team during the storming phase, encourage conversation, don't suppress it. But keep the dialogue positive. Recognize each member's value. Help members work out their differences. Continue to focus on the big picture.

Teams that are storming can sometimes meet their goals, but performance will not be up to par. As a leader, help members step back and review how the team works. Help create rules and goals everyone can agree on.

Norming

Norming is *when the team begins to work together as a whole.* As a result of their leader's patience, guidance, and role modeling, team members begin to see the advantages of teamwork. Trust grows as members share more and more experiences, training, and activities. Team members begin to feel secure. Commitment is growing.

Communication is part of the norming phase, as team members give each other feedback and share thoughts and ideas. Team standards develop. The team develops a shared work ethic. Team members begin to support one another, and individual differences become less divisive. A team spirit begins to emerge.

If you are in charge of a team that is in the norming phase, stress working together over individual performance. Reinforce an "improvement" mindset by rewarding team-based, rather than individual, performance.

Performing

Performing is *the stage at which the team works at its best.* At this stage, good things are happening, but the team continues to fine-tune its methods for working together.

You've heard the expression, "The whole is greater than the sum of the parts." That's a perfect description of an effective team. The team's vision, roles, and processes are clear. Communication is open. Members feel free to share their own views. They have a high degree of trust in the leader and each other.

At this phase, the focus is on continuing to improve performance rather than simply on completing a task. Team members are thinking about long-term goals. They make up for gaps in each other's skills and knowledge, and they help each other learn.

If you're leading a performing team, your role is to provide ongoing feedback that will help the team improve its overall long-range performance. The long-term goal is not to win Saturday's game; it's to make it to the state and national championships.

When everything clicks, teams can accomplish amazing things together. Successful teamwork laid the groundwork for Colonel Gutierrez's space shuttle missions. Likewise, in 2013, an aircrew and its medical team working smoothly together saved the life of a wounded Airman. By understanding how teams form and develop, you can help your team be successful too—no matter what its goals.

Teamwork Allows Air Evacuation Crew to Save a Life

On the battlefield of northern Afghanistan in early 2013, an Air Force combat controller was shot through the right thigh and critically wounded. The Airman was rushed to a hospital at Mazar-e Sharif, where he was operated on to save his leg and his life.

With limited medical resources at the base, however, doctors there knew he would need to be quickly evacuated to receive more advanced care.

Meanwhile, a C-130J Aeromedical Evacuation (AE) flight out of Kandahar Airfield was in the air over northwest Afghanistan. It was on a routine mission to pick up patients from remote forward operating bases. It would then transport them to Bagram Airfield, the main hub for providing medical care in the country.

The crew had already made two stops when they received an urgent message over a new communications technology in the aircraft. The message: Divert immediately to Mazar-e Sharif to evacuate a high-priority patient. There were no other details, so the crew didn't know what to expect.

The medical team on an Aeromedical Evacuation mission that transported a critically wounded combat controller to Bagram Airfield, Afghanistan, in March 2013, saving his life.

Capt. Tristan Hinderliter, Courtesy US Air Force

In addition to a four-member flight crew, the aircraft also had a five-person medical team aboard. When the aircraft landed, the young combat controller was brought out to the jet in an ambulance. Despite his injuries, he was categorized as "urgent but stable." The crew took off with orders to continue their original flight plan, which included one more stop before heading to Bagram Airfield.

Once airborne, however, the patient's condition deteriorated rapidly. He started to bleed from his gunshot wound, and his blood pressure dropped.

"I told the pilot, 'We have to go straight to Bagram,'" said Captain Adriana Valadez, a reservist deployed from Joint Base San Antonio-Lackland, Texas, and a trauma nurse in her civilian job.

"At that point we were worried about saving his leg and making sure he was … stable," she said. "We knew he needed to go straight back to surgery to figure out why he was bleeding and that he needed to get to a higher level of care very quickly."

Although the crew's orders were to continue to the next stop, their new communications technology allowed them to successfully signal that they were heading directly to Bagram to try to save their patient.

The flight, which normally takes well over an hour, took just 42 minutes. "That's the closest thing I think we'll ever get to driving an ambulance," said co-pilot Captain Eric Jones. "You call 'urgent [medical evacuation]' over the radio and they part the Red Sea for you. All the traffic gets out of your way."

In the back of the aircraft, Valadez and her team worked on the Airman, trying to control his bleeding. Valadez remained standing next to him during landing, applying pressure to the wound. She continued to work on him as he was transferred from the jet to the ambulance and all the way to the emergency room.

The injured combat controller went straight to surgery. He lived, and the medical team was able to save his leg.

"It was truly one team up there," Valadez said. "Both pilots and the loadmasters were great. When it became an emergency situation, everyone pulled together. Everyone knew their roles and was able to help out whatever way they could."

The mission was a great example of an aircrew and AE team working together to accomplish the mission and save a life, said Lieutenant Colonel Sean Barden, director of operations of the 772nd Expeditionary Airlift Squadron. "I'm really proud of the entire crew…. It's rewarding to know that our teamwork and use of technology made such a big difference for one of our fellow Airmen."

Running an Effective Meeting

Good meetings are an important team-building tool. Poorly run meetings waste everyone's time. Sooner or later, you may be the one who calls the meeting. Meetings don't have to be major productions, but a few key points can be helpful to consider:

1. **Decide if a meeting is appropriate**—You generally need to meet only when the situation requires a face-to-face discussion. This might include seeking information or advice from the team, involving the team in decision making, addressing the entire team, or coordinating the work of different groups on the team. If you're just sharing information or updating team members, an e-mail might be more efficient.

2. **Define your purpose**—Every meeting should have a purpose. If it doesn't, don't meet. Define your purpose by deciding what you want to accomplish by the end of the meeting.

3. **Decide whom to invite**—Invite only the people who are directly involved in the issues you're discussing. If you're trying to solve a problem or decide a controversial issue, make sure to invite representatives of all groups with an interest in the outcome.

4. **Decide where and when the meeting should occur**—Check the schedule of the key people you want to attend. If you have options, choose the time of day that will help you meet your objectives. Keep the meeting under an hour or plan for breaks if it must go longer.

5. **Plan how you'll record information**—Will you use a whiteboard? Do you need an easel with flip charts and butcher paper? Can you ask a team member to take notes?

6. **Send out an agenda**—Send the agenda to all the meeting participants no later than one-to-two days before the meeting. The agenda should include the date, time, location, and purpose of the meeting. This gives all participants a chance to prepare their thoughts and know where the meeting is going before they get there.

7. **Start on time, and follow the agenda**—Start on an upbeat note, and don't wait for tardy participants. Tell everyone the outcome you desire. Don't ignore your agenda—that drives people nuts.

Regularly scheduled business meetings usually follow a fixed order of business:

- Introduction and call to order
- Roll call
- Approval or correction of the previous meeting's minutes
- Reports from committees or individuals identified on the agenda
- Old business or action items from the previous meeting
- New business identified on the agenda
- New business not on the agenda
- Appointments or assignments

Remember—meetings can be canceled. Before you take your team members away from their other activities, ask yourself if the team really needs to meet. After you send out your agenda, you might get feedback that indicates an e-mail will do the job just as well. If you find that the key decision makers can't be there, reschedule the meeting.

The Leader's Role in an Effective Team

By now you know that effective teams don't win by accident. Members must trust one another and commit themselves to the effort. They have a sense of ownership. It's the team leader's role to develop that trust and commitment and to ensure that members understand their goals, carry out their assigned roles, and abide by the team rules.

Goals

Part of the leader's job is to make sure that team members understand that they are engaged in an important, valuable project—that their goal is worth the effort. Members should discuss the goal and review and refine it as time passes.

Roles

Establishing and assigning team roles is another critical part of the leader's job. Team members need to know who's in charge and who's responsible for individual tasks. When team members understand their roles, they become more confident. They can act on their own. And when the group meets a goal, each member has a rightful claim to partial credit for the success. This reinforcement shows team members the value of the positive behaviors that helped reach the goal, and it spurs them to continue to perform at the highest possible level.

Rules

Every team needs rules. At the beginning, members naturally look to their leader to set and enforce these rules. As trust and commitment develop, members themselves may want to make new rules. They also assume shared responsibility for following and enforcing the rules.

It's the team leader's role to develop trust and commitment among team members.

Monkey Business Images /Shutterstock

Using complete sentences, answer the following questions on a sheet of paper.

1. Why are team dynamics complex?

2. What team members' concerns must a team leader pay attention to?

3. What are the five characteristics of effective teams?

4. Why is the team leader's role in communication particularly important?

5. How can the team leader move the team quickly through the forming stage?

6. How can the team leader help the team in the storming phase?

7. When does a team generally need to meet?

8. When should you send out a meeting agenda, and what should it include?

APPLYING YOUR LEARNING

9. Think about your favorite team—high school, college, or pro. Where would you place it in Tuckman's model? Do you see any relationship between its development phase and the team's record?

Quick Write

_____

_____

Have you ever felt that someone had judged you based on your appearance or something you did rather than on what's inside you? Write five sentences about how that made you feel.

Learn About

- the different dimensions of respect
- the values of tolerance and understanding
- improving group effectiveness

The Different Dimensions of Respect

One key characteristic of effective teams is that the members respect each other. Respect, as you have learned, is the attention, regard, and consideration given to people and their rights, property, and ideas. For example, if you own a dog, you keep it off your neighbors' lawn out of respect for their privacy and property. If you are in a library, you don't talk out loud out of respect for the right of others to work quietly.

Respect means accepting differences—tolerating and valuing other people and their customs, culture, attitudes, and beliefs.

Establishing and Demonstrating Mutual Respect

You may have heard some people say that "respect is earned." This is true in many ways. You _do_ earn other people's respect on the basis of your words and actions. To be effective, a leader must earn respect from the members of his or her group.

But on the other hand, Americans believe that every human being has basic, inherent value and rights. People don't need to "earn" those things: They are born with them. You are obliged to respect their rights and to acknowledge their value as human beings and as citizens. They are obliged to do likewise for you.

In other words, respect must be returned. It must be mutual. Mutual respect is _the two-way relationship that develops between people or members of groups after the lines of communication are open and trust develops._

Mutual respect is what makes relationships run smoothly— between friends, student and teacher, parent and child, employee and supervisor, and police officer and citizen.

People develop respect for others when they feel that others respect their personal dignity. Personal dignity is *the internal strength that helps people feel connected, worthwhile, and valued.* Personal dignity is closely linked to a person's self-worth. A lack of respect breaks down personal dignity. Such a breakdown can lead to a number of negative social behaviors, including crime, substance abuse, child neglect, family disruption, political discontent—even suicide.

So you can see that respect is a powerful force. A society cannot function if its members don't establish mutual respect. Can you think of any examples of societies or groups in which a lack of mutual respect led to upheaval or disaster?

Ways of Showing Respect

You can show respect on the personal and professional levels. On the personal level, one of the easiest ways to show respect is simply to be courteous. In other words, use your manners. For example, you can say the following:

- "Please" when you ask for something
- "Thank you" when you receive something
- "Excuse me" if you accidentally bump into someone
- "Yes (or no) sir" or "Yes (or no) ma'am" to adults
- "Good morning" or "Good afternoon," especially to people older than you

Other examples of personal respect include:

- Holding the door for an elderly person or a child
- Standing when an older person enters the room
- Not interrupting people
- Taking off your hat or cap when you're indoors
- Taking off a glove before you shake someone's hand
- Removing your sunglasses before speaking to someone

Vocabulary

- mutual respect
- personal dignity
- tolerance
- prejudice
- discrimination
- stereotype
- diversity
- religious respect
- gender stereotypes
- justice

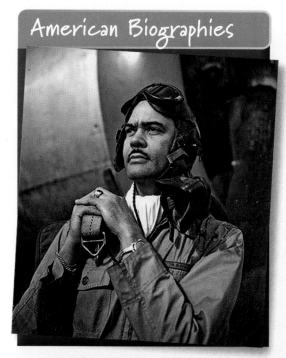

General Benjamin O. Davis Jr. as commander of the 332nd Fighter Group

Courtesy US Air Force

General Benjamin O. Davis, Jr.

Benjamin O. Davis, Jr., was a decorated military officer who led the fabled Tuskegee Airmen during World War II. He was also the first African-American to become an Air Force general.

Davis was born in Washington, D.C., in 1912 and graduated from high school in Cleveland, Ohio. His father, Benjamin O. Davis, Sr., was one of two black combat officers in the Army at that time.

From the age of 14, Benjamin Davis, Jr., knew he wanted to be a pilot. He worked hard for appointment to the US Military Academy at West Point. But once enrolled in 1932, Davis was shunned because of his race. No one would speak to him except on business matters. Although he did fine in his classes, Davis had no roommate in the dormitory, and no one would share his tent in the field. He ate his meals without a word.

But Davis persevered. "I wasn't leaving," he later said in an interview. "This was something I wanted to do, and I wasn't going to let anybody drive me out." Davis graduated from West Point in 1936—the fourth African-American to do so.

Pursuing his dream of being a pilot, Davis had applied for the Army Air Corps during his final year at West Point. He was rejected because the unit did not accept blacks. So after graduation he joined an all-black infantry regiment in Georgia.

Some other ways to show respect on a professional as well as personal basis include:

- Dealing with people in a cooperative way
- Communicating clearly
- Listening actively
- Giving constructive feedback
- Being flexible
- Creating opportunities to teach and learn
- Sharing behaviors and feelings
- Viewing situations as win-win scenarios
- Using inclusive language (for example, saying "we" instead of "you" or "they")

In 1941, responding to pressure for greater black participation as the war approached, President Franklin D. Roosevelt told the War Department to create a black flying unit. Davis was assigned to that group, which trained at Tuskegee Army Air Field in Alabama. The unit, the 99th Pursuit Squadron, went on to complete successful missions in North Africa.

Soon after, Davis became commander of the 332nd Fighter Group, a larger all-black unit. He and his men escorted bombers on 200 air-combat missions over Europe. Davis took pride in the fact that no bombers that his unit protected were lost to an enemy fighter.

By the time World War II ended, Davis had flown 60 combat missions. He was awarded the Silver Star. And he was fortunate enough to see the fruits of his struggle against racial discrimination in the military: President Harry S. Truman integrated the US armed forces in 1948. One of the major reasons for integration, historians report, was the record of Davis and his pilots. His Airmen had proved that blacks could perform as well as whites in all jobs. "I have fought all my life for the integration of blacks into the mainstream of American life," he wrote in his autobiography.

After retiring from the armed forces in 1970, Davis continued his public service. He served as assistant secretary of transportation for environment, safety, and consumer affairs in the Nixon administration.

In 1998, President Clinton awarded Davis his fourth star, advancing him to full general. "General Davis is here today as living proof that a person can overcome adversity and discrimination, achieve great things, turn skeptics into believers; and through example and perseverance, one person can bring truly extraordinary change," the president said.

Davis died on 4 July 2002 at the age of 89. In 2015, the US Military Academy announced it was naming a new cadet barracks after him.

The Values of Tolerance and Understanding

Tolerance is *respecting people's differences and values*. It means understanding and standing up for people's differences and helping ensure that everyone gets equal treatment.

You might compare tolerance and mutual respect with a two-way street. The traffic moves both ways: You show tolerance for others and they show tolerance for you.

But you might encounter barriers on this street, just as you come up against barriers when you're driving somewhere to meet a friend. Among the barriers to tolerance and mutual respect are prejudice, discrimination, and a failure to value diversity.

Prejudice

Prejudice is *an unfair opinion or judgment about a person or a group of people.* The word *prejudice* literally means "judging ahead of time." Prejudice shuts down critical thinking. It causes you to assume you have a person or a situation figured out in advance— before you even talk to the person or see the situation for yourself. It's an irrational way of thinking—it doesn't permit reflection. It's usually based on limited experience rather than on facts.

Prejudices are so common that we sometimes take them for granted. That can be not only hurtful, but downright dangerous.

Prejudices can lead you to make blanket assumptions about an entire group of people rather than looking at them as individuals. For example, how would you respond if someone said to you, "Athletes are stupid"? You could roll your eyes and nod, as if in agreement. But if overcoming prejudice were your goal, you'd respond very differently. You'd have to think logically. You'd have to ask yourself a series of questions such as:

* Who made the statement? Is it someone who plays sports or not? Does the person know any athletes?

* On what grounds did the person make the claim about athletes' intelligence? Does he or she have access to all athletes' school transcripts?

* Do you know of evidence to disprove the claim? Do you know any smart athletes? Or have you read about any great athletes who were also top scholars? If you don't personally know any athletes, is it a good idea to automatically accept another person's opinion as fact?

Reasons for Prejudice

People aren't born with prejudice any more than they are born with the ability to read. Prejudice is *learned*. You pick it up from the people around you and from the messages society sends.

People develop prejudices for several reasons. One is *fear*. People are afraid of people, ideas, and cultures that are different from their own. Another reason for prejudice is a group's belief that it's better than or *superior* to other groups— whether they are racial, ethnic, religious, or whether it's a question of men versus women. *Misunderstanding* is another source of prejudice: When people of different cultures and languages come together, all kinds of misunderstandings can erupt. An innocent gesture or word in one culture can be an insult in another.

Still another reason is perceptions of *history*. Perhaps you had a bad experience with a member of another group. You then proceed to blame *all* members of that group for what one person did. At a broader level, many ethnic and religious groups around the world have a long history of disagreements with each other over land, resources, and political power. They've sometimes fought bitter wars, with atrocities on both sides. People and groups often remember the wrongs done to them far better than they remember the wrongs they've done to others.

Discrimination

One danger of prejudice is that it leads to discrimination. Discrimination is *unfair treatment based on prejudice against a certain group*. It's prejudice in action.

Discrimination is often based on perceived traits such as skin color, age, gender, or sexual preference. But the possibilities are endless. Some overweight people, for example, claim to be victims of discrimination. Left-handers say they experience discrimination in a right-handed world. What counts are the feelings of the person being discriminated against—and your efforts to treat that individual no differently than you treat anyone else.

If someone compliments you on your new winter coat and says you have "discriminating taste," that's a good thing. It means that you tend to seek out the quality things in life. But if someone says you're "discriminatory" in your attitudes, watch out. You may be picking your friends on the basis of something other than their character, actions, or personalities. You might be judging people on the basis of stereotypes.

A stereotype is *an idea or a concept that is based on oversimplified assumptions or opinions, rather than on facts*. A stereotype can be negative or positive. It's a picture you carry around in your head about a thing or person, without ever questioning it.

For instance, if you hear that a friend just bought a pit bull, you might immediately assume that it's a vicious dog. If another friend bought a kitten, you might assume it was a cuddly little creature. Both assumptions are based on stereotypes. Are all pit bulls vicious? Are all kittens cuddly? Or are those labels that some people place on these animals on the basis of limited experience or stories in the media? How true are the stereotypes?

Diversity

Diversity means *variation or difference*. When someone says that American society values diversity, that means Americans encourage variety and live in a society that respects differences among people.

Americans live in a society that respects differences among people.

Huntstock.com/Shutterstock

Since the movement to give women the vote in the early twentieth century and the civil rights movement of the 1950s and 1960s, America has made progress in granting equal rights to all its citizens. Because of this social and legal progress, Americans today find it easier to exercise their right to vote and to have equal access to education and jobs, among other things—regardless of their gender, age, race, ethnicity, national origin, religion, family status, sexual preference, or physical ability.

But if you read the headlines or watch the news, you realize that respect for diversity is a work in progress. The United States, like all modern countries, is working to become a more tolerant and open society.

Religious Respect

Nowhere is tolerance more important than in matters of religion. Demonstrating religious respect is *honoring the right of other people to hold their own personal beliefs*. This involves individual actions to respect the beliefs of others—regardless of their faith or lack of faith. It's not condoning or condemning, but just respecting their rights. Self-discipline and self-control will allow people to refrain from demonstrating intolerance for others' beliefs.

Gender Stereotypes

Have you ever heard someone say that boys don't cry? Or that girls can't excel in science? If you're a boy, do people assume you love sports? If you're a girl, does everyone assume you like to cook? If so, you've experienced gender stereotyping.

Gender stereotypes are *limited ways of thinking about people on the basis of whether they are male or female.* Gender stereotypes cover more than just the observable physical differences between males and females. They include cultural, social, psychological, and behavioral traits.

Gender equality is a complex issue that's evolving. The nation's highest courts are still hearing cases involving gender rights. State legislatures debate them. The United States is working at how to be a just society—a society that practices justice. Justice is *the fair and equal treatment of everyone under the law.* As a free people, Americans seek justice for all.

Gender stereotypes have at least two big problems. The first one is that, like prejudices, gender stereotypes halt the thinking process. They're a trap. If you fall victim to gender stereotypes, you build your ways of dealing with people on the basis of false assumptions or misleading mental images.

The second problem is that gender stereotypes make clear communication difficult, if not impossible. Without communication, there's no understanding.

The following are some ways you can avoid stereotyping people by their gender:

- Be sensitive to language that might contain gender stereotypes.
- Don't go with your gut reaction—it's likely to be based on preconceptions.
- Take time to think.
- Avoid using hurtful words or expressions.
- Don't fall victim to peer pressure.
- View everyone as equals.

Just because you avoid stereotypes does not mean that you cannot have your own opinions about gender issues. But in the spirit of mutual respect, you need to be open-minded. Your ideas should develop as you mature. Respect the ideas of adults in your life as well as those of your friends, but don't feel that you have to go along with them 100 percent. Think for yourself.

Demonstrating Tolerance

Overcoming prejudice and discrimination begins with each individual. How do you know if you are showing tolerance and understanding towards other people? It's really very simple. Ask yourself: Am I treating them the way I would want them to treat me?

Teams are productive only when members can communicate clearly and see a common goal.

Monkey Business Images/Shutterstock

How would you feel if others made fun of your skin color, ethnic background, hair color, religion, sexual preference, or the region of the United States you are from? How would you feel if you were denied a place on the team, an education, a job, an opportunity, simply because someone decided you belonged to the wrong group? How would you feel if others refused to be friends with you, to eat in the school cafeteria with you, or to live in the same neighborhood with you because of prejudice?

If you wouldn't like someone doing that to you, don't do it to someone else. That's the foundation of tolerance and mutual respect.

Improving Group Effectiveness

Establishing mutual respect, being tolerant, and valuing diversity are important for each person on the individual level. But they're equally important at the group or organizational level.

Working Toward Common Goals

Did you ever push two bar magnets around on a tabletop? What happened as you brought them closer together? Either the magnets flipped away from each other the closer you placed them, or they snapped together, forming a bond.

All magnets are polarized—they have a south pole and a north pole. One pole is positive, and the other is negative. If you bring two positive or two negative poles together, the magnets repel each other. If you put a negative and a positive pole close to each other, the magnets attract each other.

You can compare members of a team or group with magnets. If group members can't communicate clearly and see a common goal, they tend to lack trust and respect for each other. Nothing productive will happen. They don't come together and bond. But when group or team members have a clearly defined, common goal and are able to communicate about their plan of action to achieve that goal, they come together. They bond. They're ready to produce results.

Benefits of Accepting Differences

As hard as they try, people often find it difficult to accept other people's differences. It's as if there were something in human nature that puts people at odds over racial, ethnic, religious, political, and gender differences.

If a group or team is to function effectively, however, its members must accept each other's differences. It may take a concerted effort, but the benefits of accepting other people's differences outweigh the drag that prejudicial thinking puts on team performance.

The best team is a unified whole. No team can be whole while any of its members hold assumptions, false impressions, and stereotypes about fellow team members.

Communication is key to breaking down the barriers and accepting others' differences. Tapping the talents, ideas, experiences, and ingenuity of a diverse group of people is very productive. A diverse group of people can usually come up with much better solutions than can a group of people who all think the same. But to come up with the best solutions, members must trust and listen to each other. They must not only accept but also value their differences. They must see diversity as a strength.

Evaluating and Measuring Group Effectiveness

How do you tell if your group or team is working effectively? As you have learned, the first step is to establish clear goals. The second is to decide whether the group is meeting those goals. Are team members devoting their efforts to the team's task, or wasting them arguing among themselves over issues that have little or nothing to do with it? Determining this can be difficult, especially when the team's task isn't yet done. Nevertheless, constantly seeking a measure of results—or movement toward results—is a necessary part of team building.

Remember that all effective teams *form, storm, norm,* then *perform.* Along the way, the leader must measure, evaluate, and adjust as needed. Hitting the bull's-eye might take three, six, or even ten shots, but you will finally make a direct hit. Your team will succeed.

talking POINT

For Greater Group Effectiveness:

- **Forgive mistakes**—People often learn more from failure than from success.
- **Hold members accountable**—Every team member should have a role and should be responsible for carrying it out.
- **Foster trust and commitment**—Both are essential to teamwork.
- **Don't make excuses**—Whining and placing blame are counterproductive.
- **Make the hard decisions**—Winning doesn't come easy.
- **Seek concrete answers and solutions**—You can use them to measure effectiveness.
- **Respect differences**—See them as a source of strength.
- **Constantly strive toward mutual respect**—Respect is the glue that holds the group or team together.

Remembering the Titans

T.C. Williams High School in Alexandria, Virginia, has one of the most diverse student bodies in the nation. Students from more than 80 countries, speaking dozens of languages, fill its classrooms. They pour into its football stadium every fall to cheer on their school team, the Titans.

Perhaps you don't find diversity all that unusual. Most public schools today have students from many races and ethnic backgrounds.

But this hasn't always been the case. In fact, it's happened only in the past half-century. Beginning in 1954, the US Supreme Court issued a series of rulings designed to end racial segregation in public schools across the country. In a 1971 decision, the court ruled that school districts could bus students from one neighborhood school to another to achieve racial balance in the classroom.

To comply with this ruling, the City of Alexandria restructured its public school system that year. As a result, two of the city's high schools would have only freshman and sophomore students. All juniors and seniors would attend T.C. Williams. The school, formerly all white, now had a mix of black and white students.

Strong rivalries had developed among the city's three high schools, and nowhere were these rivalries greater than in football. Football, the ultimate team sport, would be the first big test of success or failure for Alexandria's new, desegregated school system. But when the Titans came together for their first practice in 1971, little did they know that they would set the tone for the entire community in a time of racial tension.

Under the leadership of a dynamic black coach, the Titans developed a strong bond as a team. Their commitment to victory quickly overcame any prejudices based on race, economic status, or cultural beliefs. The team became a winner.

The Titans' success on the field began to extend to the rest of the school and the community. The team went on to become the division and state champion.

The Titans proved that mutual respect can be the fuel that drives not only successful teams but also strong communities. The team became the unifying symbol for the community as team members—along with adults in the community—learned to respect each other and to take pride in a joint achievement.

In 2000, the team's 1971 season was the basis of a major motion picture, *Remember the Titans*, starring Denzel Washington.

✔ CHECKPOINTS

Lesson 2 Review

Using complete sentences, answer the following questions on a sheet of paper.

1. What does respect mean?

2. What can a lack of respect lead to?

3. What are some ways to show personal respect for others?

4. What does prejudice do?

5. What are four reasons for which people develop prejudice?

6. What are some ways you can avoid stereotyping people by gender?

7. What happens if group members can't communicate clearly and see a common goal?

8. To come up with the best solutions, what must group members do?

9. What two steps should you take to tell if your group or team is working effectively?

APPLYING YOUR LEARNING

10. Think of a movie or TV show you've seen—or a book you've read—about a group or team that had to learn to work together to accomplish something. How did they work together at first? Thinking back to what you learned in a previous lesson, what "forming" and "storming" problems did they encounter? What helped them "norm" and "perform?" How did they build respect for each other's differences and individual talents?

Establishing a Common Vision

Quick Write

Write a one-sentence description of a project that would require teamwork to complete—for example, organizing a school recycling drive or a neighborhood cleanup. What would be your vision for the project?

Learn About

- the importance of a common vision
- writing a team charter
- enlisting others to work toward a common vision

The Importance of a Common Vision

If someone asked you to join a group or team, your first question would probably be, "What is its purpose?" For example, someone might ask you join a committee at school that plans to hold a class cookout over spring break. Or you might agree to help a group of neighbors who want to organize a multifamily garage sale and give the proceeds to a local shelter for the homeless.

In addition to asking about the group's purpose, you would also want to know your role on the team and the roles of other team members. Finally, you would want to know when the group would do the work.

A team works best when its members share a common vision and agree on each person's role.
Rawpixel/Shutterstock

On a broader level, you'd be interested in the team's vision. A vision is *an idea that inspires a team to perform well and accomplish its goals.* A vision sets out the shared values of the team. It states, in broad terms, what the team plans to accomplish. A team works best when its members have a common vision.

While a parent, teacher, coach, or boss might have a role in determining a team's vision at the beginning, it's up to members themselves to fine-tune the vision. This lets everyone feel like they're a part of the project. Developing this sense of ownership is an essential step in team building.

Writing a Team Charter

Every team should express its vision in a team charter. A team charter is *a document that gives direction to individual members and to the team as a whole.* A team charter helps members see the big picture and where they fit into it.

The format of the charter can vary: It can be written in a few paragraphs or expressed as a table or a flowchart. When the charter is complete, all members should receive a copy. They should refer to it as their work moves forward.

A team charter should give sufficient information to explain the team's overall vision and members' general responsibilities. The team charter, however, is not a detailed, day-to-day account of the team's activities. It includes only the main areas of responsibility— each assignment will include many tasks and duties. It's up to the team leader to assign roles for those tasks and duties and to set dates for their completion.

Who writes the charter? In some situations, the person assigning the project should develop it. In other situations, the team leader should write it. And in still other cases, team members themselves develop their charter. If the team is part of a larger organization, it may adapt the team charter to that of the organization. A 4-H club project team or a Boy Scout troop trail-maintenance team, for example, might base its team charter on the parent organization's vision or goals statement.

Every team charter should have the following elements:

- A vision statement
- Team goals
- Team members' assignments
- A timeline

In the rest of this section, you'll read about each of these four elements and how they help a team achieve its vision.

American Biographies

Walt Disney in 1950 with the wife of the prime minister of Pakistan

Department of State/Courtesy of Harry S. Truman Library and Museum

When You Wish Upon a Star

Walter Elias Disney was born in Chicago, Illinois, on 5 December 1901. In 1906, the Disney family moved to Missouri and settled on a farm. Disney's Aunt Margaret often gave him tablets, and he'd draw pictures for her. Disney clearly had a talent for art. And even in his childhood, Disney was drawn toward cartoons.

As a teenager, Disney attended the Chicago Institute of Art, worked at the family business, and drew sketches for the school paper. In the summer of 1918, he joined the Red Cross Ambulance Corps. The Red Cross sent him to France for service during World War I.

Disney returned to Missouri from France in 1919, determined to become an artist. He took a job making animated commercials, a new form of entertainment at the time. Disney read books about animation and discovered how the leading New York animators worked. He hired some apprentices and, using his gift for salesmanship, got a $15,000 loan. With the money, he started his own company, Laugh-O-Gram Films.

The company went bankrupt, despite Disney's best efforts. He decided to move to Hollywood, where the film action was. He convinced his brother to join him there. Roy Disney would take care of the financial end of things, and Walt would be the creative genius. It was a great two-person team. Working out of a rented studio with a used camera, they set out to make the Disney name famous around the world.

Creating a Vision Statement

The first element of the team charter is the vision statement, which *explains the team's reason for existing.* The writer should draft the vision statement in terms broad enough to include the team's total responsibilities. But it should be specific enough to allow team members to measure their progress as their work moves forward.

Here's an example of a vision statement for a class committee that's planning a spring cookout:

To build senior class morale and improve school spirit, our class spirit team will sponsor activities to create a sense of belonging and camaraderie among all members of our class.

talking POINT

Vision Statement Characteristics

A well-written team vision statement has the following characteristics:

- It is brief (no more than a paragraph).
- It is broadly stated.
- It explains why the team exists.
- It explains what and why, but not how.

Success didn't come quickly. But eventually Disney came up with the character that would be his key to fame: Mickey Mouse. Soon Mickey was joined by Goofy, Pluto, and Donald Duck.

By the mid-1930s, Disney had a staff of some 300 artists. Together, they created *Snow White*, the first feature-length animated film. Disney invested $3 million to build a new studio in Burbank. Meanwhile, work proceeded on films that are now classics: *Fantasia*, *Pinocchio*, and *Bambi*.

In the early 1950s, Disney took off in a new direction: He brought together some of his studio's best creative talents to plan, design, and build Disneyland Park in Anaheim, California. Although Roy Disney was worried about the risky new venture, Walt was convinced it would work. And, of course, it did.

Disney's company became a multimillion-dollar enterprise. In 1996, Disney's creative, design, planning, real estate, and project management operations united under a single name: Walt Disney Imagineering.

Today, nearly 2,000 "imagineers" representing more than 140 disciplines are responsible for all phases of a Disney project's development—from conceptualization to design, engineering, production, construction, and installation. This blending of imagination with technical know-how has produced the world's most popular theme parks and most memorable family movies.

Imagineering has inspired more than 100 Disney-owned patents in such areas as ride systems, special effects, interactive technology, live entertainment, and fiber optics. Disney Imagineers developed the first daily operating monorail system, the first computer-controlled thrill ride, and an advanced 3-D motion picture photography system.

And it all began with a boy who liked to draw.

Developing Team Goals

A team goal is *an objective the team wishes to accomplish.* Team goals express what the team will set out to do. Effective team goals have four characteristics in common:

1. They are tied to the vision statement.
2. They focus on a single issue.
3. They define the vision statement.
4. They guide the team's accomplishments.

Team Goals Are Tied to the Vision Statement

Team goals should grow out of the vision statement. Each goal must relate to that statement. If it doesn't, either the goal is off track or the vision statement is poorly written.

You read the vision statement of the class team that was planning a spring cookout above. Now look at the team's draft list of goals:

1. *Plan, organize, and hold a five-hour class cookout over spring break for 400 class members.*

2. *Order 425 theme-printed class T-shirts to sell at the cookout at $12 each. Revenue from the sale of T-shirts will contribute to the cost of the cookout.*

3. *Promote the cookout during at least three varsity sports events and during homeroom announcements.*

4. *Submit to Principal Harris a class petition of at least 250 names protesting the removal of the senior lounge soda machine.*

The team drafted these goals during a brainstorming session. Brainstorming is *a group problem-solving technique during which members contribute ideas spontaneously.* The purpose of brainstorming is to get as many ideas as possible out on the table. No one criticizes anyone else's ideas during a brainstorming session. Everyone's ideas count. After everyone has had a chance to give input, the group decides which ideas best support its vision.

Suppose you were a member of the team that had brainstormed these goals. Are all four goals related to the vision statement? If not, which one doesn't fit?

Can you see why Goal 4, while probably an important issue to some members of the team, doesn't relate to the vision statement? Perhaps that's a good goal for another team or committee, but it doesn't fit this vision statement. The team should delete this goal from the list.

Team Goals Focus on a Single Issue

The team goals should each focus on a single issue. For example, here's the vision statement for a team formed to plan, organize, and hold a multifamily garage sale to benefit a local homeless shelter.

The neighborhood will join together to help the local homeless shelter by holding community fundraising events this summer. The first event will be a multifamily sale, which will be held in the city fire station on June 30.

Now read the draft version of the team's goals:

1. *By June 15, rent 30, 8-foot-long banquet tables for one day. Pay no more than $15 per table. Have the tables delivered to the fire station at 10 a.m. on June 30.*

2. *Ensure that a bunch of community members will have a good time browsing the junk everyone puts out for sale so that we can make a difference down at the homeless shelter. This will ultimately reduce the numbers of homeless people standing on street corners.*

Goal 1 is well written. It focuses on a single issue. The team is responsible for renting and obtaining timely delivery of 30 tables of a certain style and size and at a certain cost. The team can monitor progress toward this goal and evaluate the results. Either the tables will be rented by June 15 or they won't. They will cost $15 or less, or more than that. The point is clear: Get those tables!

Goal 2 has two problems: First, it has a dual focus. Second, it's not precise. The first sentence of this goal mentions making sure that neighbors will enjoy the sale. But how many neighbors are in "a bunch?" What's "junk?" What does it mean to "make a difference?"

The second sentence in Goal 2 has problems, too. Remember that according to the vision statement, the purpose of the event was to "help the local homeless shelter." But according to Goal 2, it looks as if the main reason for the sale is not to help the homeless but to improve the appearance of the community. It sounds as if some of the planners might have their own agendas: They may be motivated by interests other than by a desire to help the homeless.

This team needs to rethink its second goal. In fact, it might divide it into two goals. The new Goal 2 should focus on community participation. It should describe the hoped-for outcome in measurable terms, such as number of buyers, sellers, and how much money the sale takes in.

The new Goal 3 should focus on how the proceeds from the sale will help the shelter. It should show how the shelter can use the money for specific improvements in services or equipment.

When goals are measurable, you can monitor your progress in reaching them. Vague language makes goals hard to attain. Finally, the goals must support the vision statement.

Team Goals Define the Vision Statement

The vision statement is broad. It emphasizes the big picture. But having seen the big picture, team members need specific information.

Think again about the cookout example. As work begins, the team forms several subteams. Each subteam will be responsible for part of the work that must be done to achieve the end result—a great, morale-building cookout. Each subteam must have its own goals. These goals are based on the vision statement. For example, one subteam might be in charge of buying food. A draft version of its goal statement might read, "Purchase the food for the class cookout."

This goal statement supports the big picture, the cookout, but it's not sufficiently detailed. At the least, members need to know what types of food and how much food to purchase. So the team needs to make the subteam's goal statement more detailed. The revised goal statement might read:

1. *Purchase 100 pounds of lean ground beef.*
2. *Purchase 5 gallons of packaged potato salad.*
3. *Purchase 5 gallons of packaged baked beans.*
4. *Purchase 100 packages of hamburger buns.*

It's important to write team goals in language that you can measure, because that's how you'll evaluate your success. The four goals above are easily measurable: For example, if the team has purchased 50 packages of buns, it's halfway to reaching Goal 4. When the team has purchased 75 packages of buns, that goal is 75 percent accomplished, and so on.

But suppose Goal 4 had stated, "Purchase a number of hamburger buns for the class cookout," or "Purchase enough hamburger buns for the class cookout." Are those goals measurable?

As worded, those two goals have no indication of quantity. How many is "a number?" If no amount is specified, any amount could be right. In the second example, the team is supposed to purchase "enough" hamburger buns. Again, how many will be enough?

The only way to measure the results of a goal stated in this way would be to hold the cookout and see what happens. If the cooks don't run out of buns, the goal is accomplished. (The team, however, might have purchased too many hamburger buns, resulting in costly waste). If the cooks run out of buns, the goal isn't attained. This would be a form of measurement, but it would be an inefficient one.

Team Goals Guide the Team's Accomplishments

Well-written goals show team members what they're responsible for accomplishing, working together. If a team's charter consisted only of assignments for individual members, the members would pursue their tasks as individuals. This is why the team goal comes before individual task assignments in the charter. In other words, first the big picture, then goals, then individual assignments.

Goals promote teamwork by emphasizing mutual assistance. Mutual assistance is *the help and support team members give each other*. Mutual assistance gets the team's work done in the best possible way.

Think about a baseball team. Each of the nine players has his or her own assignment. The outfielders are responsible for catching fly balls and running down hits that cross the infield. The infielders are responsible for stopping balls that enter areas covered by their positions and for throwing the ball to the players assigned to cover the bases.

But sometimes a player does more than just what his or her specific position, or assignment, calls for. For example, if a bunt pulls the first baseman in on the foul line, the pitcher runs to first base to catch the throw. The pitcher does this because all team members have a shared goal: to win the game.

These baseball players had a shared goal: to win the game.
Jamie Roach/Shutterstock

LESSON 3   Establishing a Common Vision

Your Dreams Are Your Only Limits

In 2005, a crew of six Airmen based in southwest Asia climbed aboard a C-130 Hercules. Their mission was to transport 151 Marines and their equipment into combat.

This was no ordinary flight: It was the first time an all-female C-130 crew flew such a combat mission. The women completed the mission successfully and went on to complete others. But as unique as this flight was, the crew members didn't want all-female teams to become standard operating procedure.

"I enjoyed flying with this crew, but I don't think we should go out of our way to have all-female crews," said Captain Carol Mitchell. "It took a long time for women to become accepted as air crew members, and now that we are, we would be taking a step back by singling ourselves out rather than blending in with the rest of the Air Force."

Airman Ci Ci Alonzo agreed. "It was a great experience not many females can say they've had. However, I don't believe the Air Force should seek out all-female crews—instead, we should focus on experience."

"[The Air Force] should have the best crews they can put together," said Captain Anita T. Mack. "Nothing other than qualification and ability should be considered." Crew members suggested that one way to avoid complacency is to mix male and female fliers to get different perspectives.

The first all-female crew to fly a C-130 Hercules on a combat mission

Master Sgt Alfred A. Gerloff Jr./Courtesy US Air Force

While the all-female crew passed a unique milestone, the members pointed out that each crew member achieved her individual goals to get there.

"I encourage any woman to do what she wants," Captain Mack said. "Too often I hear people say women can't do something. That may be because they don't realize they have the opportunity. Flying is an attainable goal for anyone who wants to work for it. You are only limited in what you can do by what you can dream."

Developing Team Members' Assignments

Team assignments are the most specific part of the team charter. A team assignment *lets each individual team member know his or her role on the team*. The assignment may be a specific task or an ongoing responsibility, depending on the team goal.

Each member must see how his or her team assignment integrates with other members' assignments. It's important to express each assignment as clearly as possible. Assignments should not be rigid, however. The team leader should change them if circumstances require it—making needed changes is the team leader's job. The charter should also make it clear that it's every member's job to step in and help another member who needs extra support.

For example, on a baseball team, each player needs to know who is assigned to play first base, second base, shortstop, and so on. They need to know who will back up whom, depending on where the batter hits the ball. Each player also needs to know when he or she will take a turn at bat.

But these assignments don't prevent the coach from moving a player to another position or to another place in the batting order for the good of the team. The coach may give a member a temporary assignment other than the designated assignment. Or the coach might ask a team member to step out of his or her assignment to assist another member. The team member returns to the charter assignment as soon he or she finishes the temporary assignment.

Creating a Timeline

Team members need to know not only *what* they're supposed to do but also *when* they need to do it. To find out this important information, they consult the project timeline. A timeline is *a table that lists the dates by which individual project tasks or activities must be accomplished.*

Timelines may have two types of tasks: *ongoing tasks* and *event-specific tasks*. A team project such as a school safety-monitoring team or a tutoring club has ongoing tasks. The timeline might say, "The team leader will meet with the vice principal every Wednesday during activity period," or "Tutors will meet with the students they are tutoring at least once a week."

Other team projects, such as a school play or the class cookout, have event-specific tasks. The team must have certain tasks finished on specific dates and times, such as, "Complete the stage platform construction by Wednesday, March 29, at 7:00 p.m."

The team leader might need to revise the timeline when one task ends and another begins, depending on whether or not the team members are meeting the task deadlines.

A deadline is *the date by which an assignment or a task must be completed*. Each team member must schedule his or her work with the deadline in mind. Looking at the deadlines also allows other team members to see where each assignment fits into the overall timeline.

Deadlines—like other measurable goals—enable the team leader and team members to monitor progress.

Enlisting Others to Work Toward a Common Vision

By now you understand how effective teams work. They unite behind a vision, write a solid team charter, establish measurable goals, make appropriate assignments, follow a timeline, and evaluate their progress.

An effective coach or team leader encourages the team to work together to achieve excellence.

Monkey Business Images/Shutterstock

But what about an exceptional team? It meets its deadlines and gets the job done, to be sure. But an exceptional team aims to exceed expectations. It strives for excellence. Excellence is *the quality teams try to achieve that inspires them to outstanding or exceptional results.* The imagineers of Walt Disney and the six women who flew the landmark mission in southwest Asia demonstrated excellence as they worked toward a common vision. Their personal commitment to excellence was reflected in the exceptional accomplishments of the teams they were a part of.

To demonstrate excellence, team members must enthusiastically support the team's vision. Enthusiasm and dedication are important elements in moving a team toward excellence.

As a leader, you can do four things to encourage the members of your team to work together to meet their common vision and to achieve excellence:

- **Assess**—Determine which factors motivate each of your team members. Among the possibilities are praise, awards, promotion, time off, and more responsibility. Every person is motivated by different things. Match each team member with the motivational factor that works best for him or her.

- **Align**—Identify team members' individual strengths. Then assign them roles that match those strengths. People are more likely to excel in tasks they can do well and that they enjoy doing.

- **Recognize**—Give quick, positive, and specific feedback. A rule of thumb is to praise publicly and criticize privately. Link recognition to what motivates each team member: Is it public praise? A half-day off? A promotion?

- **Challenge**—Set demanding but realistic standards. Unrealistically high standards demoralize people, because they feel they will never reach them, no matter how hard they try. But if standards are too low, people will get lazy. They will not be inspired to work as hard as they can. You must also make sure that each team member can see a direct connection between his or her work and the team's results.

Michelle Kwan

Mike Liu/Shutterstock

"It's Not About the Gold"

Smiling at the crowd, figure skater Michelle Kwan walked proudly with her US teammates during opening ceremonies at the Olympic Games in Turin, Italy, on 10 February 2006.

At age 25, Kwan had already won 42 championships, including five world championships and nine US championships. She was back for a third try at Olympic gold. Previous efforts in 1998 and 2002 had earned her silver and bronze medals. Kwan's millions of fans had their fingers crossed. Figure skating, everyone knows, is a dicey sport. Skaters need grace, athleticism, determination, and a little bit of luck.

This time, Kwan's luck ran out. Just a few days after the opening ceremony, Kwan had to withdraw from the Olympics. After battling a groin injury for months, she developed a new injury during a practice run in Turin.

"This injury prevents me from skating my best, and I've said all along that if I couldn't skate to the level that I expected from myself, I'd withdraw from the team," she said in announcing her decision, which allowed another team member to skate in her place.

Kwan's decision reflected her character, her sportsmanship, and her respect for her team. To those who'd traced her career, it came as no surprise. "The Olympics is the greatest sporting event in the world, and what's most important is that the United States fields the strongest team," she said in an earlier interview.

Kwan's chance for Olympic gold may have been dashed, but her spirit was not. Her fellow athletes, including 1988 Olympic gold medalist Brian Boitano, had always praised her spirit. "Michelle's a tiger underneath. She's a great fighter, a great competitor," he said.

That spirit emerged early. Born in 1980 in California to Chinese immigrant parents, Kwan started skating at age five. In 1992, she entered competition at the senior level. She started to win championships and, until Turin, she never stopped.

Michelle Kwan withdrew from Olympic competition with dignity. She put her team first. In so doing, she earned the respect of athletes and fans worldwide. Her agent, Shep Goldberg, summed it up: "Michelle's character, class, and integrity are what make her what she is, not the color of her medals."

Kwan herself said, "I've learned it's not about the gold. It's about the spirit of the Olympics… and if I don't win the gold, it's OK."

Michelle Kwan gave the world, in the words of one editor, "a legacy that glitters more than gold—a legacy of goodwill."

✔ CHECKPOINTS

Lesson 3 Review

Using complete sentences, answer the following questions on a sheet of paper.

1. What does a team vision do?

2. Whose job is it to fine-tune the vision, and why?

3. What does a team charter include?

4. What four elements should a team charter have?

5. What do team goals grow out of?

6. Why is a project timeline important?

7. What does an exceptional team do?

8. What four things can you do as a team leader to help your team work together?

APPLYING YOUR LEARNING

9. Why do you think it's important to encourage members of a team to work together to meet a common vision and achieve excellence?

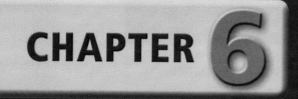

Solving Conflicts and Problems

Don't find fault. Find remedy.

Henry Ford

Identifying Conflict in Groups

Quick Write

Think about the last group or team project you worked on. Write a brief paragraph about how the group performed. Did the group have any problems? If so, what were they? How did the group resolve them?

Learn About

• types of problems in groups
• types of conflict in groups
• ways of handling conflict

Types of Problems in Groups

When a group of people works together toward a goal, many obstacles can fall across its path. Some of these obstacles—such as a thunderstorm in the middle of a class picnic—are due to simple bad luck. They're caused by forces outside anyone's control. Other problems, however, are caused by the relations among the team members themselves.

A problem is *a difficulty that a group experiences in pursuing its goals*. A conflict is *a clash among people*. This lesson looks at how groups identify and solve problems and conflicts to achieve better results. No matter what the project—schoolwork, sports, or community service—the ability to control problems and conflicts often spells the difference between success and failure.

The types of problems groups face fall into one of three types: problems with relations, problems with direction, and operational problems.

Problems with Relations

A problem with relations is *a difficulty in the way people get along with each other*. Problems with relations usually are caused by personality differences among team members. Such differences can create obstacles to group work.

Personality issues that can cause problems with relations include:

• **Overbearing members**—These people hold an unusual amount of influence in a group, often because of their high rank on the team or in-depth knowledge. Most teams benefit from their participation—but their influence can quickly dominate the team. Other members feel left out. Team spirit suffers. A team leader can deal with overbearing participants by ensuring that all members can explore any area related to the project. The leader should talk to the overbearing person in private and ask for his or her cooperation.

- **Dominating members**—These people take up too much of team members' attention. They like to hear themselves talk. They rarely give others a chance to contribute. As a result, the team cannot build a sense of joint accomplishment. A team leader can deal with dominating members by ensuring that everyone participates during discussions. A leader might say, "We've heard from you on this, Joe. I'd like to hear what others have to say." The leader should get the team to agree on the need for limits and focus in discussions.

- **Reluctant members**—Many groups have one or two members who rarely speak. These people feel unsure of themselves. They are the opposites of the overbearing members. If invited to speak, they commonly say something like, "I *am* participating; I'm listening. When I have something to say, I'll say it." A team leader can deal with reluctant members by dividing project tasks into assignments and reports. The leader should then say, "Does anyone else have ideas about this?" while looking at the reluctant participant. Or the leader could say, "Corinne, what is your experience in this area?"

- **Feuding members**—Sometimes a group becomes an arena for competition. Feuding team members can disrupt an entire team. Usually, the issue is not the subject they are arguing about but the contest itself. These people just like to compete. Other members feel like spectators. They fear that if they participate in any disagreements, they will be swept into the contest and forced to take sides. A team leader can deal with feuding team members by getting the opponents to discuss their differences privately and by offering to referee the discussion. The leader should set ground rules for managing the differences without disrupting the group.

Vocabulary

- problem
- conflict
- problem with relations
- problem with direction
- operational problem
- retreating
- standing still
- detouring
- encountering

A team leader can deal with floundering by asking the group to look critically at how it is running the project.

Monkey Business Images/Shutterstock

Problems with Direction

A problem with direction *occurs when team members want to pursue different goals.* For example, suppose a teacher of a US history course asks class teams to make presentations on a famous president. But team members can't decide which leader to focus on—George Washington, Thomas Jefferson, or Abraham Lincoln. Such a team is experiencing a problem with direction. Groups in this situation tend to flounder or wander.

Floundering

Floundering teams may have trouble at all stages of a project. At the beginning, they sometimes suffer through false starts. They waste time in pointless discussions. They engage in activities that don't lead anywhere. As the group progresses, team members may resist moving from one phase to the next. At the end, teams may put off decisions, saying, "We need something else. We're not done yet."

Each of these types of problems has a different cause. For example, start-up problems may indicate that group members are not yet comfortable with each other. They're not ready to have real discussions and make decisions. Or they may not know how to organize the task. Floundering when trying to make decisions may indicate that some members disagree with the group's work. These members don't want to admit they don't support the group's decision—but when it comes time to vote, they withhold their support.

A team that flounders after completing one phase of a project may not have a clear plan. It doesn't know what to do next. Floundering at the end of the project may indicate that team members don't want to separate. But it may also be a sign that they are reluctant to expose their work to review and possible criticism from outsiders.

A team leader can deal with floundering by asking the group to look critically at how it is running the project. The leader could say, "Let's review our mission and make sure it's clear to everyone," or "What do we need to do so we can move on? What's holding us up?"

Wandering

Wide-ranging, unfocused conversations are common in a group that is wandering. Wandering is the human tendency to stray from the subject. It can happen when team members lose track of the meeting's purpose or when they want to avoid a sensitive topic. Discussions spin off in many directions at once.

For example, suppose a group is trying to identify the reason for breakdowns in a work process. One member recalls how Sue, a classmate, solved a similar problem. This reminds someone else of how Sue solved a totally different problem. This, in turn, reminds a third group member of an incident between Sue and Ms. Long, her English teacher. This leads to a discussion of how great Ms. Long was and how everyone misses her since she moved to Florida. And so on. When the meeting ends, team members wonder where the time went.

A team leader can deal with wandering by preparing a written agenda and passing it out to members. The agenda should show how much time the group will spend on each item. The leader can then refer to the agenda when the discussion strays too far. If it's not possible to do an agenda, the leader could write the topics and time limits on large paper and post it in on the wall.

Operational Problems

When teams accept opinions as facts, rush to accomplishment, or discount input or information, they have operational problems. An operational problem is *a difficulty that is linked with conflicts over procedure, method, or approach*. Problems with operations may arise when team members want to pursue the same goals, but use different means. For example, once the group in the US history class has decided to study a particular president, members may have trouble deciding who will do which part of the project.

Operational problems may pop up when some team members express personal beliefs with such confidence that the others assume they are hearing facts. Many times team members hesitate to question self-assured statements from other members. Besides not wanting to be impolite, the reluctant members think they need more information before they challenge someone else's assertions.

A team leader can deal with unquestioned acceptance of opinions as facts by asking "Is that your opinion, or is it a fact?" or "How do you know that is true?" The leader might also say, "OK, let's accept what you say as possible, but let's also get some information to test it."

Rush to accomplishment is common to teams that are pushed by one or more members who are impatient for results. These members are unwilling to take the time needed for group problem solving or decision making. Many teams will have at least one "do something" member who is impatient or insensitive to pressures affecting the group's task, such as deadlines or project guidelines. These members reach their own conclusions on a course of action before the group has had time to consider all the options. They urge the team to make hasty decisions and discourage further discussion. Their body language and comments constantly communicate impatience.

Team members must realize that improvements don't come quickly. Quality takes patience. A team leader can deal with a rush to accomplishment by reminding team members of their prior agreements. The leader should confront the "rusher," using constructive feedback. And leaders, in their well-intentioned efforts to keep things moving, should make sure that they themselves do not pressure the group.

American Biographies

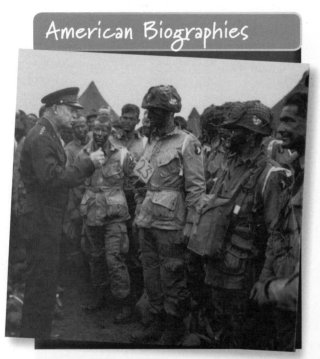

General Dwight D. Eisenhower talks with troops on the eve of D-Day in 1944.
Courtesy National Archives, photo no. 531217

Dwight D. Eisenhower: Bridging Differences to Gain Victory

Sometimes it takes a real leader to get people to work together for their own good.

During World War II General Dwight D. Eisenhower became supreme commander of Allied forces in Western Europe. One of Eisenhower's most valuable skills was his ability to create strong leadership teams—particularly among team members who didn't get along with each other to start with. Eisenhower knew that to invade Europe and defeat the Germans, he would need a united Allied force.

To create such a force, Eisenhower realized he'd have to get very different leaders from different countries to cooperate. Some of these leaders were arrogant and overconfident. Some were biased against their own supposed team members. Eisenhower had to build cooperation among the British, American, and other forces and combine land, sea, and air forces in the battle for Europe. This effort took patience, charm, and the ability to negotiate with subordinates who didn't always trust each other.

Eisenhower became general of the army in December 1944, commander of US forces in Germany in 1945, and Army chief of staff in November 1945. He resigned from the military in 1948 and took a job as president of Columbia University. In 1952, he was elected president of the United States. He served two terms.

Types of Conflict in Groups

Although groups can have any number of conflicts, they all boil down to three basic types. Each of these types relates to the problems you learned about earlier.

- Problems with relations often result from conflicts in *perspective*.
- Problems with direction are frequently tied to conflicts in *purpose*.
- Operational problems involve conflicts in *practice*.

Conflicts in Perspective

Conflicts in perspective involve people's motivations. They have to do with team members' differing beliefs and values. The student who wants the highest-possible grade point average (GPA) believes that it will help him or her get into a good college. Such a student believes that a college degree is critical for success. A student who wants only a high school diploma, on the other hand, doesn't think college is important. These two students' values are different, and those values will determine how they act and react in a group.

On a higher level, conflicts in perspective can cause international problems. For example, the conflict between the Israelis and Palestinians in the Middle East is not simply a practical issue of who will live where. Rather, it's a basic difference of perspective about who has the *right* to live where.

If people try to solve perspective-level conflicts by ignoring or working around them, the conflicts will continue. That's because the participants have not addressed the underlying issues. Even so, such conflicts are difficult, and sometimes impossible, to resolve. At times, people must agree to disagree and work out the best compromise possible.

Conflicts in Purpose

Conflicts in purpose involve what people want to achieve. These conflicts arise when members can't accept the team's goals and objectives.

For example, one team member might say, "I don't care what grade we receive on this assignment. I just want to get it done." Another member might say, "I want us to put together an A+ presentation so that I will keep the highest GPA possible."

It's easier to establish goals than it is to change team perspective. For this reason, purpose conflicts are usually easier to solve than perspective conflicts are. To deal with conflicts of purpose, the leader should set clear goals before the project begins—with input from team members.

Conflicts in Practice

Conflicts in practice have to do with the team's processes and procedures. If members can't agree on when the team will meet, where it will meet, or who will lead the meetings, they have conflicts at the practice level.

A leader's best bet in dealing with conflicts of practice is to set up operating procedures before the team begins its work. At the least, the leader can insist that practices and procedures should support the team's objectives.

Ways of Handling Conflict

In dealing with conflict in groups or teams, it's important to understand how people react to it. Generally, they react in one of two ways: *fight* or *flight*.

Some people *fight* when they perceive a conflict. They engage and may become aggressive. At their worst, they lash out, explode, argue, and become competitive. At their best, they express their own perspectives, yet continue to work with team members to arrive at a solution.

When faced with conflict, other people will resort to *flight*. These people are passive. At their worst, they pout, withdraw, passively resist, and avoid working through conflicts at all costs. At their best, they thoughtfully reflect on the issues at hand and offer their ideas to try to resolve them.

Most people have developed strategies for handling everyday conflicts. They may retreat. They may detour around the problem—a method that works sometimes, but may become habit-forming. Other situations are more difficult to deal with, however. You can't retreat. You can't pretend that the problem doesn't exist. You can't get around it. You must adjust.

What is adjustment? Does it mean giving in to avoid trouble or making a scene? Does it mean forcing others to give in to your wishes, never compromising, and relying on the other person to adjust?

Experts have identified four main methods people employ to handle conflict— *retreating*, *standing still*, *detouring*, and *encountering*.

Retreating

Retreating is *blocking or moving away from a problem or conflict*. People who retreat don't want to confront conflict head-on. Some people who retreat simply refuse to defend their point of view. They may give up without even trying. They may try to place the blame on others. In extreme cases, they may even withdraw from society to try to escape reality.

Sometimes retreat is understandable. Loss of a loved one, for example, might cause someone to retreat in fear of future loss, rejection, or loneliness.

Standing Still

Standing still is *avoiding a problem or conflict by using defense mechanisms.*
Some people prefer to stay in one place rather than to risk defeat or rejection.
They include, for example, the student with great potential who takes the easiest
course, so that he or she doesn't have to work very hard. The adult who prefers
to stand still says, "It was good enough for my parents, and it's good enough
for me. Why change now?"

Other forms of standing still include such defense mechanisms as rationalization
and projection (see Chapter 3, Lesson 2, Building a Positive Attitude) or just
daydreaming, forgetting, and regression.

Detouring

Detouring is *moving around, or avoiding, a problem or conflict.* People who
constantly avoid important issues may think they've dealt with a problem,
but the solution is temporary. The problem is bound to arise again. If your
friend Mark says, "Suzanne gets good grades because she's the teacher's pet,"
he's detouring, rather than facing the fact that he doesn't study enough.

The *displacement* defense mechanism is a detouring behavior. *Compensation*
is another way of detouring. It involves substituting traits or attributes that
give you a more pleasant picture of yourself than your undesirable traits do.
A rejected or insecure person may compensate by showing off, being sarcastic,
or misbehaving—just to get attention.

In some cases, compensation has favorable results. For example, a guy who
doesn't make the varsity basketball team might compensate by becoming a
whiz in computer science.

Encountering

Encountering is the best way to handle problems. Encountering is *facing a
conflict head-on and reaching a solution.* The person who faces problems stands
a much better chance of solving them than the person who avoids or ignores
them does. You probably find it easy to advise others about how to face their
problems, but when it's your own problem, it's a different story.

Like everyone else, you face problems and conflicts every day. You interact
with others every day. You must compromise—adjust to those around you.
To function in society, you must learn to meet, encounter, and resolve those
problems and conflicts.

Overcoming Obstacles: The Berlin Airlift

Resolving conflict takes determination, persistence, and teamwork. No group of Americans proved that better than the men and women who mounted the Berlin Airlift in 1948.

World War II was barely over when relations between the Allies and the Soviet Union began to worsen. Eastern Europe came under Soviet control. In 1946, British Prime Minister Winston Churchill warned that "an iron curtain has descended across the continent." The Soviets tightened their control of the roads leading into Berlin, the capital of Germany. After the war, the Allies had divided Germany into four zones: American, British, French, and Soviet. Berlin, which the Allies also divided into four zones, lay deep inside the Soviet zone. In June 1948, the Soviets set up a blockade to try to drive the other Allies out of Berlin. The Western Allies had to rely on an airlift if the 2 million Berliners were to survive.

The task of supplying Berlin by air fell to the US Air Forces in Europe, commanded by Major General Curtis E. LeMay. He had 102 C-47s, each with a capacity of three tons, and two C-54s, which could carry 10 tons each. He put Brigadier General Joseph Smith in charge of the operation. General Smith called it "Operation Vittles" because, "We're hauling grub."

Loading airplanes during the Berlin Airlift.
Courtesy US Air Force

The first deliveries took place on 26 June 1948. On that day, C-47s made 32 flights into Berlin with 80 tons of cargo, mainly powdered milk, flour, and medicine. As time went on, the transports delivered not only food, but also coal to heat the Berliners' homes.

The airlift's demands grew to be too much for US Air Forces in Europe to handle. So the Military Air Transport Service took over. It was created in June 1948 by combining Air Force and Navy transport units. Major General William H. Tunner, a World War II veteran, took command.

General Tunner arrived in Germany in July 1948. He quickly set about speeding up the delivery of cargo. This effort earned him the nickname "Willie the Whip." He set a goal of one landing every minute, day or night, if the cloud ceiling in Berlin was above 400 feet. At times the aircrews came close to reaching this goal, touching down just three minutes apart. To keep the aircraft going, military and civilian mechanics worked around the clock. Crews from the US Air Force, US Navy, and the British Royal Air Force flew the transports. Soviet forces harassed, but did not attack, the cargo planes.

On Easter Sunday, 17 April 1949, this system delivered 13,000 tons of cargo, including almost 600 railroad cars of coal. This "Easter Parade" set a record for a day's cargo during the operation. The Easter Parade required near-perfect teamwork.

By spring 1949, it was clear that the Soviets had not halted the airlifts. The Soviet Union signed an agreement on 5 May 1949 to lift the blockade. But this did not settle the basic issue of freedom of access to the American, British, and French zones of Berlin. Despite the return of surface traffic into the city, the airlift continued until 30 September. This built a reserve of food, fuel, and other supplies in case the Soviets resumed the blockade.

Between June 1948 and September 1949, the airlift delivered more than 2.3 million tons of cargo, about 75 percent of it in American aircraft. American aircrews made more than 189,000 flights, totaling nearly 600,000 flying hours and more than 92 million miles.

Because of the teamwork of the American and British aircrews, West Berlin remained free and democratic. The city and Germany itself were reunited under democratic government in 1990.

✔ CHECKPOINTS

Lesson 1 Review

Using complete sentences, answer the following questions on a sheet of paper.

1. What are three types of problems groups face?

2. What do groups having problems with direction tend to do?

3. What are the three types of conflict in groups?

4. What should a leader do to deal with conflicts of purpose?

5. What are the two ways people generally react to conflict?

6. What have experts identified as the four main methods people employ to handle conflict?

APPLYING YOUR LEARNING

7. How do you think an extravert would tend to react to conflict? How would an introvert tend to react? Why?

Steps for Problem Solving

Quick Write

Think of a group or team you have belonged to. Write down two or three problems that the group experienced. How did members resolve their difficulties? What was the role of the leader in helping fix problems? What were the roles of the group members?

Learn About

- common group problems
- common indicators of group problems
- the six steps of problem solving

Common Group Problems

Put human beings together in almost any setting—a family, a sports team, a class, a club, a community, or an office—and one of two things happens: Either people get along and work well together, or they have difficulties and fail to work together.

But sometimes *both things* happen. And sometimes both things happen at the same time. People have an instinct to cooperate and make progress. At the same time, something in people— for example, egos, personality differences, or cultural divides— pulls them in different directions, creating friction and tension.

All groups and teams have problems of one kind or another. One of the key responsibilities of a group or team leader is to lead the way in fixing problems that arise in the group. This role is critical if the team is to succeed.

But a leader who simply runs around putting out fires is going to be very, very busy. For example, team leader Seth finds he spends far too much time before and after meetings dealing with the fact that Carrie claims not to know how to work her cell phone—which constantly rings during the team's meetings.

The need to pay attention to details of a team's performance problems can eat up a leader's time and energy. Good leaders get ahead of the curve by anticipating the bigger problems. Anticipating a problem is *thinking about what could happen and preparing for issues before they arise.*

To anticipate problems, it helps to know the five common types of groups or teams that seem to attract them most often. These types are the following:

1. **The mismatched team**—This team has drastically differing types of people on it. Nothing it does seems to work, because team members' personalities put them on different wavelengths or performance tracks.

2. **The out-of-control team**—Like a hungry octopus, this team goes beyond its mission and purpose. It tries to do too much. It grasps at tasks beyond its reach.

3. **The bickering team**—This team can't agree on anything. Members constantly heckle one another. Effectiveness and results suffer.

4. **The stalled team**—Like a car running out of gas, this team slows down. It shows fewer and fewer results from less and less effort.

5. **The leaderless team**—Like a ship with a broken rudder, this team goes in no specific direction—or in several directions at once. It makes little progress.

Common Indicators of Group Problems

Most often, these kinds of teams show signs of stress, tension, or friction as problems develop. As a result, the team suffers *poor performance*—its members don't work well together and the team has trouble accomplishing its objectives—if it accomplishes them at all. To prevent this, leaders need to monitor their team's performance constantly.

Common signs of troubled relationships among team members include:

- Continually missing deadlines
- Producing poor work
- Frequently being absent without an excuse
- Excessively celebrating small achievements unrelated to the team goals
- Speaking rudely or bluntly to each other
- Criticizing fellow team members to outsiders
- Pursuing individual goals at the expense of team objectives
- Constantly involving the leader in putting out fires

Vocabulary

- anticipating
- root cause
- troubleshooting
- prioritizing
- specifying
- monitoring
- adjusting
- ownership trap

Team members who suffer low morale don't have positive feelings about the team.

Andrey Popov/Shutterstock

- Asking others to do their work
- Failing to contribute to meetings
- Playing the "blame game" when things don't go according to plan
- Taking individual credit for group successes or others' accomplishments

The need to intervene in petty disagreements among members can be a constant drain on a leader's energy. It forces the leader to spend time on trivial issues that have nothing to do with the team's purpose. These problems can affect not only the group's performance and results but also its morale. The effects of low morale can be slow, subtle, and devastating to the group's success. Team members who suffer from low morale perform poorly and don't have positive feelings about the team. They may stop attending meetings. If they do attend, they may refuse to contribute. Ultimately, they may give up.

Six Steps to Solving Problems

- Recognize the problem.
- Gather data.
- List possible solutions.
- Test possible solutions.
- Select the best solution.
- Implement the solution.

The Six Steps of Problem Solving

To solve these and other problems in teams and groups, it helps to use an orderly process. One such process is the six problem-solving steps that many leaders in education, business, government, and the Air Force use. When you're working alone, you can apply these steps to your problem. When you're working with a team, this process allows you to involve the team members in finding a solution. This is often more effective than having the leader simply order members to implement a solution.

Recognize the Problem

The first step is to recognize and define the problem. To do this, you need to get at its root cause. A root cause is *a significant, deeper issue that underlies problems and conflicts.*

Root causes are often complex and hard to figure out. A leader may have to troubleshoot to get at the root cause. Troubleshooting means *taking apart a problem and determining what makes it happen.* Once you know the cause, you can begin to find a solution.

Sometimes, root causes are too big or complicated for a leader to address. For example, one of your team members may constantly make sarcastic remarks about other team members. If you look closer, you may find that this person gets constant criticism at home and is merely taking out frustration on others.

A Sergeant's Persistence Led to an Act of Congress

Sometimes solutions to problems crop up in the most unexpected places and at the most unexpected times. It took one Air Force sergeant's suffering to get America's leaders to craft a solution that honored her sacrifice—and her dog's.

Technical Sergeant Jamie Dana and Rex, a bomb-detecting military dog, were coming back from a convoy patrol in Iraq on 25 June 2005. As they traveled the road, an improvised explosive device—a homemade bomb—detonated under their Humvee, blasting the vehicle to pieces.

Dana suffered severe injuries in the blast, including collapsed lungs, a fractured spine, and internal bleeding. Before she lost consciousness, she asked, "Where's Rex?" A medic told her that Rex had died. "I felt like my heart broke.... It's the last thing I remember," Dana said later in an interview.

Dana's grief was understandable: She and Rex had trained together for three years. They were deployed to Iraq side by side.

She was evacuated to Balad Air Base, where she was treated. Her injuries were so severe that she required 19 blood transfusions.

Later, while receiving care in a military hospital in Germany, Dana learned that Rex had survived the explosion with only minor burns. Dana resolved to do whatever she could to adopt Rex from the Air Force. Still critically ill herself, Dana asked Air Force officials if she could adopt the dog. She soon learned that US law prohibited the adoption of animals still considered useful to the military.

After Dana's plight became public, the US Congress changed the law to allow handlers to adopt and take home military working dogs following a traumatic event. Indeed, it took an act of Congress for this to happen. Chief of Staff of the Air Force General Michael Moseley said the adoption was a positive event. "This has been a team effort between both houses of Congress, and I'm just glad to see that there's a happy ending." Dana adopted Rex after President George W. Bush signed the special legislation in the Defense Appropriations Bill on 30 December 2005.

Technical Sergeant Jamie Dana and Rex meet with Major (Dr.) Paul Morton, who saved her life.
Courtesy US Air Force

Once you've identified the problem, you must gather information about it and list possible solutions.

antoniodiaz/Shutterstock

You can be sensitive to that person's need for positive feedback and friendship, but you cannot fix his or her home problems. One way you might deal with such tension-causing behavior is to talk to the person privately and suggest that his or her remarks may be creating a barrier to group productivity.

Gather Data

Once you've identified the problem, you must gather as much information as you can, both about the problem and about possible solutions. Depending on the nature of the problem, you might visit the library or go to the Internet to gather information. You might interview people who are familiar with the problem or who have faced similar problems. You might get team members together to discuss their views of the problem—looking at problems from different angles can often help suggest solutions.

List Possible Solutions

You've identified the problem and gathered data. Now you need to list the possible solutions. *Brainstorming* is an effective technique to use at this stage of the group problem-solving process. As you learned in the lesson on developing a common vision, brainstorming is a group problem-solving technique during which members contribute ideas spontaneously. Frequently, team leaders and members brainstorm together. Members will feel a part of the solution to a problem if they help create it.

The key here—and the key to all group problems—is communication. If you can establish open, honest, specific lines of communication with everyone on the team, you improve your chances of helping the team solve its issues. You can do this on an individual or a group basis.

As you build a list of possible solutions to a team problem, you should try to prioritize and specify as you go. An effective technique is to write all the ideas that come up during a brainstorming session on a large piece of paper or on a whiteboard. (If you're brainstorming by yourself, write them down on notebook paper, a legal pad, or on an electronic device.) Get at least one suggestion from every person. If you do this, every member of the team will feel he or she has contributed to the solution.

Once you have a good list of ideas, you must prioritize them. Prioritizing is *putting ideas in order from most to least important, significant, or effective.* When prioritizing, you put stronger, more-promising ideas at the top of the list. Put costly, impractical, far-fetched, or weaker ideas at the bottom.

With your ideas prioritized, you can begin to specify how they will work. Specifying is *assigning clear, concrete values to proposed ideas.* For example, if an idea calls for use of time, money, or human effort, your solution should specify, in writing, just how much time, money, or effort will be required.

Test Possible Solutions

Once you've listed the ideas in order of priority and expressed them as specifically as possible, you can select the most promising solutions and begin to test them. You test solutions either "offline"—outside of real-world activity, such as in a laboratory or a focus group—or by trying them out in actual practice.

Suppose you are the manager of the school store. Your problem is that sales are falling. Not enough students are coming in after school to buy. You get the staff together, brainstorm the problem, and come up with three possible solutions. One is to offer more varieties of candy, one is to print up and sell school T-shirts, and one is to open the store for a half-hour during lunch. You don't know which will work, so you decide to try each for a week.

Select the Best Solution

Once you've narrowed the list of possible solutions, you need to pick the best one to put into practice. For a leader, this might involve making a procedural change, creating a rule of order, or stating a new team policy. Your authority as leader usually allows for this, but you'll be more likely to gain your team members' acceptance if you discuss it with them beforehand. In some cases, you might even put the issue to a vote in order to get your members to buy in.

Once members agree on a solution or vote to ratify a change, you should immediately put the rule, policy, or change into effect. Formally announce the change and communicate it afterward to team members who aren't present. Everyone should know what's happening and why. Reinforce the idea that the change is for the good of the group. Bank on people's willingness to go along with reasonable change.

In the example of the school store, suppose you find that offering more varieties of candy resulted in no change in sales. Selling T-shirts led to a 10 percent increase in sales. But opening the store for a half-hour at lunch led to a 12 percent increase. So you get the members together, and most of them agree with your recommendation to change the hours so that the store is open during lunch.

Implement the New Solution

Putting the new solution into effect might be as simple as changing a meeting time, rotating responsibility for providing refreshments, or placing a marker in front of the person whose turn it is to speak.

But implementing some solutions requires sensitive, one-on-one conversations with individual group members about their behaviors and actions. Say some of the school store staff are upset with your decision—they don't want to work during their lunch hour. By talking with them, you may be able to persuade them to accept the decision. Or you may be able to make an arrangement in which they don't have to work during lunch or perhaps work only on certain days.

Arranging such conversations is part of a leader's responsibility. The conversations should be objective, straightforward, and professional in tone and content. This isn't a time to kid around. Let members know improving the team's performance and results are serious issues.

Two things good leaders do as they implement solutions are monitoring and adjusting as they go. Monitoring is *measuring whether or not a solution is truly working.* Adjusting is *making changes as needed in the solution to improve its effectiveness.*

Both monitoring and adjusting require flexibility. A leader needs to recognize that not every solution will work exactly as tested. Whenever people are involved, it's not always possible to predict what's going to happen. People will sometimes do the oddest things.

When putting a solution into practice, a leader must avoid the ownership trap. The ownership trap is *the tendency of leaders to invest too much in a solution at the expense of its effectiveness.* In other words, the leader falls in love with an idea to the exclusion of other possibilities. For example, say that for the first week or two, keeping the school store open during lunch pays off—sales are up about 12 percent. But then they start to fall off. By the end of two months, sales have fallen back to where they were before you implemented the change. Team members are unhappy because they are working extra time during their lunch and have nothing to show for it. It wouldn't be good leadership to insist on sticking to the original plan just because it seemed right at the time. Don't own a solution so much that you can't adjust when the situation calls for it.

AMERICANS *in action*

Lewis and Clark's Problem Solving

In 1804 President Thomas Jefferson sent Captain Meriwether Lewis and Captain William Clark, along with a select group of volunteers, to explore the Pacific Northwest. As Captains Lewis and Clark led their "Corps of Discovery" to explore the uncharted West, they met their first navigational test on 2 June 1805. Moving up the Missouri River, they came to a fork. Their intention was to follow the river to its headwaters, cross the mountains, and move on to the Pacific Ocean. Their problem: Which fork was the Missouri?

Lewis and Clark gathered data by sending Lewis to scout up the northwestern branch, while Clark and another group scouted the southwestern branch. When each returned, they compared their notes, reevaluated their intelligence, studied their maps, and discussed the issue with their men. Lewis and Clark decided that the southwestern branch was the Missouri. All the others disagreed. But their respect for their leaders was so great that the men agreed to follow them along the southwestern branch.

On 13 June, the party reached the Great Falls of the Missouri River. By careful problem solving and support from their team members, Lewis and Clark had chosen and implemented the correct solution.

Meriwether Lewis, portrait by Charles Wilson Peale
Everett Historical/Shutterstock

William Clark, portrait by Charles Wilson Peale
Everett Historical/Shutterstock

Lesson 2 Review

Using complete sentences, answer the following questions on a sheet of paper.

1. How do good leaders get ahead of the curve?

2. What are the five types of groups or teams that attract problems most often?

3. What are seven signs of troubled relationships among team members?

4. What are the effects of low morale on a group's success?

5. What are the six steps of problem solving?

6. What are two things good leaders do as they implement solutions?

APPLYING YOUR LEARNING

7. Explain how Lewis and Clark's actions in locating the Missouri River followed the six steps of problem solving.

Building Consensus

The Nature of Consensus

Consensus is *a mutually acceptable agreement that takes into consideration the interests of all concerned parties.* Consensus is often the product of brainstorming, which—as you have learned—involves seeking solutions to problems and selecting the best options. Consensus may sometimes involve a lot of talking, but it's not total agreement.

Let's examine how the leader of a small committee of high school students might work to build consensus, using the scenario described in the following case study.

Case Study: The Henley High Adopt-a-Road Project

At Henley High School, each year's senior class performs a community service project. In their junior year, the students vote on a project and form a steering committee. Planning for the project begins over the summer. The teams complete the project in time for Henley's homecoming weekend in October.

In May, Mr. Gundersen, the class moderator, offers a list of projects for the upcoming senior class to consider. By secret ballot, the students select one of the suggestions, a road-cleanup project.

Antoine has always been active in community service work, and he volunteers to head the steering committee for the project. With Mr. Gundersen's OK, Antoine asks five of his friends—Alessandra, George, Kim, Frank, and Bryan—to join the committee.

The steering committee decides to conduct an "Adopt-a-Road" campaign. During the campaign, groups of students will pick up trash, plant shrubs, build benches, fix up road and park signs, and install trash cans along several blocks of Henley Road, where the high school is located.

Almost immediately, the group begins to have problems among its members. Antoine finds that George questions or criticizes everything the group tries to do. Kim and Frank bicker constantly. Bryan just sits in meetings and says nothing. Alessandra is the only one who seems to want to cooperate with Antoine in moving the planning forward.

Antoine goes to Mr. Gundersen for advice.

"Before your team can move forward with anything, you're going to have to build consensus," Mr. G. tells Antoine.

"How do I do that?" Antoine asks.

"You have to teach them how to listen to each other, to negotiate, and to compromise to come to mutually acceptable decisions," he says. "You need to convince them to stop acting like a group of old friends and start acting like team members."

Vocabulary

- consensus
- unilateral decision
- negotiation
- arbitrator
- compromise

AMERICANS *in action*

Building Consensus: Welfare Reform

As early as the 1960s, politicians from both major parties began to complain that the national welfare system was broken. The program handed out checks to single mothers with children, with no requirement that the mothers do anything in return. The growing number of critics argued that it trapped welfare recipients in a cycle of dependency that kept them from escaping poverty. These critics argued that the system should require recipients to enter the workplace and gain the skills to be able to support themselves.

Defenders of the program argued that changing it would create a social disaster and push 1 million children into poverty. But gradually a bipartisan consensus developed in Washington that the system didn't work: Welfare kept people poor rather than reducing their poverty. In 1996, a Republican Congress (with some Democrats also voting in favor) and President Bill Clinton, a Democrat, agreed on landmark legislation that changed welfare. The new law gave states more freedom to set standards for who could receive assistance. It created new work requirements for those who receive benefits paid with federal dollars. And it put in place a five-year limit on federal benefits for most recipients.

By 2002, welfare rolls were half the size they had been in 1996. But the poverty rate among female-headed families with children had fallen from 42 percent to 34 percent. Two Harvard University researchers noted in 2004, "Welfare reform is now widely viewed as one of the greatest successes of contemporary social policy."

Defining Consensus

Antoine's job, according to Mr. Gundersen, is to build team consensus. If Antoine decides to follow Mr. G's advice and build consensus on the steering committee, he will have to get all six members actively participating in meetings, calmly discussing issues, and airing differences. Under his guidance, they will then decide on a course of action they all can support.

One way Antoine could do this is with a brainstorming session. During a brainstorming session, group members take part in a no-holds-barred discussion of an issue. They come up with as many ideas as possible. Once the ideas are on the table, the group discusses the pros and cons of each idea and selects the one most acceptable to everyone.

An agreement reached through brainstorming and consensus may not satisfy each participant's interests equally. It may not receive the same level of support from all participants. But it's an agreement that everyone can live with. Everyone has had a part in the discussions that led to the decision. Most important, the team can use the decision as a basis for moving forward.

By contrast, a unilateral decision is *a one-way decision usually made by the leader or a dominant team member.* For example, if George doesn't like the way Antoine and the others are planning to run the cleanup project, he could shut down and say, "Well, I'm in charge of buying supplies, and I'm going to do it my way." He's not respecting the views of the other team members, and he's creating tension by demanding his own way. Or Antoine might say, "Listen, George, I chose you for this committee. If you're not willing to go along with our plans, I think you'd better drop out of this group. We don't need your aggravation." These unilateral decisions could have a devastating effect on team morale and progress.

Benefits of Consensus

Because you've already learned about the importance of a common vision and group problem-solving skills, you can probably see why consensus has many benefits over unilateral decisions. The following are some of the benefits of consensus:

- It gives people the sense they are part of the solution.
- It leads to creative, responsive decisions.
- It increases buy-in from group members.
- It encourages participation in meetings.
- It keeps a group alive.
- It takes the burden of decision making off the leader.
- It leads to more-effective team performance.

Methods of Building Consensus

Besides brainstorming, four other methods to build consensus are *active listening*, *being a good negotiator*, *knowing how to compromise*, and *asking good questions*. Teams often need to use all these techniques to build consensus.

Active Listening

To be a good consensus builder, you must sharpen your *active-listening skills*. As you learned earlier, active listening is two-way communication. You pay full attention to what people say and ask questions if you don't understand.

Active listening actually requires active *seeing*. As you've learned, sometimes people talk even when they're not saying anything. You have to be patient and "read" people—their motions, their faces, their eyes, and their body language.

So even though Bryan isn't saying anything during the group meetings, Antoine could learn a lot just by watching him. Does Bryan seem bored? Tired? Shy? Angry? Distracted? Is his lack of participation a reaction to George's continued efforts to challenge the group? Does Bryan look at people when they speak? Does he nod or shake his head? Or is he usually gazing out the window?

And if Antoine watches and listens to Kim and Frank as they argue about whether the team should use paper or plastic bags to gather trash during the road cleanup, he can figure out what each one really wants. Are they arguing just to argue? Or does their argument have a basis— for example, is Kim concerned about the environmental effects of plastic?

Active listening produces mutual respect between listener and speaker. Remember that mutual respect is the two-way relationship that develops between people or members of groups after the lines of communication are open and trust develops.

Active listening helps build consensus, which encourages participation and leads to more-effective team performance.
Andrey_Popov/Shutterstock

Negotiating Productively

The word *negotiation* might bring to mind long, heated, and often unproductive discussions between workers and managers, or between heads of two warring nations. Maybe you've heard people talk about the "art" of negotiation. What does this mean?

Negotiation is *the process of bringing about a fair settlement through discussion and agreement.* It comes from a Latin word that means, "to carry on business." Productive negotiations are an art because leaders must oversee them with skill and sensitivity.

Techniques for Leading Negotiations

How do you lead a productive negotiation? Experts advise trying techniques such as these:

- Adopt a "win-win" attitude—assume everyone will get something of value.
- Stay flexible—be open to suggestions or offers from both sides.
- Say "we" instead of "you" and "they."
- Don't talk specifics, such as numbers or amounts, immediately.
- Let both sides fully explain their positions, needs, and offers.
- Stay as objective as possible—discourage strong emotion and focus on facts.
- Don't let parties get hung up on details.
- Use the "parking lot" approach—if members can't agree on a specific issue, "park it" and come back later.
- Don't try to fix everything in the parties' positions.

When negotiating, it's important to let people on both sides explain their positions, needs, and offers.

Andresr/Shutterstock

Negotiations can be difficult. Participants often hold strong opinions. To keep things moving, many negotiators seek the services of an arbitrator. An arbitrator is *a person chosen by both sides in a dispute who hears details of the dispute and gives a decision to settle it.* Arbitrators often undergo special training for their roles.

Most teams do not need an arbitrator, but all teams need firm leadership. The leader must not take sides. The leader's job during negotiations is to create an atmosphere in which everyone participates and feels comfortable speaking out.

Once Antoine has examined the situation with each of his team members, he can begin to get them to negotiate their differences. He understands better what motivates each of them. He respects their individual positions and, because he has listened actively, they respect Antoine as their leader. They come to trust his advice and follow his guidance. After they settle their differences, they move from the "storming" stage, then through "forming" and "norming." Finally, they're ready to "perform" as a team. They have learned how to be a working team. And they'll remain friends!

Compromising

A compromise is *an agreement between opposing parties to settle a dispute or reach a settlement in which each side gives some ground.* In a compromise, none of the parties gets exactly what it wants. Each party concedes, or yields, something to the other. Compromise involves give and take. Following a successful compromise, all parties feel they've had to sacrifice something. At the same time, they feel they got a fair deal. Like negotiation, compromise works best with the help of a skilled leader or arbitrator.

When the stakes are high, it takes insight and courage to forge compromise. But what about when the snag is a petty difference? It's still takes a good ear, a steady eye, and the ability to bring the two feuding parties together to talk about the issue. Agreements almost never happen by themselves.

Think about the argument between Frank and Kim about trash bags. How could they compromise? It's either paper or plastic, right? How can two people reach an agreement in such a situation? Antoine needs to remember what he learned when he listened actively. He may have noticed that the angrier Kim got, the more relaxed Frank seemed. He'd sit back, fold his hands, and smile at her. Was Frank simply trying to upset Kim and enjoying her emotional reaction?

Maybe Antoine needs to advise Frank to let Kim have her way on the issue of paper collection bags. In exchange, she'll agree to the team's using plastic liners in the trash cans they're about to install. Both people can act as if they've gained their point, as long as Antoine can keep them calmly talking.

Henry Clay
Everett Historical/Shutterstock

Throughout our country's history, the ability to compromise has been one of its most important traits. Sometimes the gift works superbly. And sometimes it works only temporarily.

For example, while writing the Constitution, the Founding Fathers struggled with the question of representation in Congress. The large states wanted to base representation on population. The small states, fearing the large states would constantly outvote them, wanted equal representation for all states, regardless of size. In 1787, the Constitutional Convention stalemated until Roger Sherman of Connecticut proposed the Great Compromise: Congress would consist of two chambers— a House of Representatives in which each state would have a number of representatives based on its population, and a Senate in which each state would get two seats, regardless of population. This compromise gained the convention's approval and led to the adoption of the US Constitution. The Great Compromise has served the American people well for more than 200 years.

In the nineteenth century, as the US population was growing, Congress made a series of decisions admitting new states to the Union. It admitted some states as free and some as slaveholding. Legislators from each type of state wanted to ensure that the other did not get a majority of voting power in the Senate, where each state had two senators. The admission of Alabama as a slave state in 1819 brought the number of slave and free states into balance, with equal representation in the Senate.

In January 1820, a bill to admit Maine as a state passed the House of Representatives. Members of Congress decided that by pairing Maine (a free state) and Missouri (a slave state), the balance would remain. The Senate joined the two bills. It replaced the clause forbidding slavery in Missouri with a measure that would prohibit slavery in the remainder of the Louisiana Purchase north of 36°30′ North latitude (the southern boundary of Missouri). The House rejected this compromise bill. But after spirited negotiations in both the Senate and the House, legislators agreed once again to treat the bills separately.

Speaker of the House Henry Clay worked to secure passage of the compromise. In March 1820, Congress made Maine a state and authorized Missouri to adopt a constitution that had no restrictions on slavery. Congress admitted Missouri to the Union in August 1821.

The Missouri Compromise kept the peace between the free and slaveholding states until the geographic situation changed after the Mexican War (1846–1848). The addition of new territory won from Mexico upset the balance and reopened the question of which states would be free and which slaveholding. Now serving in the Senate, Henry Clay, "the Great Compromiser," helped engineer the Compromise of 1850, which allowed slavery in the New Mexico and Utah territories, but prohibited it in the new state of California. This compromise held off civil war for another 11 years.

Asking Good Questions

To be a consensus builder, a leader must be able to ask good questions and persuade team members to express their opinions honestly. Here are some examples of the types of good questions Antoine might ask as he interacts with the steering committee of the Adopt-a-Road project.

Antoine should ask questions that:

- **Have a focus**—Ask: "What do we need to have in our supply box by Friday?" not "So what are our upcoming supply needs?"

- **Are closed ended, not open ended**—Ask: "Kim, can you tell me why you object to using plastic bags in one or two sentences?" not "Can you help me understand your point?"

- **Bear directly on the issue**—Ask: "We have six ponchos in case of rain, don't we?" not "Don't you hate picking up trash in the rain?"

- **Are objective, not personal**—Ask: "Bryan, do you have anything to add to what George said?" not "Bryan, why do you always play dumb when George talks?

Lesson 3 Review

Using complete sentences, answer the following questions on a sheet of paper.

1. What happens during a brainstorming session?

2. Why is an agreement reached through brainstorming and consensus an agreement everyone can live with?

3. What are seven benefits of consensus?

4. Besides brainstorming, what are four other methods of building consensus?

5. What is the leader's job during negotiations?

6. How do all parties feel after a successful compromise?

APPLYING YOUR LEARNING

7. Suppose you are the leader of a team that wants to plan a group activity. Some people in the group want to go to a sporting event, while others want to see a movie. As the leader of the team, what steps would you take to try to build consensus and make a group decision?

LEADERSHIP

A Leadership Model

Chapter Outline

LESSON 1
An Introduction to US Air Force Leadership

LESSON 2
Leadership Characteristics

LESSON 3
Air Force Leadership Principles

We have wonderful people in the Air Force. But we aren't perfect. Frequent reflection on the core values helps each of us refocus on the person we want to be and the example we want to set.

General Michael Ryan, former Air Force chief of staff

Quick Write

Think of a leader you admire—in the news, at school, at work, or in your community. Write a list of the five things you admire most about that person. How many of those aspects of the leader seem like personality traits? How many seem like learned behaviors?

Learn About

- the basic elements of leadership
- the Air Force Core Values
- reasons for recognizing the Core Values

The Basic Elements of Leadership

Leadership is *the art of influencing and directing people to accomplish the mission.* Being a leader means more than winning an election or receiving a title. A leader directs others toward a common goal. And although some leaders have been chosen for their roles, leadership can also be informal. Any member can be a leader when he or she influences the others to help the group reach its goal.

You may already be a leader in your school, your place of worship, or another organization. Perhaps you've been elected president of a club or captain of a team. Or maybe you exercise leadership in a less formal way—by coming up with effective solutions to problems, by creating a positive attitude that helps your team be more productive, or by helping build consensus when your team has a disagreement.

How do people interact in groups? What types of leadership do they respond to? What types of leadership turn them off? How do successful leaders work with people? By learning the answers to these questions, you can become a more effective leader. And once you think about these questions, you'll probably realize that leadership is a group function—one to which all members contribute. Knowing this will also help you develop a sense of teamwork and group cohesion. The sharing of leadership and the recognition, satisfaction, and feeling of power that accompany it ensure that your group will be productive.

As you begin this study of leadership, keep one more thing in mind: Leaders are not born; they are made. By learning from the examples of famous leaders, by learning about how leaders bring people together around shared values, and by putting these skills into practice, you can become an effective leader.

"Prepare Yourself for Leadership"

All of us know that effective military organizations must be well trained, motivated, and have a sense of confidence that can only be forged through strong leadership. The United States Air Force has a rich legacy of pioneering Airmen who provide a foundation of leadership that has made America's air arm second to none. When we look back at men like Hap Arnold, Tooey Spaatz, Jimmy Doolittle, and Billy Mitchell, we can see shared qualities of leadership that are essential to a strong Air Force.

All of our airpower pioneers and those that have followed know that an Air Force's real strength is its people. The mission is not done by machines, it is done by people. The best weapons are of little value without trained and motivated people to operate and support them. Those of us in leadership positions have a special responsibility to develop and support the high quality people who will lead the Air Force in the 21st century.

I challenge each of you to prepare yourself for leadership, and to take the time to teach those who will follow you.

—Charles A. Gabriel, General, USAF (Ret),
Former Chief of Staff

General Charles A. Gabriel, USAF (Ret) and former chief of staff, wrote this letter to the men and women of the US Air Force in 1985. His words are as meaningful today as when he wrote them.

Vocabulary

- leadership
- integrity first
- service before self
- excellence in all we do

The Air Force Leadership Concept

The Air Force's concept of leadership has two elements: *the mission* and *the people* who must carry out the mission. All facets of Air Force leadership should support these two basic elements. They are key parts of the definition of leadership.

Mission

The primary task of an organization is to perform its mission. This is paramount, and everything else must be subordinate to this objective. Thus, the leader's primary responsibility is to lead team members to carry out the mission successfully.

Former Air Force Chief of Staff General Curtis E. LeMay said, "No matter how well you apply the art of leadership, no matter how strong your unit or how high the morale of your men, if your leadership is not directed completely toward the mission, your leadership has failed." That said, a leader must never forget the importance of the team's people.

People

People perform the mission. They are the heart of the organization. Without their support, any team will fail. A leader's responsibilities include caring for and supporting team members. Successful leaders strive to meet the needs of team members promptly and properly.

Clearly, the two "simple" parts of the leadership concept—mission and people—are actually two very complicated elements. Successful leaders who have effectively dealt with this complex concept have exhibited certain characteristics or traits.

The Air Force Core Values

The Air Force Core Values form the foundation of an organization that runs on trust. They are: *integrity first, service before self,* and *excellence in all we do.* These values support the mission not only of individual teams, but of the entire Air Force. You must make a personal decision to apply these values in your everyday life. Basing your conduct on the Core Values will help make you a successful leader. It will also increase your effectiveness as a dynamic follower.

Integrity First

Integrity First reminds us we must "walk the talk"— our words and actions must be integrated in our lives. It reminds us of Thomas Jefferson's concept of moral muscles—that we build and strengthen our character through the daily exercise of words, actions, and decisions. Integrity first means not only physical courage, but moral courage as well, so that we sometimes stand up by speaking up. It means being loyal to our friends, to each other— by being loyal to our oath, our Air Force, and our Nation.

—From the "Letter to Airmen"
by Secretary of the Air Force Michael W. Wynne,
13 February 2006

Integrity First

Integrity is a character trait. Integrity first is *the willingness to do what is right even when no one is looking.* It is the "moral compass"— the inner voice, the voice of self-control, the basis for the trust imperative in today's military.

Integrity is the ability to hold together and properly regulate all of the elements of a personality. A person of integrity, for example, is capable of acting on conviction. A person of integrity can control impulses and appetites.

But integrity also covers several other moral traits indispensable to national service:

- **Courage**—A person of integrity possesses moral courage and does what is right even if the personal cost is high.

- **Honesty**—Honesty is the hallmark of the military professional, because in the military our word must be our bond. We don't pencil-whip training reports, we don't cover up tech data violations, we don't falsify documents, and we don't write misleading operational readiness messages. The bottom line is we don't lie, and we can't justify any deviation.

- **Responsibility**—No person of integrity is irresponsible; a person of true integrity acknowledges his or her duties and acts accordingly.

- **Accountability**—No person of integrity tries to shift the blame to others or take credit for the work of others; "the buck stops here" says it best.

- **Justice**—A person of integrity practices justice. Those who do similar things must get similar rewards or similar punishments.

- **Openness**—Professionals of integrity encourage a free flow of information within the organization. They seek feedback from all directions to ensure they are fulfilling key responsibilities, and they are never afraid to allow anyone at any time to examine how they do business.

- **Self-respect**—To have integrity also is to respect oneself as a professional and a human being. A person of integrity does not behave in ways that would bring discredit upon himself, the organization, or the school to which he belongs.

- **Humility**—Persons of integrity will put someone else's needs before their own. A person in the military grasps and is sobered by the awesome task of defending the Constitution of the United States of America.

Service Before Self

Service before self *tells us that a leader's duties take precedence over personal desires.* At the very least, it includes the following behaviors:

- Rule following
- Respect for others
- Discipline and self-control
- Faith in the system

Service Before Self

Service Before Self is not the same as "service," a value also claimed by some civilian institutions and corporations. Our Service requires sacrifice and commitment to our Nation. We understand we make decisions in an environment where freedoms are on the line, and lives are at stake. Service Before Self begins with duty, but it means more. It means that, in our Air Force, as we fly and fight in war and peace, going above-and-beyond-the-call-of-duty is not the exception—it is the rule.

—From the "Letter to Airmen" by Secretary Wynne

General Carl A. Spaatz (right) with the first Secretary of the Air Force, W. Stuart Symington, in 1947.

Courtesy US Air Force

General Carl A. Spaatz: Leader in Two World Wars

How can you identify a great military leader? It's someone who performs successfully in a variety of challenging, life-or-death situations. It's a person who shows a lifelong commitment to a cause. And it's someone who's earned the respect of other great leaders.

General Carl A. "Tooey" Spaatz was such a leader. He served his country with distinction in World Wars I and II. Allied Supreme Commander General Dwight D. Eisenhower once said that Spaatz and Army General Omar Bradley were the two officers who contributed most to the victory in Europe. In recognition of Spaatz's leadership skills, President Harry S. Truman in September 1947 named him the first chief of staff of the new, independent US Air Force created by the National Security Act of 1947.

Born in 1891 in Pennsylvania, Spaatz graduated from the US Military Academy at West Point in 1914. His interest in flying led him to enter aviation training in San Diego, Calif. He became one of the Army's first pilots.

Rule Following

To serve is to do one's duty, and our duties are most commonly expressed through rules. While it may be the case that leaders are expected to exercise judgment in the performance of their duties, good leaders understand that rules have a reason for being, and the default position must be to follow those rules unless there is a clear operational reason for refusing to do so.

Respect for Others

Service before self tells us also that a good leader places the troops ahead of his or her personal comfort. We must always act in the certain knowledge that all persons possess a fundamental worth as human beings.

Spaatz served in the First Aero Squadron under General John J. Pershing during the US expedition to Mexico in 1916. During World War I, he commanded the 31st Aero Squadron in France. He directed the American Aviation School in Issoudun and also saw combat. During the final months of the war, he shot down three German Fokker aircraft. In 1929 he and his co-pilot, Ira Eaker, set a new endurance record after more than 150 hours aloft.

Between the wars, Spaatz held a number of leadership positions. In 1941, as chief of the air staff under General Henry H. "Hap" Arnold, he began to plan the American air campaign in Europe.

Planning soon gave way to action. Within weeks of the December 1941 attack on Pearl Harbor, Spaatz was appointed chief of the Army Air Forces Combat Command in Washington, D.C. By mid-1942, he commanded not only the Eighth Air Force but also all US Army Air Forces in the European theater. By the end of that year, he was commanding general of the Northwest African Air Force, which he organized.

One biographer reports that Spaatz was a "doer" and "problem solver" who knew how to achieve results. He put his leadership skills to the test during three years of overseeing air combat in Europe and North Africa. Spaatz and General Eisenhower did not always agree on military issues, but they enjoyed mutual respect.

By July 1945, the war in Europe and Africa had wound down. Spaatz took command of the Strategic Air Forces in the Pacific. He oversaw the atomic bombing of the cities of Hiroshima and Nagasaki in August of that year.

Once the war ended, as chief of staff, Spaatz helped reorganize the Air Force to make it more functional. He supported research that would build a strong aircraft industry.

Spaatz retired in 1948. He continued to serve the Air Force in an advisory role until his death in 1974. This West Point graduate who loved to fly is buried at the Air Force Academy cemetery in Colorado Springs.

Discipline and Self-Control

Leaders cannot indulge themselves in self-pity, discouragement, anger, frustration, or defeatism. They have a fundamental moral obligation to the persons they lead to strike a tone of confidence and forward-looking optimism. More specifically, they are expected to exercise control in the following areas:

- **Anger**—Leaders and military professionals—especially commanders at all ranks—are expected to refrain from displays of anger that would bring discredit upon themselves and the organizations they represent.

- **Appetites**—Those who allow their appetites to drive them to drink excessive amounts of alcohol cast doubt on an individual's fitness, and when such persons are found to be drunk and disorderly, all doubts are removed.

- **Religious toleration**—Military professionals must remember that religious choice is a matter of individual conscience. Leaders, professionals, and especially commanders, must not take it upon themselves to change or by force influence the religious views of subordinates.

Faith in the System

To lose faith in the system is to adopt the view that you know better than those above you in the chain of command about what should or should not be done. In other words, to lose faith in the system is to place self before service. Leaders can be very influential in this regard: If a leader resists the temptation to doubt "the system," then subordinates may follow suit.

Excellence in All We Do

Excellence in all we do *directs you to develop a sustained passion for continuous improvement and innovation that will propel you and your organization into a long-term, upward spiral of accomplishment and performance.*

Product/Service Excellence

We must focus on providing services and generating products that fully respond to customer wants and anticipate customer needs, and we must do so within the boundaries established by the taxpaying public.

Personal Excellence

Leaders and military professionals must seek out and complete their academic and professional military education, stay in physical and mental shape, and continue to refresh their general education backgrounds.

Community Excellence

Community excellence is achieved when the members of an organization can work together to successfully reach a common goal in an atmosphere free of fear that preserves individual self-worth. Some of the factors influencing interpersonal excellence are:

An organization achieves excellence when the members can work together to successfully reach a common goal.

Monkey Business Images/Shutterstock

- **Mutual respect**—Genuine respect involves viewing another person as an individual of fundamental worth. Obviously, this means that a person is never judged on the basis of his or her possession of an attribute that places him or her in some racial, ethnic, economic, or gender-based category.

- **Benefit of the doubt**—Working hand in glove with mutual respect is the attitude that says all co-workers are "innocent until proven guilty." Before rushing to judgment about a person or his or her behavior, it's important to have the whole story.

> ### Excellence in All We Do
>
> *Excellence in All We Do reminds us, at the most basic level, of the old "Hometown Newspaper Test"—imagining our parents reading about our actions, and wanting them to be proud. But it also includes the military concept of honor—knowing our actions reflect on all Airmen—and on the Air Force itself. It reminds us that we stand on the shoulders of giants: heroes like Billy Mitchell and Doolittle, Spaatz, and Rickenbacker; heroes who faced and beat incredible odds. We have inherited a history of excellence, courage, and greatness. We must live up to that heritage, become part of it, and pass it on.*
>
> —From the "Letter to Airmen" by Secretary Wynne

Resources Excellence

Excellence in all we do also demands that we aggressively implement policies to ensure the best possible cradle-to-grave management of resources.

- **Material resources excellence**—Military professionals have an obligation to ensure that all of the equipment and property they ask for is mission essential. This means that residual funds at the end of the year should not be used to purchase "nice to have" add-ons.

- **Human resources excellence**—Human resources excellence means that we recruit, train, promote, and retain those who can do the best job for us.

Operations Excellence

There are two kinds of operations excellence—internal and external.

- **Excellence of internal operations**—This form of excellence pertains to the way we do business internal to the Air Force—from the unit level to Headquarters Air Force. It involves respect on the unit level and a total commitment to maximizing the Air Force team effort.

- **Excellence of external operations**—This form of excellence pertains to the way in which we treat the world around us as we conduct our operations. In peacetime, for example, we must be sensitive to the rules governing environmental pollution, and in wartime, we are required to obey the laws of war.

Reasons for Recognizing the Core Values

There are four reasons to recognize the Air Force Core Values. They are:

- To support personal integrity
- To support the profession of arms
- To support the ethical climate of the organization
- To support professional conduct

Personal Integrity

The first reason is that the Core Values tell us the price of admission to the Air Force itself. Air Force personnel—whether officer, enlisted, civil servant, or contractor—must display honesty, courage, responsibility, openness, self-respect, and humility in the face of the mission.

Everyone must accept accountability and practice justice, which means that all Air Force personnel must possess *Integrity first*. At the same time, a person's "self" must take a back seat to Air Force service: Rules must be acknowledged and followed faithfully; other personnel must be respected as people of fundamental worth; discipline and self-control must be in effect always; and there must be faith in the system.

In other words, the price of admission to the Air Force demands that each of us place *Service before self*. And it's important that we all seek *Excellence in all we do*—whether it be product/service excellence, resources excellence, community excellence, or operations excellence.

The Profession of Arms

The second reason for recognizing the Core Values is that they point to what is universal and unchanging in the profession of arms. Some people are bothered by the fact that different branches of the service recognize different values; other people are bothered by the fact that the Air Force once recognized six values and has now reduced them to three.

But these people need not worry. It is impossible for three or six or nine Core Values to capture the richness that is at the heart of the profession of arms. The values are road signs inviting us to consider key features of the requirements of professional service, but they cannot hope to point to or pick out everything. By examining integrity, service, and excellence, we also eventually discover the importance of duty, honor, country, dedication, fidelity, competence, and a host of other professional requirements and attributes. The important thing is not the three road signs our leaders chose. The important thing is that they have selected road signs, and it is our obligation to understand the ethical demands these road signs pick out.

Personnel must display honesty, courage, responsibility, openness, self-respect, and humility.

Mass Communication Specialist Chad J. McNeeley/Courtesy US Navy

Ethical Climate

The third reason for recognizing the Core Values is that they help us get a fix on the ethical climate of the organization. How successful are we in trying to live by the Core Values? Our answer to this question may not be the one we'd like to give. All of us have heard about the sensational scandals—senior officers and NCOs engaged in adulterous fraternization; the tragic and senseless crashes of the Ramstein CT-43 and the Fairchild B-52; contractor fraud and cost overruns; and the shootdown of the two Black Hawk helicopters over Iraq. We all have read about these incidents and experienced the shame associated with them. But these big-ticket scandals don't just happen in a vacuum, and they aren't always caused by bad people acting on impulse. The people involved knew the difference between right and wrong, and they knew what professionalism demands in these situations.

These big-ticket scandals grew out of a climate of ethical corrosion. Because we believe our operating procedures or the requirements put upon us from above are ridiculous, we tend to "cut corners," "skate by," and "get over." As time goes by, these actions become easier and they become habitual until one morning we wake up and can no longer distinguish between the "important" taskings or rules and the "stupid" ones. Lying on official forms becomes second nature. Placing personal interests ahead of the mission seems sensible. And we develop a "good enough for government work" mentality.

Ramstein CT-43 Tragedy

US Commerce Secretary Ron Brown and 34 others were killed on 3 April 1996 when an Air Force CT-43 from Ramstein AFB crashed into a mountainside in Croatia, a country in southeastern Europe. An Air Force investigation board blamed the crash on a failure of command, aircrew error, and an improperly designed instrument-approach procedure.

Fairchild B-52 Crash

A B-52 bomber crashed during an air show rehearsal on 24 June 1994 at Fairchild AFB, killing all four crew members. Investigation found that the pilot had frequently violated safety regulations and performed unsafe maneuvers. Tragically, senior officers had failed to ground him or to enforce their orders that he cease such reckless behavior.

Black Hawks Down

On 14 April 1994, two Air Force F-15s shot down two US Army Black Hawk helicopters over Iraq, killing 26 people. The F-15 pilots had misidentified the helicopters as Iraqi gunships. The Air Force secretary said the event was "a result of a tragic series of errors and unfortunate events involving numerous people.... The mishap was not the result of any one individual's actions; the conduct of numerous officers and the system itself contributed."

In such a climate of corrosion, the Core Values are like a slap in the face. How far have you strayed from integrity, service, and excellence? What about the folks with whom you work?

Professional Conduct

Fortunately, there is a fourth reason for recognizing the Core Values; just as they help us evaluate the climate of the organization, they also serve as beacons vectoring us back to the path of professional conduct. The Core Values allow us to transform a climate of corrosion into a climate of ethical commitment.

✔ CHECKPOINTS

Lesson 1 Review

Using complete sentences, answer the following questions on a sheet of paper.

1. How can you become an effective leader?

2. What are the two basic elements of leadership?

3. What are the three Air Force Core Values?

4. What are the four behaviors that reflect the Core Value of service before self?

5. What are the four reasons for recognizing the Core Values?

6. What qualities must all Air Force personnel display?

APPLYING YOUR LEARNING

7. Using the leader you wrote about in the Quick Write exercise, describe how that person's actions reflect the Air Force Core Values.

Quick Write

_____

_____

Write a brief paragraph describing the leadership qualities of a figure from American history.

Learn About

- six characteristics of effective leaders
- competence in a leader
- commitment in a leader

Integrity is the fundamental premise of military service in a free society. Without integrity, the moral pillars of our military strength—public trust and self-respect—are lost.

—General Charles A. Gabriel, former Air Force chief of staff

Six Characteristics of an Effective Leader

Effective leaders have certain distinguishing characteristics that make up the foundation of their approach to their work. These characteristics form their character. Your character defines you as a leader. It is the basis for the decisions you make and the way you treat others.

Character is not something you put on in the morning and take off at night. It is who you are 24 hours a day, seven days a week, regardless of where you are, whom you are with, or who might be watching.

Many characteristics go into building a strong character. For you, as a future leader, six characteristics are essential. They are _integrity, loyalty, commitment, energy, decisiveness,_ and _selflessness._

The most basic quality of good leadership is character—an individual's moral excellence and distinguishing ethical integrity.

—Air Force General Richard B. Myers, former chairman, Joint Chiefs of Staff

Integrity

As you learned in Lesson 1, integrity is an Air Force Core Value. Having integrity means establishing a set of values and adhering to them. Integrity means being a whole person— in mind, body, and spirit. Integrity is a total commitment to the highest personal and professional standards. A person or leader with integrity is honest and fair.

How can you spot integrity? An example of integrity in action might be the leader who has an opportunity to pass off an unpleasant task to an uncooperative team member. Instead of penalizing the team member, the leader follows the schedule and fairly assigns the task to the next person on the list. The leader decides to counsel, rather than punish, the rowdy team member. A leader with integrity treats all team members fairly, putting aside personal feelings.

Loyalty

Loyalty is faithfulness or allegiance—to superiors, peers, and subordinates. Leaders must display unquestionable loyalty to their team members before they can expect members of their team to be loyal to them.

This is what Army General George S. Patton, Jr., meant when he said, "There is a great deal of talk about loyalty from the bottom to the top. Loyalty from the top down is even more necessary and much less prevalent." Patton meant that a leader sets the example. When a leader is loyal to his or her team members, they will respond in kind. Team members' behaviors reflect the actions and attitudes of their leaders.

Loyalty motivated Air Force Lieutenant Colonel Leo Thorsness to stay in the rescue zone when his wingman was shot down over North Vietnam in 1967. Colonel Thorsness shot down one MiG-17, damaged another, and drove several others away from the rescue scene. He landed at a forward operating base rather than refuel when he learned that another aircraft was critically low on fuel and needed to rendezvous with the tanker. Eleven days later a North Vietnamese MiG shot down his F-105 and Thorsness spent six years as a prisoner of war in Hanoi, where he proved his loyalty to the United States and his fellow prisoners. When the war ended in 1973 and Thorsness returned home, President Nixon presented him with the Medal of Honor.

Commitment

Dedicated service is the hallmark of the leader. A leader must demonstrate total dedication to the United States, the Air Force, and the team. This commitment sets an example for team members. Commitment is contagious.

An example of commitment is the leader who calls on the team to rally around a team member who's having personal problems. The leader encourages other members to support their comrade. Under their leader's guidance, team members stand united to act if a fellow team member asks for help.

Vocabulary

- energy
- decisiveness
- selflessness
- competence
- technical competence
- relational competence
- enthusiasm
- empathy

No team member takes on this role of support alone. The leader asks team members to express their own commitment, not only to the team member in trouble, but to the team as a unit. This level of commitment leads to increased team unity and greater loyalty among members.

Energy

Energy is *an enthusiasm and drive to take the initiative*. Throughout history, successful leaders have demonstrated the importance of mental and physical energy. They approached assigned tasks aggressively. Their preparation included the physical and mental conditioning that enabled them to look and act like leaders. They had the perseverance and stamina to stay the course. They got the job done.

You can fail, despite your talents, if you don't use your energy to get the job done. That's what a well-known maker of running shoes means in an ad that urges people to "Just do it." Applying your energy to the team and its mission is the key to results.

The leader's commitment points the way to others.

schatzy/Shutterstock

An example of energy is the team leader who urges members to hold a scheduled outdoor training session, even during an unexpected snowstorm. The leader reminds them that the training is essential to prepare the team for its mission. Members won't be adequately prepared if they take a day off. Rather than cancel the training, the leader encourages team members to relish the opportunity to come together in adversity to perform. This kind of high-energy leadership builds respect of the team and the mission. It is the energy that wins.

Decisiveness

Decisiveness is *a willingness to act*. A leader must have the self-confidence to make timely decisions and then effectively communicate those decisions to the team.

Decisiveness includes the willingness to accept responsibility for the outcome of one's acts. Leaders are always accountable—when things go wrong as well as when they go right.

Suppose, for example, that a team leader has five team members but only three slots in a training program. The leader assesses the team members individually and decides which three will benefit most from the training. In private, the leader tells each member of the decision and gives reasons for it. Because this leader has made the decision fairly, the two team members not selected should respect the decision just as much as the members who are chosen do. All members know that the leader made the decision based on careful thought, not on personal preference.

Selflessness

Selflessness is *the ability to sacrifice personal needs and wants for a greater cause.* Leaders put accomplishing their mission and caring for their people before their own welfare or desires. Willingness to sacrifice is essential to military service.

Selflessness includes the courage to face and overcome difficulties and physical dangers. It also includes the need to make difficult decisions. This is *moral* courage. Confronting a tough situation head-on, rather than avoiding it by passing the buck to someone else, requires courage and strength of character.

> In all operations, a moment arrives when brave decisions have to be made if an enterprise is to be carried through.
>
> —Sir Roger Keyes, British admiral

> No nation can safely trust its martial honor to leaders who do not maintain the universal code which distinguishes those things that are right and those things that are wrong.
>
> —Army General Douglas MacArthur

The spirit of selflessness is closely associated with character. One of my favorite stories in this regard is about General Henry ("Hap") Arnold. During the 1920s, General William ("Billy") Mitchell became an outspoken advocate for airpower, which eventually led to court martial. Arnold decided to testify in Mitchell's defense, despite the contrary advice of senior officers. As a result, Arnold was exiled to Fort Riley and told that he would not be selected for advanced professional military education. This signaled the end of his career as an airman.

Shortly after arriving in Kansas, Arnold was contacted by an upstart airline called Pan Am. They offered him a job—not as a pilot, but as president. Arnold faced a tough decision: to stay in the Army with no future or accept a promising business opportunity. He remained in the service. His sense of selflessness—putting the interests of the Nation and his fellow soldiers ahead of his own career—motivated him to stay. In my view, that quality of leadership was instrumental in Arnold later becoming commanding general of Army Air Forces and earning a fifth star.

—General Richard B. Myers

Working to nurture these six characteristics in your own character is essential to becoming an effective leader. It will take work, but that work will be well worth it. Developing these characteristics will improve your ability to build unity, loyalty, trust, and commitment among your team members. They will imitate your example; you will stand on their success.

Competence in a Leader

Competence is *the ability to do something well*. It's the capacity—either inborn or gained through education and training—to think, plan, do, evaluate, and adjust to do better. In a leader, competence inspires trust and commitment among team members. There's nothing more demoralizing for a team member than an incompetent leader. A good leader must demonstrate two types of competence: technical and relational.

Technical Competence

Technical competence is *the ability to do your work well*. You might think of it as task excellence. People can see, measure, and respond to technical competence.

An Airman's ability to replace a turbine blade, a cowboy's ability to tackle a steer, a ballerina's ability to execute a jeté, a linguist's ability to translate a speech, an angler's ability to land a largemouth bass—all are examples of technical competence.

Leaders help their team members become proficient and competent in performing tasks. This leads to improved team performance. But to inspire others to be competent, a leader must first be able to do the task himself or herself. That means you must seek out opportunities to study and learn, as well as to demonstrate, new knowledge and skills. For an effective leader, the guideline is "Do as I do," not "Do as I say."

Relational Competence

Relational competence is *the ability to work well with people*. This kind of competence can be hard to master. It involves interacting with people, and people can be even more unpredictable than a turbine blade, a steer, or a largemouth bass.

Human beings are complex creatures. Good leaders study the techniques of motivating people that you'll learn about in upcoming lessons. Leaders make note of the skills they admire in other leaders. They try to become "people persons"—interested in, connected to, and engaged with other people.

Good leaders study the techniques of motivating people.

Rawpixel/Shutterstock

Relational competence can come from living—you learn how to get along well with others as you mature. But it can also come from education and study. Subjects you will study, such as psychology, sociology, history, literature, and philosophy, can give you the foundation you need to develop relational competence. By studying the models of history and the cases of accepted practice, you will learn to relate. While people are highly complex, there's joy and great satisfaction in dealing with them and their interests, needs, and motivations.

Commitment in a Leader

Talk to most leaders, and they'll tell you one thing: They *love* what they do. They have a passion for their work; they believe in it. Those are two good signs of commitment.

You learned earlier in this lesson that commitment is one of six essential leadership characteristics. Its importance bears repeating. Probably nothing is as important in a leader as commitment to the job. Indicators of a strong personal commitment to the calling of being a leader are the "3 Es": *enthusiasm, energy,* and *empathy.* These three forces bring you to leadership in the first place. They define you as a leader and keep you motivated to lead. Without them, you'd find no flavor or color in your work. It would be "just a job."

Secretary of State Condoleezza Rice at a 2006 meeting of foreign ministers in Berlin.

360b/Shutterstock

Dr. Condoleezza Rice: A History Maker Who Beat the Odds

Born on 14 November 1954, in Birmingham, Alabama, Dr. Condoleezza Rice grew up in the South in the days of racial segregation. She has said that to get ahead in those days, she had to be "twice as good" as others in her class.

Those childhood experiences, plus strong support from her family, shaped her commitment to succeed. And that commitment has paid off—for Dr. Rice and for the country. From 2005 to 2009, Dr. Rice served as US Secretary of State, a top leadership position in the Cabinet of President George W. Bush. She is the first black woman to hold this post. Before her appointment to that position, she was President Bush's National Security Adviser for four years.

Enthusiasm

Enthusiasm is *great excitement for and interest in a subject or cause*. It's the power that pushes people to get out of bed in the morning and to go out and try to change the world. It's the belief in something greater than yourself. It's the underlying force that pushes people to become leaders. Try as you might, it's hard to find an unenthusiastic leader who is successful.

Energy and Personality

Energy is also one of the six characteristics described earlier in this lesson. You learned that energy as a characteristic is the willingness to take on a job and see it to completion.

Rice realized early in life the importance of education to her leadership aspirations. At age 19, she earned her bachelor's degree in political science with honors from the University of Denver. She went on to earn her master's degree from the University of Notre Dame and her doctor of philosophy degree from the Graduate School of International Studies at the University of Denver.

After earning her doctorate in 1981, Rice became a fellow at Stanford University's Center for International Security and Arms Control. While at Stanford, she studied, wrote, and lectured about the politics of Europe. Her specialty became the former Soviet Union. A popular professor, Rice won two of Stanford University's highest teaching honors.

In the late 1980s, Rice took a break from her university duties to serve as Soviet affairs adviser on President George H. W. Bush's National Security Council. During this period, history-making events occurred. The Soviet Union dissolved and Germany reunified. Rice led US negotiations with Russia over missile defense and helped set the tone for the Bush presidency.

Rice returned to Stanford 1991. She became the university's youngest, first female, and first black provost. She left Stanford in 1999 to return to government service, going back to the university when her term as secretary of state ended. Since 2009 she has worked as a professor in the political science department and graduate school of business, while serving as a senior fellow on public policy at the Hoover Institution.

People who have watched Rice's career say that her belief in education and self-improvement has been key to her rise to leadership. She never let anything stand in her way. In an interview with *Newsweek* magazine, Rice said, "My parents had me absolutely convinced that, well, you may not be able to have a hamburger at Woolworth's, but you can be president of the United States."

But leaders have another kind of energy—the energy of personality. Leaders are typically serious about their individuality. They are not comfortable following the herd. They have the imagination to see what the team can accomplish with good direction, patience, and hard work.

Empathy

Empathy is *the ability to show compassion for people.* It's the capacity to feel what others feel and to act on that solidarity. People who show empathy are usually able to interact more successfully with others because they can see beneath the surface to the root causes of problems. They can address the issues that concern or bother others. They understand both the potential and the limits of those around them. Good leaders empathize with their team members. Empathy inspires trust.

Are you committed and competent? Do you have the passion to lead?

Lesson 2 Review

Using complete sentences, answer the following questions on a sheet of paper.

1. What are the six essential characteristics of a leader?

2. What do leaders put before their own welfare or desires?

3. What must a leader do to inspire others to be competent?

4. What can you study to develop relational competence?

5. What are three indicators of a strong personal commitment to the calling of being a leader?

6. Why are people who show empathy usually able to interact more successfully with others?

APPLYING YOUR LEARNING

7. Refer to your description of a leader from the Quick Write. Explain that person's leadership qualities using the six leadership characteristics from this lesson.

Air Force Leadership Principles

Quick Write

_____

_____

Read an American Biography or Americans in Action article from an earlier lesson in this textbook. Then write a list of words that indicate that person's leadership qualities. How did the person's actions reflect his or her leadership qualities?

Learn About

- key leadership principles
- know yourself and your role
- set the example
- care for your people
- communicate, educate, equip, and motivate
- accept your responsibility
- develop teamwork

Key Leadership Principles

Leadership is a complex human behavior. People who study leadership recognize there is no single formula for creating a great leader.

Ideas about leadership have changed a great deal over the past century. In the years following World Wars I and II, many businesses adopted a "top-down" management structure. It looked like a pyramid. The president or chief executive officer sat at the top, and the workers held up the bottom. Businesses borrowed this structure from the military model.

That approach to leadership went unquestioned for many decades. But by the mid-1980s, many businesses began to reevaluate this structure and to create new ones. The pyramid gave way to a flatter shape. The boundaries between the top and the bottom became less distinct. Leadership became a shared responsibility. This led to an examination of the traditional definitions of "leader" and "follower."

In its continual search for the most effective forms of leadership, the Air Force began to reevaluate its application of leadership principles. It drew on current leadership theories from business and universities to develop its own definition of leadership.

Part of your job as a future leader is to understand leadership theories and styles. By demonstrating strong values, building trust, focusing on results, and motivating, you will influence your team members. In so doing, you will help them adapt to the challenge of service in an ever-changing world.

As you learned in Lesson 1, the Air Force defines leadership as the art of influencing and directing people to accomplish the mission." To help its men and women understand the behaviors expected of its leaders, the Air Force has adopted a set of leadership principles. A leadership principle is *a rule or guide that has been tested and proven over the years by successful leaders.*

The following are the Air Force Leadership Principles:

- Know yourself and your role.
- Set the example.
- Care for your people.
- Communicate, educate, equip, and motivate.
- Accept your responsibility.
- Develop teamwork.

Vocabulary

- leadership principle
- cohesion
- cooperation

Know Yourself and Your Role

To be a successful leader, you must recognize your strengths or abilities, as well as your limitations. You must then build on your strengths and try to overcome your weaknesses.

Former Chief Master Sergeant of the Air Force (CMSAF) Robert D. Gaylor put it this way: "Sure, everyone wants to be an effective leader, whether it be in the Air Force or in the community. You can and will be if you identify your strengths, capitalize on them, and consciously strive to reduce and minimize the times you apply your style inappropriately."

As a leader, you must understand your own role. You must also understand how your team contributes to the overall mission of the organization. Finally, you must make sure that each team member understands how his or her role relates to the mission.

During the past century, the United States Army Air Corps was fortunate to have leaders such as General Henry Arnold and General Carl Spaatz. These men knew themselves well. They knew how they could enhance the Air Corps mission. Their knowledge—and self-knowledge—paid off when they accepted the task of building a force to fight and win the air battles of World War II.

Good leaders know they can't do it all by themselves. To help get their jobs done, leaders delegate responsibility to people they can trust.

> One expects a military leader to demonstrate in his daily performance a thorough knowledge of his own job and further an ability to train his subordinates in their duties and thereafter to supervise and evaluate their work.
>
> —Army General Maxwell D. Taylor, former chairman of the Joint Chiefs of Staff

The Right Place at the Right Time

Airman 1st Class Spencer Stone, Army National Guard Specialist Alek Skarlatos, and their childhood friend Anthony Sadler were enjoying a vacation together in Europe in the summer of 2015. On 21 August, they boarded a train in Amsterdam, the Netherlands, for Paris, France. Shortly after the train crossed the French boarder, a gunman, Moroccan Ayoub El-Khazzani, entered their cabin carrying an AK-47 assault rifle and several other weapons.

As the gunman passed by them, the three sprang into action. "Alek taps me on the shoulder and says 'go get 'em!' and that's when I got up and I sprinted at him," Airman Stone said. The Americans plowed into the gunman, trying to grab away the rifle. He tried to fire a pistol, but it only clicked. Then he brandished a box cutter and began slashing at Stone, cutting him in several places and nearly severing the Airman's thumb.

(*Left to right*) **Anthony Sadler, Army Specialist Alek Skarlatos, and Airman 1st Class Spencer Stone.**

Tech. Sgt. Ryan Crane/Courtesy US Air Force

Set the Example

You manage things and you lead people. You do that by being up front, honest, sincere, and visible. I've always felt strongly that you can't ask somebody to do something that either you won't do, or that you haven't done someplace along the line before.

—Former Chief Master Sergeant of the Air Force Gary Pfingston

Setting an example means giving people a strong model to imitate. As a leader, you must set the standard for your team by your actions as well as your words. People will imitate your personal conduct and appearance. They will observe your negative characteristics as well as your positive ones. If you are arrogant or domineering, you will command little respect. Leaders who violate ethical or moral standards harm their people and the mission, as well as themselves. Self-control is also essential—a leader who cannot control himself or herself cannot control others. Lack of self-discipline in a leader destroys the team's unity and its ability to perform.

As the three tackled the gunman and wrestled him to the ground, British consultant Chris Norman joined the fight. The four beat El-Khazzani unconscious and tied him up. Then Stone, badly wounded himself, rushed to the aid of another passenger, Mark Moogalian, an American living in France. Moogalian had confronted the gunman earlier and tried to take away his rifle, but was shot in the neck.

"He was spurting blood everywhere," Stone said. "So I yelled out 'I'm a medic, I'm a medic!' and took the guy and held him down. I just stuck my finger in his neck, found what I thought was an artery and just pressed down. I held that position until authorities came." Stone's actions were credited with saving Moogalian's life.

Police found that El-Khazzani was carrying multiple magazines and about 300 rounds of ammunition. French authorities labeled the incident an attempted terrorist attack and said the five men had prevented a bloodbath.

For their bravery, Stone, Skarlatos, Sadler, and Norman were awarded France's highest award, the Legion of Honor by French President François Hollande. Moogalian was to receive it after his release from the hospital. Back in the United States, Secretary of Defense Ash Carter awarded Stone the Airman's Medal and Purple Heart, Skarlatos the Soldier's Medal, and Sadler the Secretary of Defense Medal for Valor. The Airman's Medal, Soldier's Medal, and Secretary of Defense Medal for Valor are the highest commendations for non-combat bravery that the Defense Department can bestow.

"What the gunman didn't expect … was a confrontation with our very own 'Captain America,' and believe it or not, that is what Airman Stone's friends nicknamed him during Air Force technical training," said Secretary of the Air Force Deborah James. Speaking at the Pentagon, the secretary said the action of the three Americans "personified service before self, no question about it." US Airmen, she said, "bind themselves to a set of core values, which are integrity first, service before self, and excellence in all that we do."

Self-discipline also involves physical fitness. People who are in good physical condition are prepared for any mission. Setting the example in this case includes supporting a physical fitness program and enforcing Air Force weight standards. Leaders must be positive examples of professional conduct, appearance, and physical conditioning.

Team members do not expect their leaders to be saints. But they do want leaders to set a positive example.

> You are always on parade.
>
> —Army General George Patton Jr.

> A decent regard for the rights and feelings of others is essential to leadership.
>
> —General of the Army George C. Marshall

Care for Your People

Caring for people means putting others' needs before your own. To take care of people, you must know them well and be sensitive to their needs. Such concern pays off. If people are worried about their personal lives or other issues, they cannot focus fully on the task. The mission suffers. If your people believe you care for them, you will earn their confidence, respect, and loyalty.

Caring for your people involves establishing clear lines of communication between you and them. This communication must be a two-way process that allows open and honest feedback in both directions. To develop that clear line of communication, you must equip, educate, and train your people. This includes identifying and obtaining the resources they need to accomplish their mission. Once you supply them, you must prepare them to do their jobs. Taking the time to provide your people with the tools they need to succeed will, in most cases, motivate them to exceed the goals set before them. The bottom line about caring for your people is this: People who feel cared for are people who become self-motivated. Self-motivated people can accomplish the impossible.

As a leader, it's your job to keep all communication channels open.
Rawpixel/Shutterstock

A famous example of caring for people occurred 9 April 1865, at the end of the US Civil War. Confederate General Robert E. Lee met with Union General Ulysses S. Grant at Appomattox Courthouse to discuss details of the Confederate surrender. During the conversations, Lee pointed out to Grant that his men would need their horses when they returned home, as planting season had already started. Grant allowed the Confederates to keep their horses. Lee also negotiated food rations for his men. Finally, Lee and Grant agreed that Lee's men could remain in rank as they surrendered their weapons so they could retain their dignity as soldiers, even in defeat.

Lee put the needs of his troops foremost in mind. As he returned to his soldiers, tears streamed down his face. He said, "Men, we have fought through the war together. I have done the best that I could for you."

Communicate, Educate, Equip, and Motivate

Communicate

Communication and information should flow continuously throughout the organization. Successful leaders listen to their people. They are always looking for good ideas that they can pass on to their superiors. Providing feedback is also essential. The worker who is well informed about the quality of his or her work and how it contributes to the mission is more effective and motivated than a poorly informed worker. As a leader, it's your job to keep all communication channels open. The more senior leaders become, the more they must develop and use their listening skills.

> Information is the essential link between wise leadership and purposeful action.
>
> —General Thomas D. White, former Air Force chief of staff

Educate

People need training to do their jobs well. Professional military education, technical training, and on-the-job training are the formal means by which Air Force personnel receive training. Informal training, practice, and personal experience at the unit level reinforce formal training.

Equip

Part of your responsibility as a leader is to make sure your team has the equipment it needs to do its job. You would never expect an aircrew to engage in combat without a well-armed aircraft. But all team members—in the office, in the shop, or on the flight line—need the right equipment. The leader's responsibilities include identifying needs, securing funds, and obtaining the necessary supplies, tools, and equipment to accomplish the mission.

Motivate

A leader's greatest challenge is to motivate team members to achieve the high standards set for them. The ability to generate enthusiasm about the mission may be the single most important factor in leadership.

To motivate people, a leader must understand their needs and align these needs with the unit's requirements. People will work well for an organization if they believe in its mission and if they believe that the organization cares about them.

Recognition is one of the most powerful motivational forces. The leader who publicly applauds the efforts of team members builds a unified organization that will accomplish the mission.

Remember, the most powerful form of motivation is self-motivation. One of your goals as a leader should be to provide an environment that fosters and rewards self-motivation.

Accept Your Responsibility

General Curtis E. LeMay was once asked to provide a one-word definition of leadership. After some thought, General LeMay replied, "If I had to come up with one word to define leadership, I would say responsibility."

As a leader, you are responsible for ensuring that your team accomplishes its mission. If you fail, you are accountable for the consequences. If you are not willing to accept responsibility for failure, you will lose your credibility and respect. You will also lose the team's loyalty. Worst of all, you endanger the mission.

Accountability requires discipline. Just as a leader should reward a job well done, he or she must discipline those who fail to meet their responsibilities or standards.

History provides hundreds of examples of responsible leaders. But it also provides examples of leaders who have failed to meet their responsibilities. Investigators looking into the 2003 *Columbia* space shuttle accident found that NASA leaders failed to take responsibility for safety—with disastrous results.

> In no other profession are the penalties for employing untrained personnel so appalling or so irrevocable as in the military.
>
> —Army General Douglas MacArthur

> Leadership is the art of getting someone else to do something you want done because he wants to do it.
>
> —General of the Army Dwight D. Eisenhower

> Discipline is the soul of an Army. It makes small numbers formidable; procures success to the weak, and esteem to all.
>
> —General George Washington

The Columbia Disaster

On 1 February 2003, space shuttle *Columbia* fell apart during reentry into the Earth's atmosphere, killing all seven crew members. The Columbia Accident Investigation Board studied the accident and concluded that a large piece of insulating foam fell off one of the fuel tanks and struck *Columbia*'s wing during liftoff. This damaged the insulating tiles that protect the shuttle from dangerous superheated gasses when it reenters the atmosphere after space flight.

The shuttle's tiles are very fragile and easily damaged. The Board learned that during several shuttle launches, foam came loose and struck the shuttle during liftoff. But NASA leaders and managers had come to view these strikes as a minor maintenance problem instead of one that endangered the shuttle and crew.

The Board concluded that the roots of the accident lay in the space shuttle's history and culture. It found that NASA leaders had allowed cultural traits and practices to develop that endangered safety, including:

- Relying on past success instead of sound engineering practices
- Tolerating barriers that prevented effective communication of safety information and silenced disagreements about safety matters
- Permitting an informal chain of command and a decision-making process that operated outside NASA rules

A Little Story About Responsibility

This is a story about four people named **EVERYBODY**, **SOMEBODY**, **ANYBODY**, and **NOBODY**.

There was an important job to be done, and **EVERYBODY** was sure that **SOMEBODY** would do it. **ANYBODY** could have done it, but **NOBODY** did it. **SOMEBODY** got angry about that, because it was **EVERYBODY**'s job. **EVERYBODY** thought **ANYBODY** could do it, but **NOBODY** realized that **EVERYBODY** wouldn't do it. It ended up that **EVERYBODY** blamed **SOMEBODY**, when **NOBODY** did what **ANYBODY** could have done!

Develop Teamwork

The leader's job is to mold a collection of individuals into a cohesive team. Cohesion is *the ability of a team to stick together when it works toward its objective*. The team's mission will suffer if any person is "doing his own thing" rather than working together with the group.

As the leader, you should know how the various roles of individual team members fit together. You should create and maintain an atmosphere of teamwork and cooperation to meet mission demands. Cooperation is *the ability of team members to work together to accomplish the team goal*. Teamwork results when people are willing to put the team's mission before all else.

American Biographies

Lieutenant General Elwood Quesada.

Courtesy US Air Force

Visionary General Was Aviation Pioneer and Tactical Genius

Lieutenant General Elwood R. "Pete" Quesada was an aviation pioneer, an organizer of Allied victory during World War II, and a Hispanic-American.

Quesada was born in Washington, D.C., in 1904, just months after the Wright Brothers made their historic flight at Kitty Hawk, N.C. Quesada's military career spanned aviation history from the biplanes of the 1920s to supersonic jets.

He entered the Army Air Service as a flying cadet in 1924. He returned to civilian life briefly to play baseball for the St. Louis Cardinals. In 1927, he returned to the Air Service.

In 1927, along with then-Major Carl Spaatz and then-Captain Ira Eaker, Quesada developed the crucial maneuver of air-to-air refueling. Quesada's greatest contribution, however, was helping develop the concept of "close air support," in which aircraft provide support for ground forces.

Quesada was a visionary. He predicted that effective warfare in the 20th century would require "all sorts of arrangements between the air and the ground." The air-ground force he put together during World War II was the best in the world. He placed forward air observers with divisions on the ground so they could call in air support. He mounted radios in tanks so that ground commanders could contact pilots directly. He initiated the use of radar to direct planes during attacks.

Following the war, Quesada became the first commander of the Tactical Air Command. After retiring from the Air Force in 1951, he was the first head of the Federal Aviation Administration. He also held positions in private firms. Quesada died in 1993.

✔ CHECKPOINTS

Lesson 3 Review

Using complete sentences, answer the following questions on a sheet of paper.

1. How did the approach to leadership change during the 1980s?

2. What are the six Air Force Leadership Principles?

3. What must you understand as a leader about your and others' roles?

4. Why was the Army Air Corps fortunate to have leaders like General Arnold and General Spaatz?

5. What does setting an example mean?

6. What does lack of self-discipline in a leader do?

7. What happens if people are worried about their personal lives or other issues?

8. What must you do to develop a clear line of communication with your people?

9. Whose job is it to keep the lines of communication open?

10. What is a leader's greatest challenge?

11. Who is accountable when the team does not accomplish its mission?

12. Where did the roots of the *Columbia* accident lay?

13. What is the leader's job?

14. When does teamwork result?

APPLYING YOUR LEARNING

15. Write two or three paragraphs about an incident from your own experience in which a leader failed to accept responsibility.

CHAPTER 8

Empower
People

Inspire
People

Leadership

Lead
Change

Shared
Vision

arka38/Shutterstock

Adaptive Leadership

Chapter Outline

> Leadership is not something that you learn once and for all.
> It is an ever-evolving pattern of skills, talents, and ideas
> that grow and change as you do.
>
> Sheila Murray Bethel

LESSON 1

Leadership Style and Mission Demands

Quick Write

_____

_____

Write a paragraph on whether you think a leader should spend more time telling team members how to accomplish a task or training them to do it themselves.

Learn About

- the two orientations of leadership behavior
- the four leadership styles
- the primary factors of the leadership situation

The Two Orientations of Leadership Behavior

Becoming a good leader requires training and practice. But you can begin to acquire and practice leadership skills right now—at school and in your community. Suppose, for example, a volunteer team forms at your school. Its mission is to help rebuild houses devastated by a series of tornadoes. The group elects you as its leader. Now what? You need to think about the tasks ahead and the people who have volunteered to do them. It's no easy job, but it's one you can do if you understand how leaders do their jobs effectively.

This lesson provides some advice that will help. The guidelines are based on years of research about leadership. Leaders in business, in the armed forces, and in virtually every other walk of life use them successfully.

It's helpful to understand the difference between _leadership_ and _management_. You learned in an earlier lesson that leadership is the art of influencing and directing people to accomplish the mission. Management is _supervising the use of resources to achieve team objectives_. In essence, you lead _people_, and you manage _things_. While both skills are important, this lesson will concentrate on leadership.

How does a leader get people to come together to accomplish a mission? You'll find no single answer to this question. A leader must tailor his or her approach to the task and the people available to do it. The leader must base the approach on the environment and on the readiness of the team and its individual members. Readiness is _the degree to which a follower demonstrates the ability and willingness to accomplish a task_. In other words, the leader must base his or her approach on the situation in which the leader and team find themselves.

The Difference Between a Leader and a Manager

There is a difference between leadership and management. The leader and the men who follow him represent one of the oldest, most natural, and most effective of all human relationships. The manager and those he manages are a later product with neither so romantic, nor so inspiring, a history. Leadership is of the spirit, compounded of personality and vision—its practice is an art. Management is of the mind, more a matter of accurate calculation, statistics, methods, timetables, and routine—its practice is a science. Managers are necessary; leaders are essential.

—British Field Marshal Lord Slim

Vocabulary

- management
- readiness
- situational leadership
- relationship behavior
- task behavior
- telling leadership style
- selling leadership style
- participating leadership style
- delegating leadership style

Situational leadership is *a leadership model based on the concept that there is no single best way to influence and lead people.* This leadership style is flexible. It is based on the abilities, knowledge, skills, and motivational level of the team or group the leader is influencing. Situational leadership is grounded in research into how people respond to working in groups.

Two orientations on the leader's part—orientation toward people and orientation toward task—are key to understanding situational leadership. The two orientations are interactive. A leader who is people oriented focuses on interaction with his or her people. A leader oriented toward task focuses on the job to be done.

Jacqueline Cochran being sworn in as a consultant for NASA in 1961.

Courtesy of NASA

Jacqueline Cochran: Aviation and Military Leader

Jacqueline "Jackie" Cochran was a leading aviatrix who promoted an independent Air Force and was the director of women's flying training for the Women's Airforce Service Pilots program during World War II. She held more speed, altitude, and distance records than any other male or female pilot in aviation history at the time of her death.

As a test pilot, Cochran flew and tested the first turbo-supercharger ever installed on an aircraft engine in 1934. She helped design the first oxygen mask, and then became the first person to fly above 20,000 feet wearing one. In 1940, she made the first flight on the Republic P-43 and recommended a longer tail-wheel installation, which was later installed on all P-47 aircraft.

Orientation Toward People

Another name for orientation toward people is relationship behavior—*a leader's engagement in supportive, two-way communication with his or her team members.* Such behavior includes, for example, listening, praising, collaborating, and counseling. A leader who practices such behaviors can greatly improve followers' performance. If you reach a barrier that's stalling team progress, relationship behaviors can help overcome it.

And that makes sense, doesn't it? People will respond better if they feel their leader is supportive and sympathetic. A leader who simply issues orders and then criticizes team members' performance will have a hard time gaining their cooperation. Leaders should bear in mind the old expression, "You catch more flies with honey than you do with vinegar."

Cochran was hooked on flying. She set three speed records and set a world altitude record of 33,000 feet—all before 1940. With World War II on the horizon, Cochran convinced first lady Eleanor Roosevelt of the need for women pilots in the coming war effort. Cochran was soon recruiting women pilots to ferry planes for the British Ferry Command, and became the first female trans-Atlantic bomber pilot.

While Cochran was in Britain, another renowned female pilot, Nancy Harkness Love, suggested the establishment of a small ferrying squadron of trained female pilots. Almost simultaneously, General Henry H. Arnold asked Cochran to return to the United States to establish a program to train women to fly. In August of 1943, the two schemes merged under Cochran's leadership. They became the Women's Airforce Service Pilots.

Cochran recruited more than 1,000 Women's Airforce Service Pilots and supervised their training and service until they were disbanded in 1944. More than 25,000 women applied for training—1,830 were accepted and 1,074 made it through a very tough program to graduation. These women flew approximately 60 million miles for the Army Air Corps with only 38 fatalities, or about 1 for every 16,000 hours flown. Cochran was awarded the Distinguished Service Medal for services to her country during World War II.

In 1948 she became a member of the independent Air Force as a lieutenant colonel in the Reserve. She had various assignments, which included working on sensitive projects important to defense. In 1961, she became a consultant for NASA. With the assistance of her friend General Chuck Yeager, Cochran became the first woman to break the sound barrier, in an F-86 Sabre Jet in 1953. She went on to set a world speed record of 1,429 mph in 1964.

Cochran retired from the Reserve in 1970 as a colonel. In 1971, she was named Honorary Fellow, Society of Experimental Test Pilots, and inducted into the Aviation Hall of Fame. She died on 10 August 1980.

Orientation Toward Task

Task behavior is *the leader's involvement in defining the duties and responsibilities of an individual or a group.* Task behaviors include directing team members on what to do, how to do it, and when to do it. In his book *Leadership in Organizations*, Gary Yukl suggests that task behavior has limitations when used alone, because its effects on team member satisfaction and productivity are difficult to predict. That's why, as noted above, task behavior and relationship behavior must go hand in hand.

When it comes to task behavior, a leader should survey the needs and abilities of his or her followers and then choose a leadership style accordingly. If, as leader of the tornado-relief volunteers, you knew that Maria was a self-starter and needed little motivation, you could probably just make sure she understood her task and then get out of her way. You'd allow her to work independently. On the other hand, if you knew that Randy, another team member, seemed uncertain about how to accomplish his task, you would step in and use task behavior—giving Randy instructions, training, and guidance.

The Four Leadership Styles

Task behavior and relationship behavior are distinct, but complementary, leadership behaviors. Considered together, they help define four main leadership styles: *telling*, *selling*, *participating*, and *delegating*.

Telling

In the telling leadership style, *the leader provides specific instructions and closely supervises team members as they perform their tasks.* The telling leader has a high task orientation and a low relationship orientation.

Typical telling behaviors include:

- Directing others what to do
- Supervising them closely
- Following up to ensure they complete their tasks

Selling

The selling leadership style means *the leader closely supervises task completion and following up, while also providing explanations and opportunities for clarification from team members.* The selling leader has a high task orientation and a high relationship orientation.

Typical selling behaviors include:

- Supervising closely
- Following up
- Explaining relationships between tasks and team goals
- Encouraging questions
- Supporting progress

Participating

In the participating leadership style, *the leader helps and supports team members' efforts toward completing the task by sharing ideas and responsibility for decision making with his or her team members.* Participating leaders have a high relationship orientation but a low task orientation.

Participating behaviors include:

- Asking team members for ideas
- Listening
- Encouraging others to try out their ideas
- Allowing others to structure their tasks
- Sharing control and accountability

Delegating

In the delegating leadership style, *the leader turns over to team members responsibility for decision making, problem solving, and implementation.* Delegating leaders have both a low relationship orientation and a low task orientation.

Delegating behaviors include:

- Setting task boundaries
- Letting others make their own decisions
- Allowing members to chart their own courses of action
- Giving group members the freedom they need to do the job well
- Providing help when asked
- Monitoring progress

Leadership Etiquette

Successful leaders:

- Make decisions that will enhance the entire organization rather than just themselves
- Realize that they also have superiors—everyone, even a person of the highest rank, is accountable to someone
- Serve as examples of fair play, integrity, and dependability
- Listen to the needs, feedback, and suggestions of all organization members, not just a select few
- Understand that leadership is not a position of glory and popularity, but of responsibility

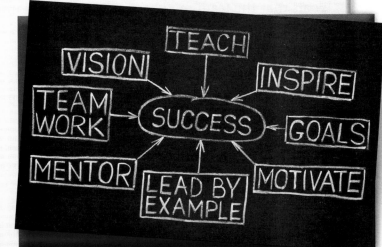

Successful leaders work for the success of the organization, not for individual gain.
Ivelin Radkov/Shutterstock

- Roll up their sleeves and help other members of the organization when the going gets tough
- Know that they cannot succeed without the work, support, and dedication of all members of the organization
- Do not seek personal recognition but rather share it equally with their followers or team members
- Work for the success of the organization, not for individual gain
- Know that the members of the organization gave them whatever power the leaders may possess—if the leader uses this power improperly, it can be taken away and given to someone else

The Primary Factors of the Leadership Situation

As noted before, you lead people and you manage things. But how do you know how much time to spend on each function? According to situational leadership theory, the situation the team finds itself in will dictate how much time the leader must devote to each activity.

Leaders should approach each leadership situation by considering four factors: *the mission*, *the people*, *the leadership style*, and *the environment*.

The Mission

Most missions involve many tasks. The team must complete each to fulfill its responsibilities. The leader must define the mission and set priorities for completing the different parts of its tasks.

In many instances, someone outside the team, such as a teacher, coach, supervisor, or unit leader, provides the mission. The leader's job is to translate this mission into goals that the team members will accept and understand. The team members must be able to relate to these goals and adopt them as their own.

When possible, involve team members in setting these goals. This will ensure their support. A team cannot succeed without the dedicated effort of each member. The goals the leader and team set must be challenging, but attainable. Unrealistic goals frustrate even the most dedicated people.

Another part of the leader's role is to set standards of job performance and to communicate them to the team. These standards must be reasonable, consistent with the mission, and clearly defined for every individual. As the work proceeds, the leader should then recognize those who meet or exceed standards. The leaders should get training for those who do not and take corrective action for those who will not. If a team member ignores the standards, the leader must determine the reason and move quickly to correct the situation through training or, if appropriate, administrative or disciplinary action. He or she gets the facts, and then acts.

The People

As a leader, you must be sensitive to people. People perform the mission. Understanding people helps determine the appropriate leadership action to take in a given situation, by determining your followers' readiness. You cannot get the most out of people on your team unless you first know their abilities.

Ability has two main elements: training and experience.

Training

You should assess each team member's level of training. If your people don't have adequate training, you must make sure they get it. No matter how committed followers are to the mission, they cannot contribute to it if they lack proper training. Medal of Honor recipient Sergeant John L. Levitow credited his heroic action under fire to the training he had received from the Air Force. He saved his plane over Vietnam by falling on and then throwing out a burning flare that had dropped into live ammunition—all while he was suffering from 40 shrapnel wounds.

Experience

As a leader, you should also be aware of the background, experience, and ability of each of your team members regarding every task you assign them. Don't base such an assessment solely on an individual's rank. While rank may be a good overall indicator, the person may have never done a certain job or been in a particular environment before. Moreover, some people learn faster than others do.

The Leadership Style

Successful leaders adapt their leadership style to meet the mission demands and to reflect the abilities and experience of their people. But in choosing a leadership style, good leaders also take into account their own individual strengths and weaknesses. For example, if you can communicate well with people on an individual basis but are uncomfortable speaking to large groups, use personal conferences as much as possible. If you write well, take advantage of this skill by writing letters of appreciation or using other forms of correspondence. If you're adept at leading discussions, bring your people together and let them solve problems.

In addition to playing to your strengths and avoiding your weakness, your leadership style must correspond to your team members' knowledge, abilities, and skills.

- When one or more of your team members lacks sufficient knowledge to do the job, you must spend much time giving that member guidance and support.

- If your team members are able but lack motivation, let them participate in planning the task. Motivate them by maintaining a professional working relationship. With this encouragement from you, they'll soon show greater motivation.

- If your team members have extensive experience and are enthusiastic about the task, provide them greater freedom. Provided they are on the track toward meeting your goals and objectives, let them complete their task in the way they choose. As the leader, you are still responsible for the mission, so be sure to monitor the group's progress.

Command Chief Master Sergeant Rocky Hart with Secretary of the Air Force Deborah James

Marvin Krause/Courtesy US Air Force

First Sergeant Has Heart

"It's good enough" was not a phrase Senior Master Sergeant Rocky Hart, first sergeant for the 83rd Aerial Port Squadron in Portland, Oregon, wanted to hear when it came to his Airmen.

"When someone says something like 'It's good enough for government work,' it fires me up," Sergeant Hart said. "My troops deserve the best, and I'm going to do everything I can to get it for them. I have a high expectation of my troops. I want them to do the best, I want them to have the best, and I want them to be the best."

The job of a first sergeant is to take care of people.

"The first sergeant is an integral part of this mission," said Major Connie Jenkins, 83rd APS commander. "The first sergeant maintains the morale and discipline of the troops while being an excellent liaison between the enlisted troops and the commander."

"The work we do is done at an accelerated tempo, with millions of dollars of equipment and many lives depending upon us," Major Jenkins said. "Sergeant Hart is the one who consistently remembers the troops whenever an issue or mission comes up that is 'all-consuming.' He never loses focus on what is important...."

Sergeant Hart would begin his weekend duty on Thursday mornings before the unit training assembly. He arrived around 4:30 a.m. to get everything set up and to check for last-minute phone calls.

"First thing in the morning, I get phone calls from people who can't come in to the UTA or who are having problems," Sergeant Hart said. "I start formulating a list of who is not going to make it, why they aren't going to make it, and how I'm going to fix any problems, all before the formation begins...."

On any given day, Sergeant Hart worked several issues simultaneously—meals, lodging, physical fitness, training, urinalysis testing, family care, promotions, enlisted performance reports, government travel card issues and more. Yet he still found time to advise Airmen on their careers and help supervisors with counseling on positive as well as negative issues.

During lunch, he would eat with his troops.

"I want to eat with my troops and spend time with them to find out what's going on in their lives," Sergeant Hart said. "It's amazing how much they will tell you personally and professionally when you care about them. If I can help take care of their personal life, they'll be better able to take care of their military life."

Sergeant Hart also kept involved with squadron operations.

"I like being an aerial porter, so I want to make sure training is going on and we're not cutting corners," he said.

At the end of the day, the first sergeant would catch up with all of his paperwork.

"I don't like being in my office at all," Sergeant Hart said. "I want to be out with the troops, visiting, looking at the records, helping them, and talking to them. I don't want to be in my office during the day because I can sit at my desk and do paperwork after hours."

The first sergeant faced a gamut of emotions daily working with his troops. All in one morning, Sergeant Hart talked to a sergeant who told him she was dying of breast cancer, had to raise his voice to effectively communicate with another Airman on how to fix a problem, and then congratulated an Airman and his wife on the birth of their baby.

"Never let them see you sweat," must have been this first sergeant's motto. The degree of stress in this job is evident, yet Sergeant Hart remained level-headed. Oftentimes, first sergeants are seen as "caregivers"—treated as if stress and hard work are only part of the job description. Sergeant Hart said he enjoyed the behind-the-scenes action the most.

"I like the light you see in a troop's eyes and the enthusiasm on their face when you are able to help them with something," Sergeant Hart said.

In 2006, Sergeant Hart was promoted to chief master sergeant. He spent almost two years from 2011 to 2013 as Command Chief Master Sergeant at Kandahar Airfield in Afghanistan. In 2013, he became Command Chief Master Sergeant, 440th Airlift Wing, Pope Army Airfield, Ft. Bragg, North Carolina.

The Environment

There's no way to plan for every eventuality. You'll always have surprises, and some of them won't be pleasant. One way to prepare for the unexpected is to begin by carefully considering the environment. Good leaders do this constantly. They know the leadership methods that worked in one situation with one group may not work with the same group in a different environment.

Think again about the volunteer team formed at your school to help the tornado victims. Even if the team had a great leader, super team members, and a commendable mission, it might still encounter problems. Housing or food-service difficulties, equipment or parts shortages, bad weather, and many other problems might arise. Any of these problems would create a new and unpredictable environment that the group's leader would have to deal with.

As a leader, you must alter your leadership behavior, as necessary, to accommodate changes in the mission's environment. Be sensitive to your surroundings.

The key is to stay flexible—and to adapt to the situation you face!

✔ CHECKPOINTS

Lesson 1 Review

Using complete sentences, answer the following questions on a sheet of paper.

1. What is the difference between leadership and management?

2. What are the two primary orientations of leadership behavior?

3. What are the four leadership styles?

4. What are two things that successful leaders know?

5. What are the four factors in every leadership situation?

6. What must a leader do to accommodate changes in the mission environment?

APPLYING YOUR LEARNING

7. Analyze Senior Master Sergeant Rocky Hart's leadership based on the material you have covered in this lesson. How would you characterize his leadership orientation and leadership style?

LESSON 2

Followership

Quick Write

_____

_____

Pick a figure from American history, a sports figure, or any other well-known person, and explain how he or she demonstrated the qualities of a good follower.

Learn About

- the importance of good followership
- the readiness factors of followers
- building effective relationships with leaders
- being an effective follower

The Importance of Good Followership

Here's a piece of good advice: "Before you can lead, you have to learn to follow." Good leaders emerge from the ranks of able followers. As a member of various teams and groups throughout your life, you'll have many chances to practice good followership. Followership is *displaying the attitudes, behaviors, and actions that help a leader succeed at leading.*

Why do you need a lesson about following? To be a follower, you simply do what you're told, right? Well, the role of a good follower is more than that. The role of the follower is often missing in studies of leadership. Yet a dynamic follower who shares the leader's goals and values is an invaluable team member. Followers are the heart and soul of a team.

The Follower Relationship

Throughout your life you will be a follower in one role or another. On a sports team, you follow the lead of the captain or coach. On a school project, you help the team leader. In your unit, you follow higher-ranking people. In the military, as a captain, you would follow majors and colonels. And even if you became an Air Force general, you would still have to follow the directions of the country's civilian leaders.

The relationship between follower and leader sometimes blurs. During a single day, a team member's role might flip back and forth from leader to follower many times. For example, suppose that your principal asks the Adopt-a-Road team, which you lead, to clean up the school parking lot. Wearing your follower hat, you say, "No problem, ma'am. Our team can handle it!" Later, with your leader hat on, you assign certain parts of the job to various members of your team.

A group of business leaders was asked to list traits they looked for in leaders and followers. The traits they chose in both cases were similar. The most commonly named were:

Leader: honest, competent, forward-looking, inspiring
Follower: honest, competent, dependable, cooperative.

Why are the two lists so similar? It's because the roles of leader and follower are closely related. In fact, followership and leadership are sometimes so closely connected that a person may not even realize when he or she is switching roles.

Followers Have Power

Individual followers can play different yet crucial roles in helping their team achieve its goals or mission. As a member of a group or team, you probably possess certain skills or knowledge that no one else does. To the degree that the team needs your knowledge and skills, you as a follower can affect team behavior and exert considerable power. Your skill may even be the power of your personality. A popular follower, as an individual, can change the behavior of a group. It's up to the team leader to decide how to use the individual strengths of each follower for the team's overall good.

Vocabulary

- followership
- ability
- willingness
- confidence
- proactive

The US Air Force Band: Followers play different yet crucial roles in helping their team achieve its goals.

Courtesy US Air Force

The Readiness Factors of Followers

In Act 5, Scene 2, of Shakespeare's *Hamlet*, the prince remarks, "the readiness is all." Hamlet was right. Understanding the readiness of followers is a key element of leadership. As you learned in the last lesson, *readiness* is how prepared and willing a team member is to carry out a particular task or tasks. Confidence also plays a role in readiness. Team members are naturally at different levels of readiness as they face each task or mission. The leader's job is to help followers or team members gain the knowledge and skills they need to perform at the highest level they can.

Let's look at the three factors that determine readiness: *ability*, *willingness*, and *confidence*.

Ability of Followers

Ability is *the knowledge, experience, and skill a team member or a team brings to a task.* It is partly based on the experience a team member has gained from doing previous tasks.

If you are a leader and need to assess the ability levels of your followers or team members, first consider the task you will be assigning and its desired outcome. Then decide which followers are best suited, by knowledge, skill, and experience, to handle that task.

Willingness of Followers

Willingness is *the degree to which a team member or a team shows confidence, commitment, and motivation to accomplish a task.* Willingness consists of the ability to do the work, a sense of duty in doing it, and a desire to do it. A team member might show unwillingness if he or she isn't comfortable with a task and isn't confident that his or her performance will meet the standard.

Ability and willingness work in tandem. A change in either factor will affect the way the two factors operate together.

Confidence of Followers

As team members' competence and abilities change, so will their attitudes, levels of enthusiasm, and commitment. As they learn more and become more competent, their confidence level will increase. Confidence is *a team member's belief that he or she can perform the task, along with the member's level of energy, enthusiasm, and commitment.* This level can shift and change. As a leader, you must be aware of your followers' changing levels of confidence and competence. Followers usually become increasingly confident as work proceeds. In any case, never label a team member. Be aware of members' growth, and intervene if they start to slip.

Readiness Levels

Readiness levels are the combinations of ability and willingness that a person brings to team tasks. Follower readiness breaks down into four levels. Each level represents a different combination of follower ability, willingness, and confidence.

Low Readiness

Readiness Level 1: Unable and unwilling—The team member lacks ability, commitment, and motivation. This level may also apply to a team member who is both unable and insecure, lacking the confidence to perform a task to standard.

Moderate Readiness

Readiness Level 2: Unable but willing—The team member lacks ability, but is motivated and makes an effort to complete the task. The person may also be unable but confident, as long as you are there to provide guidance.

Readiness Level 3: Able but unwilling—The team member is able to perform the task, but is unwilling to use that ability. Or the team member is able but insecure—showing ability but acting insecure about doing the job.

High Readiness

Readiness Level 4: Able and willing—The team member has the ability and commitment to perform the job. The team member is confident about completing the task.

Building Effective Relationships With Leaders

People often think that a good leader-follower relationship is a matter of luck. Many followers say they have a "good" leader or a "bad" leader, and assume they can't do anything to change it. They're wrong: The leader alone does not determine the quality of the relationship between leader and follower.

Effective followers know how to strengthen their relationship with their leaders. They also know how to enhance the support they provide their leaders and the team.

As a follower, how can you strengthen the leader-follower relationship? The following five suggestions can help.

Always Help the Leader Succeed

Part of the leader's job is to help his or her followers succeed. But it works both ways: Followers also need to help their leaders succeed. That doesn't mean you should be an "apple polisher" or play politics. You just need to remember that you and your leader are part of the same team. If the team succeeds, everyone benefits. If the team fails, the blame should fall on the followers as well as the leader.

Understand the Leader's World

Effective team members must know the leader's and the organization's objectives so they can share that vision. Loyalty and support are a two-way street. Just as a leader can help followers attain their personal goals, a follower can help a leader in that pursuit. Knowing his or her leader's values, preferences, and personality can help a follower understand the leader's actions and decisions. Such understanding gives followers insight into how to strengthen their relationships with their leaders.

Educate Your Leader

Leaders don't have all the answers. Followers can make a great contribution to a team's success by recognizing, and trying to help overcome, a leader's human shortcomings.

American Biographies

Astronaut Leroy Chiao
Courtesy of NASA

Leroy Chiao, Spacewalker

Astronaut Leroy Chiao, Ph.D., has demonstrated on many occasions the qualities of both an effective follower and leader. He flew as a crew member on three space shuttle missions and commanded an expedition to the International Space Station.

Dr. Chiao graduated from the University of California, Berkeley, with a bachelor's degree in chemical engineering. He earned his master's degree and a doctorate from the University of California, Santa Barbara. NASA selected him as an astronaut in 1990.

On the shuttle *Columbia* in 1994, Chiao and his fellow crew members conducted 80 experiments on materials and life sciences research in microgravity. In 1996 he flew on the shuttle *Endeavor*, performing two spacewalks to demonstrate tools and hardware and to evaluate techniques for building the space station. On this mission, he became the first Asian American and the first ethnic Chinese to walk in space. As a crew member aboard the shuttle *Discovery* in 2000, he took two more spacewalks, during which he helped attach equipment to the International Space Station.

From October 2004 to April 2005, he changed roles from follower to leader, commanding Expedition 10 to the space station. Launching aboard a Russian Soyuz TMA-5 from Kazakhstan, he performed 20 experiments and two installation and repair spacewalks over six months at the station. With this mission, Chiao became the first Asian American and ethnic Chinese mission commander.

A new leader almost always needs team members' help. Such a leader may have a great deal of knowledge and experience, but may not be familiar with the operations or needs of the team to which he or she has just been assigned. It's up to followers to orient and educate a new leader about team members' expertise and experience. This is especially important if the leader comes from a different field or activity.

Keep Your Leader Informed

Few people like surprises—especially if it's bad news. As a follower, never put your leader in the embarrassing situation of having someone else know more about the team's business than he or she does.

Adapt to Your Leader's Style

It's the follower's responsibility to adapt to the leader's style, not vice versa. Followers need to be flexible. They need to adapt to the leader's decision-making style, problem-solving strategies, methods of communication, and styles of interaction. If your leader does not set clear expectations, ask for clarification. If you are the leader, clarify your expectations about followers' roles and responsibilities.

Being an Effective Follower

Besides working to build a supportive relationship with your leader, you can take these additional actions to be an effective follower:

- **Be honest**—Followers need to be honest and dependable. If a follower does not have integrity, it doesn't matter how many other great qualities or talents he or she might have. No one wants to work with someone who isn't trustworthy. After integrity, leaders value dependability. They value workers who have reliable work habits, accomplish assigned tasks at the right time in the right order, and do what they promise.

- **Don't gripe**—Part of a follower's job is to help the team work well. Ideally, the leader does this, but sometimes the team must carry on despite its leader. Poor leadership is an enormous burden. But complaining about policies and poor leadership is never productive. A follower who gripes only further undermines the leader's authority and the team's ability to function.

- **Be proactive**—Being proactive means *taking the initiative and assuming part of the responsibility to make things happen.* This includes building a good relationship with your leader. A proactive follower critically considers policies and presents suggestions to the leader that will contribute to team success. A follower must buy into the task of making the team better.

Senior Airman Kyara Johnson
Courtesy US Air Force

Life Motto Drives First Woman on F-22 Raptor Demo Crew

Senior Airman Kyara Johnson, 94th Aircraft Maintenance Unit weapons loader, enlisted in 2013. Now she's a member of the F-22 Raptor Demonstration Team, the first female to earn a spot on the crew.

"I've had people come up to me and tell me they just had to talk to me because they are happy that a female is on the team," said Johnson, whose wide smile illuminates her face. She adds that while she is working she doesn't see gender; she is just a person, the same as everyone else.

"She is definitely a breath of fresh air for the team," said Technical Sergeant Jonathan Billie, F-22 Raptor Demonstration Team maintenance team chief. "Her work ethic is astounding. You never have to ask her to do anything because she is already three steps ahead of you, and she does it with a smile on her face."

Before Johnson began as a member of the Demo Team, her days consisted of loading bombs and missiles onto the F-22 Raptor—the world's only operational fifth-generation fighter aircraft—as well as ensuring the weapons system remained up-to-date.

On the road with the Demo Team, however, Johnson's life is far from ordinary. Since the performance aircraft isn't equipped with weapons, and no weapon systems need to be checked, Johnson welcomes the opportunity to branch out of her career field, while remaining in the F-22 community. She also added that being a people person helps her with her new tasks as well.

During air shows, the Demo Team has a tent set up to give the local community the opportunity to interact with Airmen, as well as learn about the Air Force and the aircraft.

"We get a lot of people that come by, asking questions about the [F-22]. How it works and how fast does it go," said Johnson. "You have to engage in conversation and make sure they are pumped up and ready for the demo."

While Johnson remains modest in how she interacts with the crowds, her team chief, Billie, sees much more than Johnson lets on. "You can never show the American public when you are having a bad day, and Kyara never has a bad day," added Billie. "It's awesome to have her on the team, and we love her to death."

The ability to bring a smile to someone's face isn't something that Johnson finds hard. By applying her life motto—Live, Love, Life—to her daily routine, she said, she can accomplish almost anything.

"You can't let any and everything get you down. You have to look at the positive," said Johnson. "Things could be going so wrong, but you have to think about it: There's somebody who is worse off than you. So you have to count your blessings and be thankful."

- **Make sound decisions**—Once you have taken a proactive approach to followership and are confident in your role, you will need to make sound decisions. Your decisions will affect those around you. Step up and use your expertise.

- **Be enthusiastic**—Enthusiasm is contagious energy. An enthusiastic follower can have a great influence over the team and its leader.

  Suppose your leader gives you a task. You may like the task or you may think it's boring or even useless. As far as the team's welfare goes, that's not important. No matter how you feel about a task, approach it with a positive attitude. Your enthusiasm will have a ripple effect on the group's or the leader's feelings concerning the task. Be upbeat and energetic when performing and promoting tasks. Success rests with the followers' enthusiasm as well as the leader's.

- **Be versatile and flexible**—Hitting your head repeatedly against a brick wall isn't the most efficient way to get to the other side. When a problem comes up, take a few minutes to reevaluate a task. Use your brain rather than your skull. A second look will often reveal a better way around the wall.

Whenever you're a follower, learn as much as you can about effective leadership by watching good leaders in action. In brief, use your experience as a follower to help you become an effective leader. Remember that the differences between a leader and a follower are quite small. This is because good leaders and good followers share a goal—to be part of an excellent team.

The Follower Becomes a Leader

One of the students from the high school yearbook committee asked a senior aerospace science instructor (SASI) from Florida for some words about AFJROTC to put on the AFJROTC pages—and of course, the student needed it right away. The SASI passed the request to her cadet public affairs officer, with very little guidance, and promptly received this the next morning:

"The AFJROTC is a program with one thing on its mind—a mission. A mission 'To Build Better Citizens for America.' This program will prepare cadets (students in the corps) physically and mentally for the future as citizens of the United States. This is not just another program. It's a family—a family of marvelous, unique kids on an extraordinary learning experience: from leadership camps, drill competitions, dining-ins, dining-outs, military balls, air shows, even to helping out our community with football games, band concerts, cheerleading competitions—and not to mention our sincere hearts lending a hand to the victims of the hurricanes, Relay for Life for the American Cancer Society, and collecting school supplies for Iraqi children with our fun-filled fundraisers. We are AFJROTC, inspired by our fallen troops, guided by our corps' values, and motivated by our ability to **never** say 'CAN'T.' WE ARE THE FUTURE."

When the SASI finished reading this, she realized her cadet public affairs officer— the SASI's follower—had just become a leader.

Lesson 2 Review

Using complete sentences, answer the following questions on a sheet of paper.

1. Where do good leaders emerge from?

2. Why does a follower have power?

3. Which three factors determine readiness?

4. How do ability and willingness operate together?

5. What do effective followers know?

6. What are five suggestions for how a follower can strengthen the relationship with a leader?

7. What are some additional actions you can take to be an effective follower?

8. As a follower, how can you learn more about effective leadership?

APPLYING YOUR LEARNING

9. Write a paragraph or two describing how you can show good followership for your teachers, coaches, bosses, or other leaders or people who supervise you.

LESSON 3

Leadership Preparation

Quick Write

_____

_____

Write down five steps you think you can take now to prepare for a leadership role. Which of the steps can you take yourself? Would you need help from a coach, a teacher, or another adult for some of the steps? If so, which ones?

Learn About

- preparing for leadership
- key elements of effective coaching and mentoring
- ways to practice leadership
- leadership maxims

Preparing for Leadership

The United States has always had strong leaders in all walks of life, but particularly in the armed forces. As a result, today's leaders carry on a tradition of leadership. In the case of the Air Force, this tradition began with pioneers such as Billy Mitchell, Jimmy Doolittle, Carl Spaatz, Eddie Rickenbacker, and other leaders you've read about in this book. These heroes left a legacy of excellence, courage, and service.

Now that you've learned some of the basics of leadership, how do you best prepare yourself to lead? You develop your leadership style by starting now to apply it in ordinary situations at school and in the community. Seek opportunities to lead and guide others, so you can build the experience and strength of character to lead effectively.

The steps for preparing yourself to lead include _thinking, observing, studying,_ and _practicing._

Think About Leadership

To be a good leader, you must think about what leadership is. What would you do in a given situation, and why? If you took charge of the Adopt-a-Road Recycling Team tomorrow, how would you act? Remember the characteristics and principles of leadership you learned in previous lessons. How would you apply them to lead your team?

Observe Leaders Lead

One of the best ways to learn to be a good leader is to observe other leaders in action. Ask yourself these questions: How does your parent or guardian, teacher, coach, counselor, or boss handle a given situation? Why did a particular action succeed or fail? How does the leader deal with team members who balk or question authority? How does the leader praise good performance?

Study

History is full of good examples of effective leadership. Study leadership and the profession of arms. The military has a long tradition of leadership. Read about America's war leaders. Read about the successful political, civic, and government leaders in US history, and study how they led.

Navy Rear Admiral Alfred Thayer Mahan wrote, "The study of history lies at the foundation of all sound military conclusions and practice." A detailed knowledge of leadership as a profession is essential to developing your perspective on the leadership challenges of the future.

Practice

Whenever you get the chance, practice leading. Look for opportunities to exercise leadership—they're all around you. It can be as simple as taking the initiative and leading one person to complete a task. Always lead by positive example. Make a plan, gather your team, and get the job done.

Vocabulary

- coaching
- mentoring
- protégé

AMERICANS *in action*

Eisenhower on D-Day

In his book *D-Day: June 6, 1944: The Climactic Battle of World War II*, historian Stephen E. Ambrose described Army General Dwight D. Eisenhower's situation just after he issued the order to begin the assault on the Normandy beaches in France: "Then the commanders rushed from their chairs and dashed outside to get to their command posts. Within thirty seconds the mess room was empty, except for Eisenhower. His isolation was symbolic, for, having given the order, he was now powerless. As he put it, 'That's the most terrible time for a senior commander. He has done all that he can do, all the planning and so on. There's nothing more that he can do.'"

Eisenhower knew that the success or failure of the invasion now rested on the skill and determination of his followers. But he had trained them. Each of his subordinates—from headquarters all the way down to the beaches—knew his or her duty, role, and orders. The confidence Eisenhower showed in his people reflected his leadership ability.

Key Elements of Effective Coaching and Mentoring

At some point you may find yourself serving as a coach or mentor—helping others develop their individual talents and skills.

Coaching is *a method of helping people grow and improve their competence by providing suggestions and encouragement.* Mentoring is *counseling people to help them develop in their profession or career.* Both mentors and coaches often lead by example. They help build a person's self-esteem and self-confidence. A mentor is an individual with advanced experience and knowledge who is committed to giving support and career advice to a less experienced person. A primary role of a mentor is to be a listening ear, a trusted confidant, and an adviser.

A person who's lucky enough to have a mentor is called a protégé. A protégé is *a less experienced person who benefits from a mentor's guidance and advice.*

Mentors realize that it takes time to build trust with their protégés. So they are patient. They take a gradual approach to developing the relationship.

The Role of a Mentor

A mentor should act as a:

- Trusted adviser
- Clearinghouse for questions, problems, and leadership issues
- Sounding board for decision making and problem solving
- Leadership role model
- Resource provider
- Patient, caring, listening guide

A mentor should *not*:

- "Police" the protégé's day
- Criticize or lecture the protégé
- Make decisions for the protégé
- Try to transform the protégé
- Be judgmental
- Try to "fix" the protégé, the protégé's problems, or the protégé's environment

A coach helps people grow and improve their competence by providing suggestions and encouragement.

dotshock/Shutterstock

Understanding the Mentor's Role

As a mentor, you try to put yourself in your protégé's shoes. You try to understand the world from his or her perspective. That requires putting aside preconceived ideas. It also means being nonjudgmental. A mentor does not impose his or her own values on a protégé.

For example, mentors might give general information about grants, scholarships, contests, competitions, and special programs that might help a protégé further his or her education and career. But mentors try to be objective. They do not recommend a specific course of action but rather encourage the protégé to explore options. They avoid taking sides when a protégé has a conflict with his or her parents or guardian, teacher, or peers. Mentors advise their protégés on conflict resolution, but they don't replace the roles of a school counselor, spiritual leader, social worker, or team leader. For example, if a protégé is having a family conflict, the mentor will not advise him or her directly. Instead, the mentor will suggest that the protégé consult a guidance counselor, leader, or another trustworthy and experienced adult.

A mentor will always keep a positive, upbeat, professional tone in the relationship. The relationship will be confidential. The mentor will ordinarily not share any personal information about the protégé, including address, phone number, e-mail address, photos, or files.

Mentors and coaches donate their time and energy. They typically don't give or accept money or gifts. Their protégés' heartfelt thanks—and successful careers as students and leaders—are their reward.

Barriers to Mentor-Protégé Relationships

Good mentors remain aware of the purpose of the mentor-protégé relationship. They know that their role is to advise, rather than to change or reform, the protégé. They know the potential, as well as the limits, of their role.

In some cases, a well-meaning mentor may push too hard and too quickly on a protégé's problems and issues. That makes the protégé feel ill at ease.

The protégé should feel totally comfortable with the mentor. A good mentor will not press the protégé to talk about issues before he or she is ready.

Some mentors fail because they focus on their own agendas and not on the protégé's needs. As a good mentor, you set the agenda for the relationship *with* the protégé, not *for* the protégé.

The key to an effective relationship between mentor and protégé is creating mutual trust.

Monkey Business Images/Shutterstock

What Makes a Mentor-Protégé Relationship Successful?

The key to an effective mentor-protégé relationship is creating trust between the two people. People volunteer to be mentors because they want to help their protégés develop their leadership skills. Building trust requires time and is not always easy. It requires ongoing and open communication. But without mutual trust, a mentor can never truly help a protégé.

An important way for the mentor to build trust is through *active listening*. Recall what you learned about listening in Chapter 1, Lesson 2: Active listening is two-way communication. You pay full attention and think about what people say, asking questions if you don't understand. Active listening actually requires active seeing, too. That's because sometimes people talk even when they're not saying anything. You must be patient and "read" people—their motions, their faces, their eyes, and their body language.

Active listening skills include avoiding distraction, making good eye contact, and letting the other person speak. Active listeners listen for both fact and feelings. They use body language effectively and acknowledge what's said. They ask good questions and smile appropriately.

Ways to Practice Leadership

You can practice leadership every day and in many situations, whether you are the chief leader, a subordinate leader, or a team member. You can volunteer to serve on a committee at school, in your place of worship, or in a civic organization. You can find ways to assist school officials, teachers, coaches, and fellow students. Leadership opportunities abound in school clubs, Boy Scout and Girl Scout troops, Boys and Girls Clubs—and even at home, where you can take the lead in helping with household chores and responsibilities.

The following are some ways you can lead in any circumstance.

Lead by Example

There is no better way to lead than to set a good example for others. Live the Air Force core values. Practice the leadership traits and characteristics you have learned. Be a good follower, and support the people who are leading you. Be faithful to your religious values or philosophy of life. Always do what is right.

The more you lead, the better leader you will become. If you continually seek out and take on opportunities to lead, your confidence in yourself and your abilities will grow. Moreover, other people—teachers, supervisors, and other adults, as well as your followers—will gain confidence in you.

This effect will snowball. People will regard you as a leader and will seek your advice.

Lead by Imitation

As a leader in training, you wear two hats. In some situations, you can serve as an example for others. But you can also continue to imitate leadership behaviors you admire in others. Watch and study other leaders carefully. Then copy their successful actions and behaviors. Put into practice what you learn.

Try to be like successful leaders and to lead as they do. But at the same time, be aware of your own leadership style. Don't try to copy something that doesn't feel comfortable to you. Although leaders share certain characteristics, each leader expresses them in an individual manner.

Lead by Consensus

As you gain experience in leadership, you'll become more comfortable in leading by consensus. You'll relax and be willing to let your followers help you lead. Your followers will be flattered that you've asked for their input, and their productivity and interest will rise.

The best leaders don't work too hard at trying to keep control. They establish their authority, define the mission, and then let their followers do their assigned jobs. They intervene only when asked or if they see the project going off course.

Leading by consensus means sharing the leadership load. It gets team members to cooperate and pull their weight. The entire team benefits—including the leaders.

Hazards of Leadership

When things are going well and your team is accomplishing its goals, being a leader is a rewarding experience. But being a leader does have risks. For example, a leader might:

- Begin to love the experience of being in charge and become an autocratic leader—one who takes complete authority and control and misuses his or her position
- Become carried away with his or her own importance and lose sight of the group's goals
- Fail to listen to others
- Try too hard and take on too much responsibility—leaders who spread themselves too thin cannot accomplish any individual task well and become frustrated
- Fail to organize—a leader who is not well organized cannot get tasks done in a timely way
- Get upset by the performance of some group members—despite a leader's efforts, not every follower will give 100 percent, and a realistic leader accepts this

To overcome these potential hazards, it's not enough to know which kind of leadership style you want to develop. A leader must bear in mind one key thing: *The leader's purpose is help the group reach its goals.*

Evaluate Your Leadership Behavior

How do you know if you're an effective leader? You have to evaluate your leadership skills. The following techniques can help you determine whether you are leading effectively.

- First, seek input and feedback from your own leader, other leaders, or the adults around you. Ask your parents or guardian, teachers, coaches, boss, counselor, unit leader, and other adults how you are doing as a leader.

- Second, talk with your team members and ask them for feedback, too. Try to get honest and critical information on how your leadership style works in each project.

- Third, continue to learn from your efforts. Use your successes as a basis for refining your leadership technique. Use your mistakes and failures as a means for addressing larger areas for improvement.

- Finally, have a conversation with yourself. Think about your leadership experiences—what seems to work, and what doesn't. Evaluate your leadership in light of your team's goals: How far along is the team to achieving its goals? What obstacles stand in the way? What can you do to help the team overcome these obstacles? Is your leadership style one of the obstacles?

Seek opportunities wherever and whenever you can to practice leadership. Also, look for opportunities to measure yourself—against the set standard, against other leaders, and against yourself. You will not always succeed. But you can learn to become a better leader by evaluating your failures as well as your successes.

> The mistakes we make are usually temporary, but the lessons they teach us are permanent.
>
> —Colonel Peter A. Land, USAF Retired

President George Washington
Everett Historical/Shutterstock

George Washington: Leader in War and Peace

George Washington. Ulysses S. Grant. Dwight D. Eisenhower. All were military leaders who served their country in time of war and who went on to become president of the United States. They were great leaders of the eighteenth, nineteenth, and twentieth centuries, and each has earned a prime place in US history.

But George Washington was a leader among leaders. Americans today still call him "the father of our country." He learned from his setbacks and overcame his challenges, earning the respect and love of the men and women he led. He set the standard for other leaders to follow.

Washington was born on 22 February 1732. His parents were moderately wealthy Virginia planters. Like all young men of his class in that time, Washington studied mathematics and the classics while in school. His mother discouraged George's early interest in going to sea, so he began a career as a surveyor at age 16.

When the French and Indian War erupted in 1754, the ambitious young Virginian saw an opportunity. He became commander of the Virginia militia. He saw battle—four bullets once ripped through his coat and two horses were shot out from under him. By age 22, Washington had earned a reputation among his officers and fellow soldiers. He learned quickly and was a good problem solver. He combined boldness and initiative with inborn ability.

By the late 1750s, Washington had returned to Virginia. He married and was elected to Virginia's House of Burgesses. He became a leader in expressing Virginia's opposition to British policies concerning the American colonies. The legislature named him a delegate to the Continental Congress in 1774.

In 1775, as hostilities between British troops and colonists became intense, the Second Continental Congress unanimously chose Washington as commander in chief of the continental forces.

Washington found himself the head of a force of unorganized, poorly disciplined, short-term enlisted militia. His officers were often insubordinate. Failing to be discouraged, Washington spent a few months training his troops and trying to get supplies. But soon it was time for action.

Despite enormous odds, including an uncooperative Congress, Washington occupied Dorchester Heights and forced British forces to evacuate Boston in March 1776. At the request of Congress, he tried to defend New York City. This effort was a failure, and he retreated to Pennsylvania. He lost many of his men because their enlistment periods had expired. Others simply deserted. Supplies were always short, as were funds. Washington even served without pay. During this difficult period, Washington was indeed learning. But without books or a mentor, he was learning mainly by trial and error. Washington's record would show that experience is an excellent teacher for those who will heed it.

Washington and his troops faced a bitter test during the winter of 1777–1778 at Valley Forge, Pennsylvania—one of the grimmest in military history. Washington's most important tasks during those difficult days were to hold the American army together, boost his troops' morale, and improve their training.

Over the next six years, Washington was courageous and persistent. He lost battles, but he also won some important ones. By this time he'd become a skilled and imaginative military leader, known for making quick and unexpected attacks.

The turning point came when France recognized American independence. In October 1781, with the aid of French allies, Washington forced the surrender of General Charles Cornwallis at the Battle of Yorktown, effectively ending the war.

Washington retired from the army 1783. He wanted nothing more than to return to family life at Mt. Vernon. But his sense of civic duty remained strong. He became a prime force in planning the Constitutional Convention in Philadelphia in 1787. After the Constitution was ratified, the new Electoral College unanimously elected Washington president in 1789.

Washington knew how to use power well. Realizing the importance of consensus, he chose talented men from all factions for his Cabinet. Realizing that no leader is above the law, he respected the separation of powers between the presidency and the Congress. He was unanimously reelected in 1793. At the end of his second term, he performed an act almost unheard of in that day and age—he voluntarily stepped down from office.

Washington retired to Virginia in 1797 to resume farming. He died on 14 December 1799. The nation he had helped create as a military and peacetime leader was well established. Americans mourned his loss for months.

Leadership Maxims

You've learned a good deal about leadership in these last two chapters. The following leadership maxims reflect much of what you have studied. They're based on the experience of scores of successful business executives and military leaders.

Make people want to do things. Making people want to do something is a subtler process than "selling" them on doing it. The latter is usually just another name for forceful persuasion and is no more effective. In thinking about this rule, consider the term *want*. The words *need* and *want* are synonymous. Think about people's acquired needs. Then think of the characteristics of needs, behavior, and goals.

Study team members, and determine what makes each tick. Most of your dealings are with "others" in general. But some of your dealings are with Joe, Tomás, and Aisha as individuals. What kinds of things must you know about each person working with you? Most experts say that knowing one's team members is the main tool of leadership.

Delegate the responsibility for details to subordinates. Delegating responsibility is the essence of leadership. You are not a leader if you do not delegate, just as you are not a machinist if you cannot run a machine.

Be a good listener. Effective leaders know their people. The easiest way to learn about people is to encourage them to talk, to draw them out, and to ask them questions. A *teller*, by contrast, only encourages people to keep quiet. Never dominate a conversation or meeting without a good reason. A good trick: Always give the other person the right-of-way when you both start to speak at the same time.

Criticize or correct constructively. Get all the facts. Review them and get agreement on them. Then suggest a course of action. Or better still, have the person whom you're correcting suggest a remedial action. When you criticize, be sure to criticize the method, never the motive. Precede criticism with praise, but be careful. When this becomes routine, people get wise and resent the technique.

Criticize or correct in private. This is among the most obvious of rules, but people break it constantly. Why is a public reprimand such a poor human relations practice? Think about the effect of public criticism on the average person. Try to think of a situation in which public scolding would be justifiable and effective.

Praise in public. This is a result of the preceding rule. But when praising, take a few precautions. Make certain the person deserves the praise. Make sure to praise everyone involved in the task. And avoid praising so frequently that the group is unimpressed.

Be considerate. Nothing contributes more to building a strong, hard-working, and loyal team than a considerate, courteous leader. Such leaders put themselves in the team members' place before making decisions that affect them. These leaders realize that team members have personal problems in school, on the job, and at home. They know that people have personal and social needs, and that team members will work effectively when others recognize and respect—not trample on—those needs.

Give credit where it is due. The leader who takes credit for followers' work is something of a tyrant. In the military, superiors sometimes impose taking credit on a subordinate leader. The leader is responsible, and the leader's boss is concerned with mission accomplishment, not how and by whom the mission was accomplished.

Credit for new ideas, special projects, and the like, however, belongs to the person who developed them. As a leader, you must ensure that if you or the team receives recognition for such achievement, the individual concerned gets recognition, too. In turn, you get credit for building a good team and for representing the individual members well.

Avoid domination or forcefulness. Effective leaders think of the team as working *with*, not *for*, them. Dominant, overly forceful leaders stifle people who have initiative. Such leaders do their teams no favor: If the chief runs everything, the best people will try to get out. The weaker people will let the chief do all the work.

Show interest in and appreciation of the other person. Be a human being. Not everyone is warmhearted, but even the most self-centered and coldest leader can take steps to maintain warm relationships with subordinates. For example, use first names in private conversations, talk about hobbies and family news, and arrange occasional friendly bull sessions. Keep informed on workloads and hours of overtime, and investigate any evidence of fatigue and unhappiness.

Occasionally it's a good idea to say, "Joe, you look tired; knock off a few hours early." Gestures of this sort pay great dividends in loyalty and accomplishment. But avoid going too far in such matters. Don't violate the unwritten law of effective leadership: Keep your professional and personal lives separate.

Make your wishes known by suggestions or requests. If your people are not hostile and resentful, requests and suggestions are more effective than orders or commands. When a leader must frequently order team members to take action, the situation is a sorry one.

Be sure to explain the reasons for your requests. People want to know both what they are doing and why they are doing it. This is a "must" in the American culture.

Let your assistants in on your plans and programs as early as possible. Sometimes you cannot discuss plans too far in advance. But you should talk them over with followers or team members before you finalize them. The sum of your assistants' ideas, plus your own, will ordinarily be better than your ideas alone. Getting the group involved in planning is a significant undertaking in leadership. Participation by subordinates in planning is a valuable leadership tool. When people know what is coming and why, they can gear their thinking more realistically to the goal.

Never forget that leaders set the style for their people. If your habits are irregular, if you're consistently late for appointments or careless about facts, or if you usually look bored, you can expect your followers to follow suit.

It's not easy to explain this reaction. You might simply think, "Well, that's the way people are." But researchers have identified a scientific basis for this phenomenon. A way of behaving may become a need. For example, the craftsperson acquires a need to do excellent work. Most of us have acquired the need to imitate. And most likely this need has become generalized to many goals. People learn to talk by imitating the members of their family. People learn to express happiness or approval by copying their parents' or guardian's behavior. People are especially likely to imitate the behavior of those they are dependent on.

Play up the positive. For most people, praise is a better stimulant than criticism. Appreciation is better than a lack of appreciation. Ambition is a more effective motivation than punishment.

Be consistent. A leader who flies off the handle, sets off fireworks, or gyrates wildly in mood, reaction, and manner bewilders and frightens followers.

Show your people that you have confidence in them and that you expect them to do their best. People tend to live up to what you expect of them. When goals and standards are realistic, most people do a first-rate job. If a leader shows confidence in his or her team members and expects high standards of efficiency and production, that is usually what will happen.

Ask those who work with you for their counsel and help. This gets them involved. The mission of the group becomes their "baby," and people tend to consider their "babies" to be important. Equally significant, team members have good ideas that may never see daylight unless someone asks for the members' advice and help.

Give people a chance to take part in decisions, particularly those affecting them. When people have had a say in a decision, they are much more likely to go along with it enthusiastically. If they agree with the decision, they will go along. If they had a part in making it, the decision is their own "baby." Even if they don't agree, they will go along, since they had a part in it. They know the leader considered their views. Many experts in leadership believe that group dynamics is the major determiner of success or failure of all leadership activity. You are on the right track if you consider the group to be the most powerful single factor in influencing human behavior.

Listen courteously to ideas from your followers. Even far-fetched ideas deserve a full hearing. Never disparage or ridicule an idea. An original idea is valuable to the team, to the leader, and especially to the originator. Even a very bad idea is the originator's own "baby."

If you adopt a team member's idea, tell him or her why. If the originator knows why you approve of his or her idea, it reinforces that person's line of thought. The team member will likely apply it to other problems. If you do not adopt an idea that a team member suggests, you should also explain why. If your reasons are good, the person will accept them. If you never respond to your followers' ideas, your followers will become discouraged and perhaps even resentful.

Give weight to the fact that people carry out their own ideas best. When two ideas of equal merit appear, choose the one presented by the person who will carry out the project. Here again, the project is someone's personal "baby." Carry this point one step further to a subtle technique of leadership: It is a good tactic to plant seeds of ideas in others' minds. The person who executes the idea will feel that it is his or her own. He or she then is responsible for proving that the idea is workable.

When you are wrong or make a mistake, admit it. No one expects a leader to be perfect. Leaders don't lose face by admitting they are wrong, provided they aren't wrong too often. By admitting mistakes, you gain the confidence of your team in your fairness and honesty.

Plan what you say and how you say it. When you talk to your team members as a group or individually, your words have a dramatic impact. Why? Think this one through carefully. Consider the impact of words and tone of voice in people's lives. For example, people associate harshness and curtness with anxiety, reprimand, disapproval, and hostility. You can acquire the most beneficial leadership skills in this area of communication. Even an artless person can learn to say things in a pleasant, encouraging, and stimulating way. You can speak in an atmosphere of approval even when you are criticizing someone.

In any event, effective communication is a significant leadership and human relations tool. Carelessly chosen words, an unintended inflection of the voice, or dismissal of a subject that someone has raised can breed unhappiness and misunderstanding. Words that you forget the moment you speak them can cause unproductive days and sleepless nights for those who hear them.

Perhaps you think that such sensitive souls make poor team members. Perhaps you're right. But your value judgment doesn't alter the nature of the American teenager or adult. You are not going to break down a lifetime of acquired motives just because you think it is easier to be curt and inconsiderate. Your job is to get the best out of your team. You do this by capitalizing on human nature. And in the realm of communications, a pleasant voice, well-chosen words, approval, and understanding get better results than harshness, curtness, apathy, and impersonal speech.

Don't let moderate complaining upset you. In small doses, griping serves as a safety valve. It helps people let off steam. Frustration is part of the very nature of life. This is true of any work situation. Someone once said that if a leader were perfect, people would gripe because he or she was perfect. Accept mild complaining as a normal outlet for frustration. Vicious personal griping is another story, however. Try to determine the cause for such complaints and eliminate them.

Use every opportunity to build up in team members a sense of the importance of their work. People like to consider their roles in life and on the job to be important. Many people even have a need to feel they are essential to a particular job. Without this, they are unable to click.

Give your people goals, a sense of direction, and something to strive for and achieve—keep them informed. People need to know where they are going, what they are doing, and why they are doing it. People can't stay interested simply in working from hour to hour and day to day. They must see how their day-to-day work fits into the framework of larger goals. On the other hand, long-range goals mobilize less energy than immediate goals. This may seem paradoxical, but it isn't. Consider carefully the nature of complex motivated behavior. Remember that immediate goals are only a means to an end. For example, consider the long-range and immediate goals in the following situations:

- The Marine recruit undergoes harsh treatment, vigorous physical training, and long hours of classroom work.
- A potential Rhodes scholar is drafted. He chooses to go to radar training. Then he asks to be assigned to an isolated radar defense installation.
- A sick man undergoes an operation.
- An overweight person goes on a diet.
- A business executive takes an honorary government post at reduced salary.

Let your people know where they stand. The day of "Treat 'em rough and tell 'em nothing" is gone. Leaders should always let their team members know their strong and weak points. Both regularly scheduled and informal ratings of people are a must in sound human relations. The most devastating work situation is one in which an employee doesn't know where he or she stands with the boss.

Your team members must know what you expect. They will inevitably try to please you. Your good opinion is their bread and butter. Evaluating your people is among the most difficult human relations problems a leader must deal with. Ordinarily, if a person has a weakness and knows it, he or she probably considers the weakness to be a matter of minor importance. If you as a leader believe this weakness is of major importance, that person will be very unhappy when you bring up the matter.

Such situations demand real skill in human relations. Criticism or evaluation must never place the person in a position that prevents him or her from regaining the leader's confidence and approval. As a general rule, evaluations that involve both praise and criticism are the most effective form of long-range motivation. But the criticism must be constructive. The individual will want to correct weaknesses when this change will satisfy more-important needs.

As a leader and a follower, practice these leadership maxims on a daily basis. Continue this tradition of leadership excellence and pass it on to others.

In this book you have studied how to learn and communicate. You have read about understanding your attitude and actions. You have reviewed how groups and teams succeed or fail. Finally, you have studied the basics of leadership and followership. The grand lesson is that these are all related: Good leaders and followers have this knowledge and these skills, and they put them into practice.

It's impossible to overstate the importance of good leadership—not just in the military or in government, but in society as a whole. Whether it's in your family, at your place of worship, at your school, in a volunteer organization, or in business, good leadership is always needed. Remember that leadership is not primarily about getting the group to do what you want. It's about helping the group achieve its goals.

During this year, you have studied the successes and failures of some of the nation's greatest leaders. These men and women brought the United States to where it is today. They won independence, ended slavery, fought for justice, won two world wars, went to space, and peered into the far reaches of the universe. They created the nation and the society you have been privileged to grow up in.

But the story is not over. New challenges lie ahead for the United States and the rest of humanity. Meeting those challenges won't be easy—good leaders and critical thinkers will be needed in every field. You now have the tools to practice leading. The time to begin is now.

Lesson 3 Review

Using complete sentences, answer the following questions on a sheet of paper.

1. What four actions can you take now to prepare yourself to lead?

2. What questions should you ask yourself when observing a leader?

3. What is a mentor?

4. Why do some mentors fail?

5. What is the best way to lead?

6. What techniques can you use to determine whether you are leading effectively?

7. What action is the essence of leadership?

8. What happens when you admit your mistakes?

APPLYING YOUR LEARNING

9. Pick a leader you know personally—it could be a teacher, coach, religious leader, family member, youth group leader, or someone else—and list the leadership lessons you can learn from his or her example. Relate these to the leadership maxims in this lesson.

References

CHAPTER 1 Learning and Communication

LESSON 1 Learning to Communicate

Bartelby.com. (1989). *Respectfully Quoted: A Dictionary of Quotations*. Retrieved 27 January 2015 from http://www.bartleby.com/73/1914.html.

Hersey, P., Blanchard, K. H., & Johnson, D. E. (2001). *Management of Organizational Behavior: Leading Human Resources* (8th ed.). Upper Saddle River, NJ: Prentice-Hall, Inc.

Robbins, S., & DeCenzo, D. (2004). *Fundamentals of Management* (4th ed.). Upper Saddle River, NJ: Pearson Prentice Hall.

US Air Force. (2004). AFH 33-337, *The Tongue and Quill*. Washington, DC: Department of the Air Force.

LESSON 2 Learning to Listen

Academic Skills Center, Dartmouth College. (2001). Taking Lecture Notes. Retrieved 6 February 2015 from http://www.dartmouth.edu/~acskills/success/notes.html.

Hersey, P., Blanchard, K. H., & Johnson, D. E. (2001). *Management of Organizational Behavior: Leading Human Resources* (8th ed.). Upper Saddle River, NJ: Prentice-Hall, Inc.

Kline, J. (1996). Listening Effectively. Air University Press. Retrieved 6 February 2015 from http://www.e-booksdirectory.com/details.php?ebook=9264.

Kline, J. (2003). *Listening Effectively*. Upper Saddle River, NJ: Prentice Hall.

LESSON 3 Learning to Think Critically

Critical Thinking Model 1. (2007). Retrieved 10 February 2015 from http://www.criticalthinking.org/ctmodel/logic-model1.htm.

Kurland, D. K. (2000). What Is Critical Reading? Retrieved 9 February 2015 from http://www.criticalreading.com/critical_reading.htm.

Paul, R., & Elder, L. (2001). *Critical Thinking*. Upper Saddle River, NJ: Prentice-Hall, Inc.

Sherfield, R., Montgomery, R., & Moody, P. (2005). *Cornerstone: Building on Your Best* (4th ed.). Upper Saddle River, NJ: Prentice Hall.

Three Types of Questions[PowerPoint slides]. (n.d.). Retrieved 10 February 2015 from www.criticalthinking.org/files/3%20types%20of%20Questions.ppt.

University of Massachusetts at Dartmouth. (2015). Decision Making Process. Retrieved 9 February 2015 from http://www.umassd.edu/fycm/decisionmaking/process/.

YouthLearn. (2012). Asking Questions. Waltham, MA: Education Development Center. Retrieved 10 February 2015 from http://www.youthlearn.org/learning/teaching/techniques/asking-questions/asking-questions.

CHAPTER 2 Communicating Effectively

LESSON 1 The Basic Checklist for Writing

US Air Force. (2004). AFH 33-337, *The Tongue and Quill*. Washington, DC: Department of the Air Force.

LESSON 2 Writing Effectively

US Air Force. (2004). AFH 33-337, *The Tongue and Quill*. Washington, DC: Department of the Air Force.

Hersey, P., Blanchard, K. H., & Johnson, D. E. (2001). *Management of Organizational Behavior: Leading Human Resources* (8th ed.). Upper Saddle River, NJ: Prentice-Hall, Inc.

LESSON 3 Speaking Effectively

US Air Force. (2004). AFH 33-337, *The Tongue and Quill*. Washington, DC: Department of the Air Force.

Kline, J. (2004). *Speaking Effectively*. Upper Saddle River, NJ: Prentice-Hall, Inc.

CHAPTER 3 Understanding Your Attitude

LESSON 1 Interpreting Events and Experiences

Hersey, P., Blanchard, K. H., & Johnson, D. E. (2001). *Management of Organizational Behavior: Leading Human Resources* (8th ed.). Upper Saddle River, NJ: Prentice-Hall, Inc.

Paul, R., & Elder, L. (2001). *Critical Thinking*. Upper Saddle River, NJ: Prentice-Hall, Inc.

Sherfield, R., Montgomery, R., & Moody, P. (2005). *Cornerstone: Building on Your Best* (4th ed.). Upper Saddle River, NJ: Prentice Hall.

LESSON 2 Developing a Positive Attitude

Bee, H., & Bjorklund, B. (2004). *The Journey of Adulthood* (5th ed.). Upper Saddle River, NJ: Pearson Prentice Hall.

Hersey, P., Blanchard, K. H., & Johnson, D. E. (2001). *Management of Organizational Behavior: Leading Human Resources* (8th ed.). Upper Saddle River, NJ: Prentice-Hall, Inc.

Paul, R., & Elder, L. (2001). *Critical Thinking*. Upper Saddle River, NJ: Prentice-Hall, Inc.

Peale, N. V. (1993). *Positive Thinking Every Day: An Inspiration for Each Day of the Year*. New York: Fireside, Simon & Schuster Inc. Retrieved 3 February 2003 from http://www.motivationalquotes.com/People/peale.shtml.

Sherfield, R., Montgomery, R., & Moody, P. (2005). *Cornerstone: Building on Your Best* (4th ed.). Upper Saddle River, NJ: Prentice Hall.

LESSON 3 What It Takes to Be a Leader

Air Force Public Affairs Agency. (2014). Louis Zamperini. Veterans in Blue, Vol. V. Retrieved 29 May 2015 from http://static.dma.mil/usaf/veterans/43zamperini.html.

Arlington National Cemetery website. (n.d.). Daniel "Chappie" James, Jr., General, United States Air Force. Retrieved 16 February 2006 from http://www.arlingtoncemetery.net/djames.htm.

Brown, E. (2012). Daniel K. Inouye, U.S. Senator, Dies at 88. *The Washington Post*, 17 December 2012. Retrieved 4 June 2015 from http://www.washingtonpost.com/local/obituaries/daniel-k-inouye-us-senator-dies-at-88/2012/12/17/61030936-b259-11e0-9a80-c46b9cb1255f_story.html.

National Aeronautics and Space Administration. (2005). Eileen Marie Collins. *Biographical Data*. Retrieved 23 February 2006 from http://www.jsc.nasa.gov/Bios/htmlbios/collins.html.

Studio Melizo. (2006). Rosa Parks and the Montgomery Bus Boycott. Retrieved 28 January 2006 from http://www.holidays.net/mlk/rosa.htm.

Unbroken: Louis Zamperini. (n.d.). Retrieved 29 May 2015 from http://www.louiszamperini.net.

US Air Force Historical Studies Office. (n.d.). Lieutenant General (USAF Ret.) James Harold Doolittle. Retrieved 7 February 2006 from https://www.airforcehistory.hq.af.mil/PopTopics/MOH-bios/Doolittle.html.

US Army Center for Military History. (2014.). Medal of Honor Recipients: Inouye, Daniel K. Retrieved 4 June 2015 from http://www.history.army.mil/moh/wwII-g-l.html.

United States Senate. (n.d.). Daniel K. Inouye: A Featured Biography. Retrieved 4 June 2015 from http://www.senate.gov/artandhistory/history/common/generic/Featured_Bio_Inouye.htm.

Vietnamwar.com website. (n.d.). John McCain. Retrieved 28 January 2006 from http://www.vietnamwar.com/johnmccainbio.htm.

Williams, R. (25 November 2003). Oklahoma Brigadier General LaRita Aragon: Proud of Her Cherokee, Choctaw Heritage. *American Forces Press Service*. Retrieved 28 January 2006 from http://defendamerica.mil/profiles/ dec2003/ pr120103a.html.

CHAPTER 4 Understanding Your Actions

LESSON 1 Integrity and Character

Cannon, J. (n.d.). Gerald R. Ford. Retrieved 21 February 2006 from http://www .pbs.org/newshour/character/essays/ford.html.

Cannon, K., (2014). Lieutenant continues legacy started by great uncle, Medal of Honor recipient. *Air Force News Service*. Retrieved 17 June 2015 from http:// www.af.mil/News/ArticleDisplay/tabid/223/Article/473303/lieutenant-continues -legacy-started-by-great-uncle-medal-of-honor-recipient.aspx.

City College of New York. (n.d.). Colin Powell School for Civil and Global Leadership. Retrieved 17 June 2015 from http://www.ccny.cuny.edu/powell/.

National Commission on Terrorist Attacks on the United States (9/11 Commission). (2004). 9/11 Commission Report. Retrieved 9 February 2006 from http://www .9-11commission.gov/.

Powell, C. (with Persico, J.). (1995). *My American Journey*. New York: Random House, Inc.

The White House. (n.d.). Gerald R. Ford. Retrieved 22 February 2006 from http://www.whitehouse.gov/history/presidents/gf38.html.

LESSON 2 Personality and Actions

Briggs Myers, I. (revised by Kirby, L. and Myers, K.). (1998). *Introduction to Type*. Mountain View, CA: Consulting Psychologists Press, Inc.

Cherry, K. (2015). Personality Psychology Study Guide. Retrieved 24 June 2015 from http://psychology.about.com/od/psychologystudyguides/a/personalitysg.htm.

Cunningham, L. (2012). Myers-Briggs: Does It Pay to Know Your Type? *The Washington Post*, 14 December 2012. Retrieved 24 June 2015 from http://www.washingtonpost .com/national/on-leadership/myers-briggs-does-it-pay-to-know-your-type/2012/ 12/14/eaed51ae-3fcc-11e2-bca3-aadc9b7e29c5_story.html.

McCrae, R. R., & John. O. (1992). An Introduction to the Five-Factor Model and Its Applications. *Journal of Psychology, 60*, 175–215. Retrieved 24 June 2015 from http://psych.colorado.edu/~carey/courses/psyc5112/readings/psnbig5 _mccrae03.pdf.

New York State Department of Labor. (n.d.). Career Zone: Assess Yourself. Retrieved 25 June 2015 from https://www.careerzone.ny.gov/views/careerzone/guesttool/ qa.jsf.

LESSON 3 Consequences and Responsibilities

Bacon, L. M. (16 June 2005). Thunderbirds to get first female pilot. *Air Force Times*. Retrieved 13 February 2006 from http://www.airforcetimes.com/story.php?f=1 -292925-918312.php.

Bee, H., & Bjorklund, B. (2004). *The Journey of Adulthood* (5th ed.). Upper Saddle River, NJ: Prentice Hall.

Buzanowski, J. G. (2010). WASPs awarded Congressional Gold Medal. *Air Force News Service*. Retrieved 7 July 2015 from http://www.af.mil/News/ArticleDisplay/tabid/ 223/Article/117355/wasps-awarded-congressional-gold-medal.aspx.

Freeman, D. S. (1934). *R. E. Lee: A Biography*. New York: Charles Scribner's Sons.

Howell, J., & Costley, D. (2006). *Understanding Behaviors for Effective Leadership* (2nd ed.). Upper Saddle River, NJ: Pearson Prentice Hall.

Larlee, J. (2008). Pilot inducted into women's aviation hall of fame. *Air Force Print News*. Retrieved 7 July 2015 from http://www.af.mil/News/ArticleDisplay/tabid/ 223/Article/124058/pilot-inducted-into-womens-aviation-hall-of-fame.aspx.

CHAPTER 5 Developing Vision and Teams

LESSON 1 Group and Team Dynamics

Gutierrez, S. (2015). LinkedIn profile. Retrieved 16 July 2015 from https://www .linkedin.com/pub/sidney-gutierrez/3/b67/197.

Hinderliter, T. (14 April 2013). Teamwork, technology allows [sic] Kandahar C-130J crew to save a life. *Air Force News Service*. Retrieved 16 July 2015 from http://www .af.mil/News/ArticleDisplay/tabid/223/Article/109358/teamwork-technology-allows -kandahar-c-130j-ae-crew-to-save-a-life.aspx.

National Aeronautics and Space Administration. (1996). Biographical Data: Sidney M. Gutierrez. Retrieved 7 March 2006 from http://www.jsc.nasa.gov/Bios/htmlbios/ gutierrez-sm.html.

Shapiro, L. (1980). US Shocks Soviets in Ice Hockey, 4–3. *The Washington Post*, 23 February 1980, page D1.

The Space Agency website (2004). Sid Gutierrez. Retrieved 7 March 2006 from http://www.thespaceagency.org/bios/gutierrez.html.

Tuckman, B. W. (2001). Developmental Sequence in Small Groups. *Group Facilitation: A Research and Applications Journal*. Number 3, Spring 2001. (Reprinted from Psychological Bulletin, (1965). 63, 384–399). Retrieved 2 March 2006 from http://dennislearningcenter.osu.edu/references/ GROUP%20DEV%20ARTICLE.doc.

US Air Force. (2004). AFH 33-337, *The Tongue and Quill*. Washington, DC: Department of the Air Force.

LESSON 2 Building Mutual Respect

Arlington National Cemetery website. (n.d.). Benjamin O. Davis, Jr., 89, Dies; First Black General in Air Force. Retrieved 7 March 2006 from http://www.arlingtoncemetery.net/bodavisjr.htm.

Gropman, A. (Fall 2004). Gen Benjamin O. Davis Jr.: American Hero. *Air & Space Power Journal*. Retrieved 7 March 2006 from http://www.findarticles.com/p/ articles/mi_m0NXL/is_3_18/ai_n6361633.html.

Lilley, K. (17 March 2015). West Point barracks to honor Tuskegee Airmen leader. *Army Times*. Retrieved 28 July 2015 from http://www.armytimes.com/story/ military/2015/03/17/benjamin-davis-academy-general/70288760/.

Original Titans.com. (n.d.). History of the 1971 Titans. Retrieved 3 March 2006 from http://www.71originaltitans.com/history.html.

LESSON 3 Establishing a Common Vision

Disney.go.com. (n.d.). Walt's Biography. The Walt Disney Family Museum. Retrieved 9 March 2006 from http://disney.go.com/disneyatoz/familymuseum.

Disney.go.com. (n.d.). Walt Disney Imagineering Overview. Disney College Overview. Retrieved 9 March 2006 from http://disney.go.com/disneycareers/ college/wdi.

Goetsch, D. L. (2004). *Effective Teamwork: Ten Steps for Technical Professions*. Upper Saddle River, NJ: Pearson Education, Inc.

Johnson, M. (27 September 2005). First All-female Crew Flies Combat Mission. *Defend America*. Retrieved 8 March 2006 from http://www.defendamerica.mil/ articles/sep2005/a092705wm3.html.

Kwan's graceful withdrawal. (14 February 2006). *Deseret News*. Retrieved 20 March 2006 from http://deseretnews.com/dn/view/0,1249,635184121,00.html.

Our View: Kwan's graceful exit. (14 February 2006). *The Patriot Ledger*. Retrieved 20 March 2006 from http://ledger.southofboston.com/articles/2006/02/14/ opinion/opin01.txt.

Phillips, B. (2005). Graceful Kwan still seeking gold. *ESPN Classic.com*. Retrieved 20 March 2006 from http://sports.espn.go.com/espn/classic/bio/news/story ?page=Kwan_Michelle.

CHAPTER 6   Solving Conflicts and Problems

LESSON 1   Identifying Conflict in Groups

Air Force Historical Studies Office. (n.d.). The Berlin Airlift. Retrieved 20 March 2006 from https://www.airforcehistory.hq.af.mil/PopTopics/berlin.htm.

Bell, A. H., & Smith, D. M. (2002). *Developing Leadership Abilities*. Upper Saddle River, NJ: Prentice Hall.

Bell, A. H., & Smith, D. M. (2003). *Learning Team Skills*. Upper Saddle River, NJ: Prentice Hall.

Columbia Electronic Encyclopedia (6th ed.). (2006). D. D. Eisenhower: General during World War II. New York: Columbia University Press. Retrieved 24 March 2006 from http://www.infoplease.com/ce6/people/A0857927.html.

Goetsch, D. L. (2005). *Effective Leadership: Ten Steps for Technical Professions*. Upper Saddle River, NJ: Prentice Hall.

Roberson, P. (ed.). (1998). *Leadership Education II: Intercommunication Skills*. Maxwell Air Force Base, AL: US Air Force Reserve Officer Training Program, Junior Program Branch.

LESSON 2   Steps for Problem Solving

Bell, A. H., & Smith, D. M. (2002). *Developing Leadership Abilities*. Upper Saddle River, NJ: Prentice Hall.

Bell, A. H., & Smith, D. M. (2003). *Learning Team Skills*. Upper Saddle River, NJ: Prentice Hall.

Giles, T. (December 2005). Wounded Airman meets doctor who saved her life. SG Newswire. US Air Force Medical Service. Retrieved 3 April 2006 from http://www.airforcemedicine.afms.mil/sg_newswire/dec_05/WoundedAirma n.htm.

Gilreath, M. (18 January 2006). Handler Adopts K-9 Partner. Defend America website. Retrieved 4 April 2006 from http://www.defendamerica.mil/profiles/jan2006/pr011706ms1.html.

Goetsch D. L. (2005). *Effective Leadership: Ten Steps for Technical Professions*. Upper Saddle River, NJ: Pearson Education, Inc.

Hogan, D. & White, C. (2003). The U.S. Army and the Lewis and Clark Expedition. Washington, DC: US Army Center for Military History. Retrieved 3 April 2006 from http://www.army.mil/cmh-pg/LC/The%20Mission/ Expedition/page_6.htm.

Language in Defense Bill Paves Way for Jamie Dana to Adopt Rex. (12 December 2005). Press release from Office of Congressman John E. Peterson. Washington, DC: U.S. House of Representatives. Retrieved 25 March 2006 from http://www.house.gov/johnpeterson/press/dec05/122205rex.htm.

Reardon, M. (n.d.). With Resolute and Thorough Planning: Captain Meriwether Lewis' Preparations for the Journey to the Pacific Ocean. US Army Center of Military History. Retrieved 13 August 2015 from http://www.history.army.mil/LC/The%20Mission/planning_and_preparation.htm.

St. George, D. (11 November 2005). Wounded vet wants Air Force dog. *The Washington Post*. Retrieved 30 March 2006 from http://www.sfgate.com/cgi-bin/article.cgi?file=/chronicle/archive/2005/11/20/MNGVDFRDHU1.DTL.

LESSON 3 Building Consensus

Columbia Encyclopedia (6th ed.). (2005). The Missouri Compromise. New York, NY: Columbia University Press.

The Constitution and the Art of Compromise. (2002). *Rediscovering George Washington*. The Claremont Institute. Retrieved 10 April 2006 from http://www.pbs.org/georgewashington/classroom/index3.html.

Dubrin, A. J. (2005) *Coaching and Mentoring Skills*. Upper Saddle River, NJ: Prentice Hall.

Winship, S. & Jencks, C. (2004). Understanding Welfare Reform. *Harvard Magazine*, November–December 2004. Retrieved 17 April 2006 from http://www.harvardmagazine.com/on-line/110489.html.

CHAPTER 7 A Leadership Model

LESSON 1 An Introduction to US Air Force Leadership

Arana-Barradas, L. (1995). Black hawk incident "tragic series of errors." *Air Force News Service*. Retrieved 4 April 2006 from http://userpages.aug.com/captbarb/blackhawk.html.

Camden, J. (20 May 1999). Officer pleads guilty in Fairchild B-52 crash. *The (Spokane, Wash.) Spokesman Review*. Retrieved 4 April 2006 from http://www.findarticles.com/p/articles/mi_qn4186/is_19950520/ai_n11510856.

Carl A. Spaatz. (2006). The Spaatz Association website. Retrieved 5 April 2006 from http://www.spaatz.org/gen/spaatzbio.html.

Carl Spaatz. (2006). Answers.com. Retrieved 5 April 2006 from http:// www.answers.com/topic/carl-spaatz.

General Carl A. Spaatz. (n.d.). *Air Force History Link*. Retrieved 2 April 2006 from http://www.af.mil/history/person.asp?dec=&pid=123006494.

Kozaryn, L. (14 January 2003). Air Force Releases Brown Crash Investigation Report. *Armed Forces Press Service*. Retrieved 4 April 2006 from http://www.defenselink.mil/news/Jun1996/n06131996_9606132.html.

US Air Force. (1985). AFP 35-49, *Air Force Leadership*. Washington, DC: Department of the Air Force.

US Air Force. (1997). *United States Air Force Core Values*. Washington, DC: Department of the Air Force.

LESSON 2 Leadership Characteristics

Biography of Dr. Condoleezza Rice. (July 2004). White House website. Retrieved 4 April 2006 from http://www.whitehouse.gov/nsc/ricebio.html.

Myers, R. (2002). A word from the chairman. *Joint Force Quarterly*, Autumn 2002. Retrieved 11 April 2006 from http://www.findarticles.com/p/articles/mi_m0KNN/is_32/ai_105853005.

Stanford Graduate School of Business. (n.d.). Condoleezza Rice. Retrieved 10 September 2015 from https://www.gsb.stanford.edu/faculty-research/faculty/condoleezza-rice.

US Air Force. (1985). AFP 35-49, *Air Force Leadership*. Washington, DC: Department of the Air Force.

Wright, B. (25 September 2001). Profile: Condoleezza Rice. *BBC News*. Retrieved 6 April 2006 from http://news.bbc.co.uk/2/hi/americas/1561791.stm.

LESSON 3 Air Force Leadership Principles

Appomattox Court House, Virginia: General Robert E. Lee Surrenders to General Ulysses S. Grant. (n.d.). Retrieved 7 April 2006 from http://americancivilwar.com/appo.html.

Columbia Accident Investigation Board Report. (2003). Retrieved 12 April 2006 from http://caib.nasa.gov/.

Crane, R. (23 August 2015). US Airman recognized as 'hero' in Paris. *Air Force News Service*. Retrieved 11 September 2015 from http://www.af.mil/News/ArticleDisplay/tabid/223/Article/614530/us-airman-recognized-as-hero-in-paris.aspx.

Ellis, R., Karimi, T., Frantz, A. & Robertson, N. (25 August 2015). Train heroes 'gave us an example of what is possible,' says French President. *CNN.com*. Retrieved 11 September 2015 from http://www.cnn.com/2015/08/24/europe/france-train-shooting/.

Fielder, S. I. (4 April 2006). Moody troop earns ACC Airman of Year. *Air Combat Command News Service*. Retrieved 4 April 2006 from http://www.acc.af.mil/news/story.asp?id=123018541.

Garamone, J. (2000). Hispanic-American General Was Aviation Pioneer. *American Forces Information Service*. Retrieved 6 April 2006 from http://www.defenselink.mil/news/Sep2000/n09112000_20009114.html.

Gibbons-Neff, T. (14 September 2015). Airman wounded in train attack in France to receive Purple Heart. *The Washington Post*. Retrieved 16 September 2015 from https://www.washingtonpost.com/news/checkpoint/wp/2015/09/14/airman-wounded-in-train-attack-in-france-to-receive-purple-heart/.

Knickerbocker, B. (22 August 2015). Attack aboard a French train, and the three American friends who stopped it. *The Christian Science Monitor*. Retrieved 11 September 2015 from http://www.csmonitor.com/USA/2015/0822/Attack-aboard-a-French-train-and-the-three-American-friends-who-stopped-it.

Mulrine, A. (25 August 2015). France train attack: why heroes probably won't get US medal for valor. *The Christian Science Monitor*. Retrieved 11 September 2015 from http://www.csmonitor.com/USA/Military/2015/0825/France-train-attack-why-heroes-probably-won-t-get-US-medal-for-valor?cmpid=addthis_email.

Schogol, J. (25 August 2015). Hero airman nominated for Airman's Medal. *Air Force Times*. Retrieved 16 September 2015 from http://www.airforcetimes.com/story/military/2015/08/24/hero-airman-nominated-airmans-medal/32286247/.

Spacy, B. (27 January 2006). Looking at future of security forces in combat. *The Beam*. Bolling AFB. Retrieved 8 April 2006 from http://www.dcmilitary.com/airforce/beam/11_13/commentary/39339-1.html.

US Air Force. (1985). AFP 35-49, *Air Force Leadership*. Washington, DC: Department of the Air Force.

Weckerlein, J. (9 March 2006). Heritage to horizons: Advice from former chiefs spans generations. *Air Force Print News Today*. Retrieved 12 April 2006 from http://www.af.mil/news/story_print.asp?storyID=123017036.

CHAPTER 8 Adaptive Leadership

LESSON 1 Leadership Style and Mission Demands

440th Airlift Wing. (August 2015). Biography: Command Chief Master Sergeant Rocky Hart. Retrieved 16 September 2015 from http://www.pope.afrc.af.mil/library/biographies/bio.asp?bioid=16807.

Hersey, P., Blanchard, K. H., & Johnson, D. E. (2001). *Management of Organizational Behavior: Leading Human Resources* (8th ed.). Upper Saddle River, NJ: Prentice-Hall, Inc.

Jacqueline Cochran. (n.d.). *Air Force Link*. Retrieved 13 April 2006 from http://www.af.mil/history/spotlight_print.asp?storyID=123016819.

Yukl, G. (2006). *Leadership in Organizations* (6th ed.). Upper Saddle River, NJ: Pearson Prentice Hall.

Zarzyczny, R. (13 April 2006). First sergeant has heart. *Air Force Link*. Retrieved 13 April 2006 from http://www.af.mil/news/story.asp?storyID=123018960.

LESSON 2 Followership

Hersey, P., Blanchard, K. H., & Johnson, D. E. (2001). *Management of Organizational Behavior: Leading Human Resources* (8th ed.). Upper Saddle River, NJ: Prentice-Hall, Inc.

National Aeronautics and Space Administration. (2005). Biographical Information: Leroy Chiao, Ph.D. Retrieved 12 April 2006 from http://www.jsc.nasa.gov/Bios/htmlbios/chiao.html.

Newman, K. (17 July 2015). Life Motto Drives Airman. 633rd Air Base Wing. Retrieved 18 September 2015 from http://www.jble.af.mil/news/story.asp?id=123454765.

Roberson, P. (ed.). (1998). *Leadership Education II: Intercommunication Skills*. Maxwell Air Force Base, AL: US Air Force Reserve Officer Training Program, Junior Program Branch.

LESSON 3 Leadership Preparation

Ambrose, S. E. (1995). *D-Day: June 6, 1944: The Climactic Battle of World War II*. New York: Simon and Schuster.

Durbin, A. J. (2005). *Coaching and Mentoring Skills*. Upper Saddle River, NJ: Pearson Prentice Hall.

George Washington. (n.d.). Retrieved 14 April 2006 from http://sc94.ameslab.gov/TOUR/gwash.html.

Roberson, P. (ed.). (1998). *Leadership Education II: Intercommunication Skills*. Maxwell Air Force Base, AL: US Air Force Reserve Officer Training Program, Junior Program Branch.

The White House. (n.d.). George Washington. Retrieved 14 April 2006 from http://www.whitehouse.gov/history/presidents/gw1.html.

Glossary

A

ability—the knowledge, experience, and skill a team member or a team brings to a task. (p. 304)

accountable—answerable for the outcomes of their words and actions. (p. 154)

achievements—attainment of goals and accomplishment of objectives that are in line with established standards of performance or behavior. (p. 116)

acknowledging—letting the speaker know that you have understood the message and that you appreciate the speaker's point of view. (p. 22)

acting out—using actions rather than words to express the emotional conflict. (p. 123)

active listening—genuine, two-way communication. (p. 16)

active voice—the subject is the actor, or doer, of the action. (p. 72)

adjusting—making changes as needed in the solution to improve its effectiveness. (p. 240)

affiliation need—a desire to be and feel a part of a group. (p. 112)

analysis—breaking an issue or problem into parts and studying each one and how it relates to the others. (p. 30)

antecedent—the noun a pronoun refers to or replaces. (p. 76)

anticipating—thinking about what could happen and preparing for issues before they arise. (p. 234)

appreciation—the admiration, approval, or gratitude that you express to others and receive from them. (p. 129)

arbitrator—a person chosen by both sides in a dispute who hears details of the dispute and gives a decision to settle it. (p. 249)

argument—a series of statements intended to persuade others. (p. 50)

articulation—the art of expressing words distinctly. (p. 98)

attitude—a thought, feeling, or belief. (p. 107)

audience—the people to whom you are writing. (p. 43)

audience demographics—the receiver's key characteristics—age, race, gender, education level, status, or role in the community. (p. 5)

B

the basic checklist—a set of guidelines that can help you tackle any writing and speaking project with confidence and competence. (p. 42)

behavior—an action that others can see you doing. (p. 107)

belief—a strong and deeply held idea that forms the basis for much of your thinking. (p. 113)

bias—a belief, judgment, or prejudice that gets in the way of impartial thinking. (p. 32)

black hole—a period of time that eats into your productivity and prevents you from reaching your goals. (p. 130)

brainstorming—a group problem-solving technique during which members contribute ideas spontaneously. (p. 210)

C

channeling—putting an encoded message into a medium of delivery. (p. 6)

character—the inner strength you show through your actions. (p. 148)

clarifying—asking specific questions to ensure you have understood the message. (p. 21)

clarity—the quality of clearness that lets your reader understand your meaning quickly. (p. 64)

coaching—a method of helping people grow and improve their competence by providing suggestions and encouragement. (p. 314)

cohesion—the ability of a team to stick together when it works toward its objective. (p. 285)

commitment—the dedicated focus on an idea, cause, issue, plan, or task to the exclusion of any interruption, distraction, or compromise. (p. 154)

communication cues—the signals that a person sends in addition to the message that may affect how the receiver interprets your meaning. (p. 7)

competence—the ability to do something well. (p. 272)

competitive listening—takes place when the receiver is not listening closely. (p. 16)

compromise—an agreement between opposing parties to settle a dispute or reach a settlement in which each side gives some ground. (p. 249)

confidence—a team member's belief that he or she can perform the task, along with the member's level of energy, enthusiasm, and commitment. (p. 304)

conflict—a clash among people. (p. 222)

consensus—a mutually acceptable agreement that takes into consideration the interests of all concerned parties. (p. 244)

consequences—the outcomes, or results, of your actions and decisions. (p. 168)

continuity—in writing, every part works toward the goal of communicating meaning clearly and quickly. (p. 65)

cooperation—the ability of team members to work together to accomplish the team goal. (p. 285)

courage—the mental and moral strength to withstand danger, fear, or difficulty. (p. 139)

credibility—a quality of character that inspires others to trust and have confidence in you—when you say or do something, people believe you. (p. 125)

critical reading—not just passively accepting what you read, but thinking about what you are reading, asking questions about the material, and interpreting what the writer is saying. (p. 30)

critical thinking—making sure you are thinking, reflecting, and reasoning the best you can in any situation. (p. 30)

D

deadline—the date by which an assignment or a task must be completed. (p. 216)

decision making—the process of setting goals, considering your options, and choosing the one you think best, given what you know. (p. 28)

decisiveness—a willingness to act. (p. 270)

decoding—turning a channeled, encoded message into meaning for you. (p. 6)

defense mechanisms—behaviors and mental processes people use to deal with mental or emotional pain—with anxiety, shame, loss of self-esteem, conflict, or other negative feelings and thoughts. (p. 122)

definition—the precise meaning or significance of a word or phrase. (p. 49)

delegating leadership style—style in which the leader turns over to team members responsibility for decision making, problem solving, and implementation. (p. 295)

denial—refusing to acknowledge some painful aspect of external reality or one's own experience that would be apparent to others. (p. 123)

desire—something you deeply want for yourself and those close to you. (p. 113)

detouring—moving around, or avoiding, a problem or conflict. (p. 229)

discrimination—unfair treatment based on prejudice against a certain group. (p. 199)

displacement—transferring a feeling about a person or an object to another, less threatening object. (p. 123)

distraction—anything that takes you away from your planned activities. (p. 130)

diversity—variation or difference. (p. 199)

drafting—a quick first writing of a paper, focused on ideas and not style. (p. 54)

dynamics—interactions. (p. 181)

E

editing—the slow, careful examination of a piece of writing to correct and clarify ideas and to ensure proper form. (p. 54)

e-mail—a message sent electronically over a computer network or the Internet. (p. 77)

empathy—the ability to show compassion for people. (p. 275)

encoding—turning a message into symbols that will have meaning for the receiver. (p. 6)

encountering—facing a conflict head-on and reaching a solution. (p. 229)

energy—an enthusiasm and drive to take the initiative. (p. 270)

enthusiasm—great excitement for and interest in a subject or cause. (p. 274)

example—a specific instance chosen to represent a larger fact to clarify an idea or support a claim. (p. 49)

excellence—the quality teams try to achieve that inspires them to outstanding or exceptional results. (p. 217)

excellence in all we do—an Air Force Core Value; directs you to develop a sustained passion for continuous improvement and innovation that will propel you and your organization into a long-term, upward spiral of accomplishment and performance. (p. 262)

explanation—makes a point plain or understandable or creates a relationship between cause and effect. (p. 50)

extemporaneous presentation—one that you carefully plan and outline in detail, and deliver with only minimal notes. (p. 90)

external noise—happens outside your own head; a siren, a phone ringing, a dog barking. (p. 8)

extravert—a person who draws energy from people, things, activities, or the world outside themselves. (p. 159)

extrinsic motivation—a force that drives people to act that is based on factors outside the individual. (p. 115)

F

feedback—the receiver's response to the sender's message. (p. 4)

followership—displaying the attitudes, behaviors, and actions that help a leader succeed at leading. (p. 302)

forming—the period when team members meet and begin to create relationships among themselves and with their leader. (p. 185)

framing—can let you see whether the speaker is open to hearing your ideas; it can also let you draw suggested solutions from the speaker. (p. 23)

G

gender stereotypes—limited ways of thinking about people on the basis of whether they are male or female. (p. 201)

gestures—the purposeful use of your hands, arms, shoulders, and head to reinforce what you are saying. (p. 96)

goal—an external aim, or end, to which you direct effort. (p. 115)

H

hierarchy—a ranking, or series of steps, that follows a specific order—for example, largest to smallest, oldest to newest, most important to least important. (p. 108)

humility—not thinking you are superior to or better than other people. (p. 126)

I

impromptu—speaking without preparation. (p. 90)

integrity—a commitment to a code of values or beliefs that results in a unified, positive attitude and approach to life. (p. 125)

integrity first—an Air Force Core Value; the willingness to do what is right even when no one is looking. (p. 258)

interaction—a situation that involves you with other people in school, at work, at home, and in social life. (p. 162)

internal noise—happens inside the receiver; daydreaming, worrying, hunger, reminiscing, and strong emotions. (p. 8)

intrinsic motivation—a drive people feel that is based on internal factors such as the need for affiliation, achievement, power, wisdom, and security. (p. 115)

introvert—a person who draws energy from ideas, information, explanations, imagination, or their inner world. (p. 159)

intuition—the feeling that you know something without any reasoning or proof. (p. 28)

J

jargon—the overly specific or technical language used by people within a specialty or cultural area. (p. 64)

justice—the fair and equal treatment of everyone under the law. (p. 201)

L

leader—someone who can influence or guide other people toward a shared goal. (p. 134)

leadership—the art of influencing and directing people to accomplish the mission. (p. 256)

leadership principle—a rule or guide that has been tested and proven over the years by successful leaders. (p. 278)

learning curve—the time necessary to get better at a task or to reach a goal. (p. 122)

listening—a focused, conscious, hearing activity. (p. 15)

logic—a way of thinking that seeks to build on facts and the conclusions you can draw from them. (p. 32)

loyalty—allegiance or faithfulness. (p. 154)

M

management—supervising the use of resources to achieve team objectives. (p. 290)

maturity—the state of being fully grown or developed. (p. 107)

mentor—a life coach who guides, advises, and advocates for you in your individual life path (p. 125)

mentoring—counseling people to help them develop in their profession or career. (p. 314)

mirroring—using the speaker's words or your own and repeating what you think the speaker has said. (p. 21)

monitoring—measuring whether or not a solution is truly working. (p. 240)

morale—a mental and emotional state of enthusiasm, confidence, and loyalty in team members and followers. (p. 135)

motivation—the inner force that drives people to act. (p. 108)

mutual assistance—the help and support team members give each other. (p. 213)

mutual respect—the two-way relationship that develops between people or members of groups after the lines of communication are open and trust develops. (p. 194)

N

negotiation—the process of bringing about a fair settlement through discussion and agreement. (p. 248)

noise—anything that interferes with communication. (p. 8)

nonverbal communication—the unconscious ways in which people communicate their true intentions and meaning, regardless of what they are actually saying. (p. 7)

norming—when the team begins to work together as a whole. (p. 187)

note taking—jotting down words, phrases, diagrams, or the occasional sentence that will remind you of the speaker's main points. (p. 23)

O

operational problem—a difficulty that is linked with conflicts over procedure, method, or approach. (p. 225)

orator—someone who is known for his or her skill and power as a public speaker. (p. 84)

outline—contains your main points and supporting ideas arranged in a logical order. (p. 52)

ownership trap—the tendency of leaders to invest too much in a solution at the expense of its effectiveness. (p. 240)

P

paraphrasing—using the speaker's words or your own and repeating what you think the speaker has said. (p. 21)

participating leadership style—style in which the leader helps and supports team members' efforts toward completing the task by sharing ideas and responsibility for decision making with his or her team members. (p. 294)

passive listening—a one-way communication in which the receiver does not provide feedback and may or may not understand the sender's message. (p. 16)

passive voice—the subject receives the action or is acted upon. (p. 72)

patience—the ability to bear difficulty, delay, frustration, or pain calmly and without complaint. (p. 126)

pause—a brief halt in your presentation. (p. 98)

performing—the stage at which the team works at its best. (p. 187)

perseverance—the quality of being determined and steadfast, never giving up or straying from your goal. (p. 135)

personal dignity—the internal strength that helps people feel connected, worthwhile, and valued. (p. 195)

personality—what you are inside and what you show to others. (p. 107)

personality trait—a characteristic that causes an individual to behave in certain ways. (p. 160)

personality type—a recognizable set of functions that some psychologists believe can help you understand who you are. (p. 159)

perspective—your way of seeing the world. (p. 111)

pitch—the highness or lowness of a sound. (p. 97)

potential—your promise—what you are capable of doing or becoming. (p. 106)

prejudice—an unfair opinion or judgment about a person or a group of people. (p. 198)

premise—the foundation on which you build a logical conclusion. (p. 32)

principles—your moral and ethical standards. (p. 153)

prioritizing—putting ideas in order from most to least important, significant, or effective. (p. 239)

proactive—taking the initiative and assuming part of the responsibility to make things happen. (p. 307)

problem—a difficulty that a group experiences in pursuing its goals. (p. 222)

problem solving—thinking through a problem or an issue to come up with a solution. (p. 29)

problem with direction—occurs when team members want to pursue different goals. (p. 224)

problem with relations—a difficulty in the way people get along with each other. (p. 222)

procrastination—the process of putting things off. (p. 130)

projection—falsely attributing to others your own unacceptable feelings, impulses, or thoughts. (p. 123)

pronoun—a word that replaces a noun and refers to a specific noun. (p. 76)

pronunciation—the ability to say words correctly. (p. 98)

protégé—a less experienced person who benefits from a mentor's guidance and advice. (p. 314)

purpose—what you want your audience to think, do, say, or believe after they've read what you've written. (p. 44)

R

rate—the speed at which you speak. (p. 96)

rationalization—concealing the true motivations for one's thoughts, actions, or feelings by offering reassuring but incorrect explanations. (p. 123)

readiness—the degree to which a follower demonstrates the ability and willingness to accomplish a task. (p. 290)

receiver—the person who receives the sender's message. (p. 4)

reflection—the act of thinking seriously about the world around you. (p. 26)

reflective listening—the receiver not only actively listens to the speaker but also tries to interpret the speaker's feelings. (p. 16)

relational competence—the ability to work well with people. (p. 272)

relationship behavior—a leader's engagement in supportive, two-way communication with his or her team members. (p. 292)

religious respect—honoring the right of other people to hold their own personal beliefs. (p. 200)

repression—pushing disturbing thoughts, wishes, or experiences from one's conscious awareness while the feeling continues to operate on an unconscious level. (p. 123)

research—the process of digging up information that supports your purpose. (p. 46)

respect—the esteem, regard, and consideration that you pay others and that you earn from them. (p. 128)

restating—using the speaker's words or your own and repeating what you think the speaker has said. (p. 21)

retreating—blocking or moving away from a problem or conflict. (p. 228)

role—the specific job or task assigned to a team member. (p. 184)

role model—a person with integrity and credibility on whom others base their own attitudes and actions. (p. 125)

root cause—a significant, deeper issue that underlies problems and conflicts. (p. 236)

rule—a guideline for membership, conduct, or performance. (p. 183)

S

scapegoat—someone who is made to take the blame for others. (p. 169)

self-actualization—the process of becoming what you are capable of becoming. (p. 109)

selflessness—the ability to sacrifice personal needs and wants for a greater cause. (p. 271)

selling leadership style—style in which the leader closely supervises task completion and following up, while also providing explanations and opportunities for clarification from team members. (p. 294)

sender—the person who originates and sends a message. (p. 4)

service before self— an Air Force Core Value; tells us that a leader's duties take precedence over personal desires. (p. 259)

situational leadership—a leadership model based on the concept that there is no single best way to influence and lead people. (p. 291)

slide transitions—effects such as sound, animation, or movement that take you from one slide or part of the talk to the next. (p. 94)

social media—websites and applications on which members of an online community share messages, photos, and other information. (p.78)

specifying—assigning clear, concrete values to proposed ideas. (p. 239)

stage fright—the nervousness you feel when appearing in front of an audience— seen in misdirected energy, excitement, and anxiety displayed in your behavior. (p. 99)

standing still—avoiding a problem or conflict by using defense mechanisms. (p. 229)

statistics—provide a summary of data in a numerical format that allows your audience to interpret the information. (p. 49)

stereotype—an idea or a concept that is based on oversimplified assumptions or opinions, rather than on facts. (p. 199)

storming—a period during which personalities begin to clash as team members try to overcome their natural tendency to focus on their own needs. (p. 186)

style—how you communicate in your own personal way, through the words you choose, the order in which you place them, and their level of formality. (p. 62)

subject-verb agreement—the subject and verb are the same number. (p. 74)

subordinate—a lower-ranking leader or individual. (p. 170)

summarizing—a way to review progress in a conversation; you touch on the main ideas or conclusions, not on each individual point; you restate the main ideas briefly and set the tone for the next subject or conversation. (p. 22)

synonym—a word that has nearly the same meaning as another word does. (p. 64)

T

task behavior—the leader's involvement in defining the duties and responsibilities of an individual or a group. (p. 293)

task completion—the process of doing things expected of you in a timely, orderly, accurate, and honest manner. (p. 129)

team—a collection of individuals who are identified by others and by themselves as a group and who work together to accomplish a common goal. (p. 181)

team assignment—lets each individual team member know his or her role on the team. (p. 215)

team charter—a document that gives direction to individual members and to the team as a whole. (p. 207)

team goal—an objective the team wishes to accomplish. (p. 210)

technical competence—the ability to do your work well. (p. 272)

telling leadership style—style in which the leader provides specific instructions and closely supervises team members as they perform their tasks. (p. 294)

testimony—the comments of authorities that you use to support a claim. (p. 49)

text messaging (texting)—a message sent using the Short Message Service (SMS) protocol, usually on a cell phone or other mobile device. (p. 77)

thinking—what happens when your mind tries to make sense of what is happening to you and leads you to conclusions and judgments. (p. 26)

timeline—a table that lists the dates by which individual project tasks or activities must be accomplished. (p. 215)

tolerance—respecting people's differences and values. (p. 197)

tone—the way you say something. (p. 46)

topic sentence—one sentence that captures the central idea of the paragraph. (p. 57)

trait—a distinguishing feature of your character. (p. 148)

transitions—words, phrases, or sentences that bridge gaps and help move the reader from one idea to another. (p. 66)

troubleshooting—taking apart a problem and determining what makes it happen. (p. 236)

trust—the degree of confidence and belief you have in others and they have in you. (p. 185)

U

unilateral decision—a one-way decision usually made by the leader or a dominant team member. (p. 246)

V

vision—an idea that inspires a team to perform well and accomplish its goals. (p. 207)

vision statement—explains the team's reason for existing. (p. 209)

visual aids—objects or displays that give emphasis to and illustrate your ideas. (p. 93)

voice—a property of a verb that shows whether the subject of a sentence is acting or being acted upon. (p. 72)

volume—how loudly or softly you speak. (p. 97)

W

willingness—the degree to which a team member or a team shows confidence, commitment, and motivation to accomplish a task. (p. 304)

cues
    communication, 7
    nonverbal, 17

D

Dana, Technical Sergeant Jamie, 237
Davis, General Benjamin, Jr. 196
Davis, Jefferson, 174
D-Day: June 6, 1944 (Ambrose), 313
deadline, 216
decision making, 28, 309
decisiveness, 270–271
decoding, 6
defense mechanisms, 122–124
    affect actions and decisions, 172–173
definition, 49
delegating leadership style, 295
Demosthenes, 86
denial, 123
desire, 113
detouring, 229
differences, benefits of accepting, 203
direction, problems with, 224–225
discipline, 284
Discovery space shuttle, 306
discrimination, 199
Disney, Roy, 209
Disney, Walt, 208
displacement, 123, 229
Distinguished Flying Cross, 138, 140
Distinguished Service Cross, 143, 293
distraction, 130
diversity, 199–200
Doolittle, General James, 139–140
drafting, 54
    body (of text), 65
    conclusion, 65
    introduction, 65
    paragraphs, 66
    writing, 65
dynamics, 181

E

Eaker, Captain Ira, 261, 286
editing, 54–57
    three-step approach to, 55–57

educate, 283
effective speaking, 84–101
effective teams
    characteristics of, 183–184
    communication and, 184
    goals and, 183, 191
    leader's role in, 191
    participation and, 184
    roles and, 184, 191
    rules and, 183, 191
Eisenhower, General of the Army Dwight,
        226, 260, 284, 313
    followers and, 313
electoral college, 321
El-Khazzani, Ayoub, 280–281
e-mail, 77–81
Emancipation Proclamation, 23, 30
empathy, 275
    in a leader, 275
encoding, 6
encountering, 229
Endeavor space shuttle, 306
energy, 270
    and personality in a leader, 274–275
enthusiasm, 274
    in a leader, 274
    leaders and, 309
environment, leadership situation and, 300
equip, 283
events and experiences, interpreting, 106–117
example, 49
excellence, 217
excellence in all we do, (Air Force Core
        Value), 262–263
explanation, 50
extemporaneous presentation, 90
external noise, 8
extravert, 159
extrinsic motivation, 115–117

F

F-22 Raptor Demonstration Team, 308
Fairchild AFB B-52 crash, 266
fear, 126
Federal Aviation Administration, 286
feedback, 4, 10–12
    fighting for, 58

Y

Z